Shinohata

Titles in Pantheon's series of reports from
villages throughout the world are

Shinohata

A Portrait of a Japanese Village

Ronald P. Dore

Pantheon Books
New York

Library of Congress Cataloging in Publication Data

Dore, Ronald Philip.
    Shinohata: A portrait of a Japanese village.
    Includes index.
    1. Villages—Japan—Case studies. 2. Rural
families—Japan—Case studies. I. Title.
HN723.5.D67 1978   301.35′2′0952   79-3279
ISBN 0-394-73843-8 pbk.

Manufactured in the United States of America

9876

About the Author

Ronald P. Dore is a Fellow of the Institute of Development Studies at Sussex and a Fellow of the
British Academy. A leading authority on contem-
porary Japan, he is the author of *Land Reform in
Japan, City Life in Japan, Aspects of Social
Change in Modern Japan, Education in Tokugawa, Japan, British Factory/Japanese Factory,*
and *The Diploma Disease.*

For Tomiyo, Hiromasa, Chieko, Yoshihide
and in memory of Atsushi

Contents

List of Illustrations

(between pages 194 and 195)

Preface

I first visited Shinohata in 1955, and spent six weeks doing a once-over-lightly social survey as part of a general study of the post-war Japanese land reform. Over the next decade I went there again twice for several months at a time, not explicitly for research (although I did spasmodically keep a diary) but because I found it a pleasant and undistracting place to write books and because I found the Yamamoto family extraordinarily congenial to live with. In the late sixties I agreed to write about it for Allen Lane.

In retrospect, I rather wish I had not. Having embarked on a project of this sort one is reluctant to abandon it, and having finished a book one is reluctant to tear it up and not publish. What is more I much enjoyed the two months I have since spent in Shinohata with the purpose of writing this book in mind, and many parts of the book itself were a pleasure to write. But still I have some misgivings – on two counts.

The first is about making fun of people. I like to think that I have a sense of humour, and in spite of some years of immersion in Japanese life it is largely an English sense of humour. Many of the things I notice and record I do notice and record because they tickle that English sense of humour. There are many things that people in Shinohata do rather seriously and solemnly which when described dead-pan do seem a little bizarre. To point up those elements makes for more interesting reading, but it does sometimes run close to making fun of people. Now there are some people in Shinohata whom I feel no compunction in depicting as figures of fun; they are figures of fun to some of my Shinohata friends too. But there are three problems. One is to avoid a tone of knowing superiority. The second is to protect my sources – the friends who told me some of the less flattering anecdotes about their fellow villagers. The third is to avoid the danger of presenting also as figures of fun those Shinohata friends whom I do hold in affection and esteem. I hope I have succeeded. Fictitious names, locations and circumstances will, I trust, protect everybody in Shinohata from being actually bothered as a result of anything I have written, but one would like to feel that even if an assiduous detective were to penetrate some of the disguises I would have nothing to be really apologetic about. One can never be quite sure.

The second problem is less serious. For someone who has been a sober social scientist all his life, concerned with scholarship and sociological generalization, a bedside-reading, human-interest kind of book is not an easy one to write. In the end I could not do it, of course. I had to smuggle in a few tables and digress into the mechanisms of income redistribution and the social origins of egalitarianism. The resulting mix of anecdote and what some people might be pleased to call structural analysis does reflect fairly accurately what I want to say about Shinohata, to the general reader rather than to my fellow sociologists. But I fear that being neither a scholarly production nor sufficiently remote from scholarship to be forgivable (an academic does better to write detective stories) it is not going to do much for my scholarly reputation. I once thought of giving the book the sub-title 'A Sociographic Entertainment', but who am I to give myself the pretensions of a Graham Greene? It also occurred to me to use a pseudonym, but the Japanese studies world is a small world and it could only be a mere dissociative gesture – which I suppose, in fact, is what this preface is.

I should explain one convention concerning the direct speech which I use rather liberally. The few passages which bear quotation marks are taken straight from a tape recording. Otherwise they are reconstructed from memory. Tape recorders are all very well if one is very explicitly 'getting someone's story'. A lot of my quotations come from more casual encounters, sometimes on occasions when it was natural for me to have a notebook and pencil in hand, sometimes not. I did try, however, whether on the basis of notes or not, to do the reconstruction as soon as possible after the event; often within minutes, otherwise within a few hours. A few of the quotations represent a splicing together of more than one conversation, but the vast majority are presented 'straight', as they came.

Many thanks are due to Ethel Royston for some resilient typing, to Jonathan Unger and Peter Carson for reading the typescript and making many excellent suggestions and to Nancy Dore for help with the index and many other things. The Japan Foundation kindly financed the last of my longer visits. What I owe to the people of Shinohata, and especially to the Yamamoto family, for their ability to describe and make sense of their own society as well as for their friendliness and openness, will be obvious to every reader of this book.

I

Town and Country

Some seventy miles or so along one of the main routes which
fan out from Tokyo, you will come to Sano Plain. It is a wide
basin surrounded by mountains, steep but wooded to the top,
a serration of smallish peaks, above which the cap of one of
Japan's elegant volcanoes, white for several months of the year,
adds the final tourist-poster touch. Here and there, in the dark
evergreen of the wooded mountain sides, are a few gashes of
yellow where the erosion which followed reckless war-time
logging has not yet been repaired. On the lower slopes are the
large square patches of the upland fields, light green in June,
darker in September, sere in the autumn and white for the rest
of the year from the acres of vinyl sheeting which farmers have
recently learned to use. There is nothing very traditional about
any agricultural practice in Japan today, least of all about the
new crops imported from Europe in the last century.

The railway line across the mountains from Tokyo was a
considerable engineering feat in its day. Now, beside it, sweeping across valleys, gouging out mountain sides, banked on the
vast mounds of raw spill, are the concrete masses of a new four-
lane express-way due to be opened in a few years. Whichever
way one approaches it, it is hard to say where the city of Sano
begins, so tightly packed are the surrounding villages in this
intensively cultivated and increasingly industrialized plain, and
so continuous, now, the settlement between one former village
centre and another. But the Sano city centre is unmistakably

a city centre, and one that befits a prefectural capital. The station forecourt is a broad expanse of tarmac with flower beds and fountains and a great knobbly globe of concrete topped by chunky crystals of coloured glass – the city's homage to modern art. The broad street leading down from the station to the shabby 1950-vintage prefectural offices and a glittering 1970s prefectural library, past the two six-storey department stores and countless souvenir shops, is a divided highway with flower beds down the centre. In the middle of them, just below the station, stands the city's homage to representational art and to history – a great green-bronze figure of the sixteenth-century warrior whose family ruled the district for centuries and who might, had he not finally lost to the Tokugawa in the wars of the late sixteenth century, have made Sano the capital of Japan. Three times life size he sits in full armour on a low stool, legs planted wide apart, the horns of his fearsome helmet tilted forward, glowering at his decadent descendants.

Shinohata, the village of this book, is some twenty-five miles further on from Sano, northwards up the valley of the Isokawa river. The train, followed once by a five-mile walk, nowadays more often by an eight-mile taxi ride, is one way of getting there. The electric trains of today are a far cry from the battered coaches and leaky steam locomotives of twenty years ago. And the expresses – painted bright red, to distinguish them from the yellow and green semi-fast and the dull blue stoppers – take less than half the time to climb the thirty miles up the valley to the water-shed and over the next prefecture. Everything about them is trim and dapper; the stylized flourishes of the white-gloved guard, for instance, as he waves the flag for the train to start from Sano station, or the precise unfumbling way the conductor, in equally clean white gloves, clips one's ticket, arms slightly raised, ticket held at correct angle and correct distance from the body, clipper engaged and operated in a sharp single movement. Equally neat and trim are the uniform dresses of the girls who come round with their refreshment baskets, equally exact the way in which each of their packed rice lunches has its strips of pork and fish pâté and pickled radish and ginger laid in a tasteful pattern on the rice. Even the aerosol-scrawled slogans from last week's strike have been nearly scrubbed off from the sides of the coaches and now only faintly proclaim the solidarity, and eventual certain victory, of the working class. And last week's striker is now today's conductor, carefully adjusting a slipped antimacassar in one of the 'green coaches' – what used to be first-class coaches until, fifteen years ago, the railway authorities decided that 'green' and 'ordinary' sounded better than first and second class in this egalitarian age.

Progress is slower if one travels northwards up the valley by bus. Ten years ago, when the trunk road was first completely metalled all the way into the next prefecture, there were express buses, but no longer. Now, the roads are so crowded that 'express' would be a mockery. No society in history has ever been so rapidly motorized, and few societies have had such trouble adapting to the motor-car, as Japan with its dense population and tightly packed settlements. Sano and its surroundings show all the signs of improvised adaptation. No other road in the city has the amplitude of the central station road. The ones through which one edges out to the suburbs are just wide enough for two streams of traffic. Pedestrians need better protection than a mere sidewalk can provide in these narrow streets. Steel girders, set on stout iron posts, run along a couple of feet from the ground to mark a yard-wide strip on either side reserved for their safety. Some of the main crossroads have what is here known to everyone as a Sukuramburu – what American traffic experts apparently call a 'scramble', but here with a difference. When all traffic stops and all pedestrian lights go green and the crowds at the corners surge forward in all directions, loudspeakers play the tune of a well-known children's song about walking home hand-in-hand in the sunset, a tune redolent of innocence and safety and the benevolence of kindly paternal authority.

Paternal authority is also evident in the banners across the roads which proclaim what 'drive' is being urged on the citizenry this week – what particular form of exhortation, whether to protect wild birds, to buy savings bonds, to help the aged or to promote international friendship. In road safety week, the volunteer from the local ward's Crime Prevention Co-operation Group will be manning each of the pedestrian crossings which punctuate the steel barriers every two hundred yards or so. With yellow cap and yellow flag he is there to reinforce the message of the crossing lights (which people seem not much inclined to disobey in ordinary weeks anyway), alternately holding out his flag at a ninety-degree angle to stop the flow of cars or people and then energetically waving them forward as if there was not a moment to be lost.

Every other shop in these streets glitters with plate glass, aluminium frames and often automatic sliding doors of a kind which less affluent or less gadget-minded societies reserve for airports and supermarkets. Shoe shops, electric appliance shops, motor accessories shops, chemists, jewellers and farm implements shops – even farm implements shops – are the most glittery ones with spinning, revolving, flashing neon strips shouting for attention in broad daylight.

Interspersed are the more traditional shops with open counters when the shutters are removed, built in the plain unpainted timbers which were the staple of Japanese traditional architecture. There are greengrocers and fishmongers; a carver of the wooden seals which each householder registers at the town hall and uses in place of the European's signature; a shop specializing in all kinds of traditional papers, for pasting on screens, for wrapping gifts, for presentation scrolls; a Japanese cake shop whose tasteful creations in rice flour and bean paste represent a still entirely distinct tradition from that of the bakery with its cream puffs and eclairs next door.

As one jerks and crawls out through the suburbs and the first rice fields come in sight, the road broadens somewhat, but still the new extensions to the town stretch out on either side. Clusters of tiny houses with roofs of bright blue and magenta and post-office red snuggle behind the ornamental trees planted in their few square feet of garden. There are tall blocks of flats; a two-storey golf practice driving range, a bowling alley whose neon says 'BOWL' just like its American original, a yard with wrecked cars piled six high. There are even a few used car lots to complete the momentary illusion that it is an American town one is leaving. But the rice fields ensure that such illusions *are* momentary. Glistening squares of water in May, a shimmer of the lightest green in June, rippling yellow in autumn and well-drained dry stubble for the rest of the year, these could only be Japanese rice fields. Nowhere else are rice fields banked with expensive concrete blocks, and nowhere else are rice fields, banked with such expensive concrete blocks (some of them in this valley entirely re-created after a typhoon washed them away fifteen years ago – at a cost to public funds of over £1,000 an acre), left to grow weeds throughout the year. Until 1974 the government paid a sizeable non-cultivation subsidy to reduce production, and even two seasons after the policy was reversed their owners had not adjusted to the new situation.

The Isokawa river which gulped in those rice fields in 1959 becomes that kind of raging torrent only once in a generation or so. In August and September, when most of the water coming off the hills is trapped and dammed and gently led off into rice fields, it is the thinnest of trickles and only in the June monsoon or in the autumn typhoon season does it cover much of its broad bed – about 300 yards from dike to dike, even at the narrow point where it comes closer to the cliffs it has carved out of the valley's east side and forces the road to cross over to the west. The bed is a mass of boulders and rough mounds covered with miscellaneous rank vegetation interspersed with the tall screens and conveyor belts and storage heaps of numerous gravel works. Trucks clamber up make-shift roads over the dikes – concrete dikes in many places, thanks again to the Typhoon Disaster Recovery Grants – taking load after load away to feed the insatiable needs of Japan's construction industry. Japan's *per capita* consumption of cement has in recent years been the highest in the world. The face of nature is being changed. So much aggregate has been taken out of the river bed that some of the riparian villages are demanding compensation from the gravel companies because the water table has been lowered and their wells have dried up. 'They should worry!' would have been the reaction of the samurai official who wrote the official gazetteer of the district in 1814. Explaining that the river's name referred to its lack of a central channel, he went on, 'the river is the great curse of the district. It brings down so much sand and rocks that it fills up all its channels and the bed is constantly rising. The dikes have to be constantly raised. In some places the water level can rise to six or ten feet above the level of the surrounding fields and inevitably, sometimes, it breaks through, pouring sand and rocks onto the rice fields which it takes years to remove.'

As the valley narrows further up one sees ahead on the east side, above the line of the brown sandstone cliff tops, the broad clean slopes of a volcano. Several tens of thousand years older than the more famous smooth-peaked volcanoes, its top has already fallen in to leave a jagged array of lesser peaks. Its lower slopes, though, still have a magnificently expansive sweep to them. The steep wooded foothills of another mountain chain gets closer to the west. Little signs pointing off the road announce the starting point of the route up to Buddha Peak, to Phoenix Peak, to Pony Peak. The frequent 'doraivuin' ('drive-in' restaurants) show that this is the holiday route – as do the equally frequent little three-or-four-hut motels, whose advertisements proclaim the comforts which young couples can expect to find. Some of them are uncompromisingly modern, with Motel Monte Carlo or Motel Arizona written in bold Roman letters. Others get the best of both worlds. Moteru Romansu is written in Japanese script. And it has the traditional shingle too – the 'upturned jellyfish' sign; a little circle with waving tentacles of steam which once meant a hot spring and then, because of the erotic mixed-bathing-and-pillow-geisha associations of hot springs, came to mean any hotel where one could take a girl for an illicit afternoon. There are garages and agricultural co-operative granaries, a factory recently established to employ the local sons who prefer to stay at home and make their future as part-time farmers rather than migrate to the industrial centres. Is it the holiday-makers or the commuters to the factory who are the reckless drivers? A barrier across the road bears a slogan in the seventeen syllables of a traditional haiku:

> Crowded Japan.
> Where are you going,
> in such a mad hurry?

There are fewer rice fields, more steeply terraced, as the valley gets narrower: more dry fields climbing up the slopes, many of them planted with mulberry for silkworms. The small town centres which the main road passes through, or more often bypasses, get smaller now as the hinterland they serve contracts. A few miles from the head of the valley a side road turns off westward up towards the hills. It follows the little stream through some rice fields for about three-quarters of a mile until it turns round the corner of the plantation of young pine trees

to reveal a cluster of sixty houses nestling in the foothills o
mountains ahead – the hamlet of Shinohata.

My first visit to Shinohata was in 1955. I was doing a study or
the effects of the land reform on Japanese villages. I had already
spent some time in a northern village in a predominantly rice-
growing area, formerly dominated by a single powerful landlord. I planned another spell in a western village with a more
diversified agriculture and a strong owner-farmer tradition. To
complete what inevitably had to be a rather small sample, I
wanted to find a village in central Japan with several landlords
of medium-sized holdings, in an area where forest land played
a larger part in the village economy. Forest land not having
been redistributed in the land reform, one might expect landlord power to be less diminished in such a village and older
'feudal traditions' to remain stronger. I went to the agricultural
department of the prefectural offices in Sano and explained myself. Maps were brought out. The village at the top of the valley
was declared the most likely to meet my requirements. I set off
up the valley; two officials, kindly but slightly puzzled and still
not quite convinced that a foreigner should actually want to live
for a month in a Japanese village, remembered a land dispute
which had to be checked up on in that direction and promised
to follow a little later.

It was a very different road then. The tarmac stopped before
it was out of Sano city. Between towns there was little traffic;
groups of school-children going home from school stepped off
the road at the approach of the occasional battered, jam-packed
bus or a three-wheeled truck, and held handkerchiefs to their
mouths until the dust had settled. Cyclists, taking home enormous loads of grass from the river banks to feed their cow,
wobbled uncertainly around the potholes; bullocks plodded
slowly along drawing carts piled high with farm produce, only
a few of them with rubber wheels. There were few new houses
to be seen, and those close to the roadside were made to look
older and shabbier by their coating of dust. Shopkeepers of the
village centres on the way threw buckets of water on the road
to keep the dust off their goods in the open shop fronts, but to
little avail. There were no drive-ins or motels; only, occasionally, a modest tea house-hotel in traditional Japanese style. The

roadside advertisements were not for colour television and cheap foreign holidays, but for durable farmers' footwear and for curry powders that made a little go a long way.

The officials, whose car could manage the wash-board corrugated road better than my scooter could, got there just before me, so that my arrival caused less consternation in the village office than it might have done. Of the seven hamlets which made up the administrative unit, it was soon decided that Shinohata was the one for me. The people there were known to be calm and equable in spirit, unlikely to be too disconcerted by the arrival of a foreigner or too busy to talk to him. I checked up on the land-ownership situation and decided it would do. But where would I stay? 'You mean you actually want to stay in the village?' Eventually my protestations about my familiarity with Japanese food and Japanese toilets were accepted, if still with some scepticism. In that case, the most obvious place, it was decided, was the house of the biggest former landlord. He would know all about looking after foreigners. Not quite the thing, I explained, to be closely identified with the landlords, if one wanted to get frank accounts of the land reform. Wasn't there a temple? Yes, there was, but that was out of the question. The office clerk who lived in Shinohata explained with some embarrassment that the old priest was deaf and morose, his wife a great trouble-maker and unreliable. The solution was the village shop. A pleasant family, generally liked. The old man would be tickled pink to have a foreign lodger, and since the daughter stayed in to mind the shop, there would be no problems about meals. The clerk got on his bicycle and went ahead to negotiate. Word came back that all was well and at dusk that evening I had my first glimpse of Shinohata, with the smoke from evening cooking fires curling out of the roof vents of sixty houses, and nothing to be heard when I stopped my scooter engine but the croaking of frogs, the sizzle of a late cicada, the rustling of the water in the irrigation ditches, the crackling of the fire in the bath-shed where it had just been lit under the iron bath tub, the whispering of the children who gathered at the gate through which the strange foreigner had just come, and the cheerful, if slightly apprehensive, greetings of the Yamamoto family.

2

Time Past

Men have been living in this area for a long time, though nobody knows much about the people who were here four thous-
and years ago. Fragments of their pots with their swirling
designs and the baroque elaboration of their handles are still
occasionally dug up by local farmers, but these Jómon people –
who did not have rice and whom it is hard to think of as real
Japanese, so integral is rice to Japanese culture – may or may
not be among the direct ancestors of the present inhabitants.
Koma, the county name which the district has borne since the
first historical records of the seventh century, was the Japanese
name for the Korean kingdom of Kudara. In the early centuries,
rather as between France and Britain in the eleventh and twelfth
centuries, both countries were divided into a number of centres
of local power, and the sense of Koreanness and Japaneseness
was not all that strong. Hence it was quite natural, when the
Kudara kingdom was wiped out by its enemies at the end of
the seventh century, for some of the survivors to come across the
water as refugees. Koma was probably one of the places where
they settled, but records are fragmentary. There was certainly a
rich 'continental family' in the area in the middle of the eighth
century because there was litigation about one of its slaves who
in 761 had been sent to a temple in the capital, Kyoto, nearly
300 miles away to work as a copyist on Buddhist sutras. He
broke bond and fled, and so did a second slave sent to replace
him.

Perhaps it was the Koreans who introduced horse-breeding. At any rate the district five miles down the valley from Shinohata still has the name 'Grazing Fields' and is recorded in 927 as having the honourable obligation of sending fifteen fine horses every year as tribute to the court in Kyoto.

Shinohata itself first appears in records of the late thirteenth century. By then the central authority of the Kyoto court had dwindled to nothing. It was the locally resident feudal barons who had the power to squeeze tax rice out of the farmers, and the constant temptation to expand their estates at the expense of their neighbours was one which neither greed nor their military-heroic cultural traditions prompted them to resist. It was in one of the intermittent periods of relative peace, when the victory of one warring league established something like a stable order over large tracts of the country, that the local baron enfeoffed one of his sons in Shinohata, though where he had his mansion, how strongly fortified it was, how many his retainers and how many farming families he could exact tribute from, nobody now knows.

Almost certainly, here as in other parts of Japan, the distinction between warrior retainers with a claim to some kind of aristocratic lineage and bonded tax-paying farmers with no claims to be other than 'common people' became increasingly fluid. The warriors farmed, or at least directed closely the farming labours of hereditarily bonded farmers. Likewise, when the chance of a battle arose, an enterprising and courageous farmer could hope to distinguish himself enough to be recognized as a warrior, to receive a feudal grant of land and the right to tax the people who worked it.

Thus, for centuries, farming and fighting went hand in hand. Real peace came to the district, as to the rest of Japan, only at the end of the sixteenth century. Helped by the new weapons which the Portuguese had brought, the Tokugawa family at last achieved what its predecessors had all sought – stable hegemony over the whole country; enough overwhelming power and enough legitimacy to settle boundaries between fiefs and confine their vassal barons within their allotted areas, to unify currencies and weights and measures, to control inter-fief commerce and external trade.

Part of the pacification policy was a sharp separation between warriors and farmers. The latter's swords were impounded. Their land was surveyed and registered and the tax assessment of each plot fixed. Cultivation was an obligation as much as a right. The farmers were bound to the land and in principle could not sell or mortgage it. The samurai warriors no longer lived in the villages but in the castle towns. Their annual stipends were paid in rice – so many bales per family according to rank – from the taxes collected in kind from the villages. They busied themselves with guard duties, with practice of the military arts and study of the Chinese classics, above all with ceremonial pomp and circumstance. Occasionally they took spells of duty in the fief branch offices, supervising the collection of the tax rice, settling disputes between villages over rights to irrigation water or the boundaries between the tracts of forest land which villages were allotted for communal use, supervising riparian works and the upkeep of bridges and roads and important shrines and temples.

During the two and a half centuries of the Tokugawa regime, from 1600 to 1870, the province of which Sano city was the centre frequently changed hands. Sometimes it was given in fief to relatives and close retainers of the Tokugawa family; at others it was directly administered Tokugawa land. It made little difference to the 'common people'. As far as they were concerned they were governed by 'the authorities' in the castle town of Sano. Shinohata came under the branch office at Nakatani, half way up the valley, but there was a small detachment of troops stationed a little way away at the head of the valley, at the inspection barrier where the road passed over into the neighbouring fief. Shinohata's land survey was completed in 1603, though the only remaining record of it is the 'black-ink seal' warrant which exempted from taxation the half-acre of rice land registered in the name of the village's Shinto shrine. The proceeds of renting that land were used for the upkeep of the shrine and the expenses of its festivals. (Only the Tokugawa Shōgun himself issued 'red seal warrants'; his officials' ink was a less imperious black.)

Villages like Shinohata were largely left to govern themselves – or rather to be governed by the 'three ranks of officials'. 'Headman', the 'representative of the farmers', and 'senior farmer(s)' were the titles used in Shinohata: elsewhere the last were sometimes called 'neighbourhood group chiefs'. These offices, certainly the first one, seemed to have run in the same rich families for several generations. It is unlikely, though, that any of these officials exercised anything like dictatorial power. There were, probably, informal councils of older farmers of fairly well-to-do families who would expect to be consulted in most matters. But as far as the samurai authorities were concerned the three ranks of officers were the responsible officials. It was they, for example, who signed the documents from which the 1814 gazetteer of the district was compiled – documents still preserved in Sano by a descendant of the Confucian scholar who edited the compilation. One of them is a somewhat crude schematic map of the village – generally rather uninformative except about such things as the location of a curious rock with a perpetual rust-red pool of water which was good for curing warts. Even that was signed in the bottom corner by some of these officials as an assurance that this was a true likeness of their village. More consequentially, they were the people who could expect especially dire punishment if their village was guilty of rebellion, or the sheltering of secret Christians. But generally their job was to keep law and order, to supervise communal village work – the repair of roads and the irrigation system, the sharing out of water in dry years – and, above all, to see to the collection and delivery of the tax rice.

The rice tax was a collective village responsibility although tax assessments were fixed for individual farmers' holdings. Gontarō, who is arguably Shinohata's most eminent and certainly its most bizarre inhabitant, and who until 1946 was its biggest landowner, is the descendant – the present house-head – of the family which held the headman position in the latter part of the Tokugawa period. He will proudly show visitors a hanging bamboo screen which his great-grandfather was given by the local samurai Intendant by way of reward and encouragement for his prompt delivery of the rice tax. Like many other head-men towards the end of the period when the power of the samurai was weakening vis-à-vis the peasants and merchants, he had been given quasi-warrior status – allowed, that is, to use a family surname just like a samurai and to wear both a long and a short sword, privileges denied to ordinary farmers ever since swords were impounded at the end of the sixteenth century.

Surnames, historically deriving from place names, implied landed property rights. They were therefore inappropriate for peasants, who had property obligations rather than rights. Peasants were known by their personal names, which generally ran in the family. A son would give up his 'young man's name' and take his father's when his father died or 'abdicated' (and moved out of the main house to the 'old people's annex'), leaving him the headship of the family.

The tax burden – the number of bales of rice the village had annually to deliver – probably fluctuated. Apart from occasional *ad hoc* remissions in years of bad harvests there were also periodic re-surveys. In the 1688 revision, two lesser shrines in Shinohata lost the exemption they had received in 1602, which indicates a general tightening. There were other attempts to increase the tax yield in the areas of directly administered Tokugawa land in the early eighteenth century, but they were prosecuted with a good deal less vigour from the middle of the century onwards. Altogether, with rice strains and cultivation practices gradually improving, it is generally thought that the tax burden fell considerably in the Tokugawa areas – for rice land from perhaps as much as 60 per cent of gross yields at the beginning of the period, to something closer to 40 per cent by the middle of the nineteenth century.

Apart from the slow improvement of rice yields, there were also some new sources of income. Silkworms were reared and more land planted out to mulberry. The cocoons were sold to merchants who ran the filiatures where the silk was reeled, and organized the cottage weaving industry for which the more advanced part of the province, closer to Edo – the modern Tokyo and then the capital of the Shōgun – was famous. The mountains, too, provided various exotic mushrooms which could be dried and sold in Edo. For it was in Edo that the purchasing power for luxuries was concentrated. One of the ways which the founder of the Tokugawa dynasty invented for keeping the feudal lords under control was to make them build mansions in his capital and spend half their time there – and in most years, probably, a good deal more than half their feudal revenues, such was the round of conspicuous ceremonial consumption in which the lords and their large samurai retinues spent their days. Edo was also the destination of much of the timber and charcoal which also came from the mountains. Like the tax rice they were punted down the valley to the sea and then sent by ship to Edo. In the village next to Shinohata there was a rich timber merchant who owned a large timber yard in Edo.

With these new economic developments, the villagers of Shinohata were probably rather better off by the end of the Tokugawa regime than they were at the beginning. Certainly the gravestones in the village graveyard get rather bigger after about 1800, though whether that reflects greater wealth or greater piety is a moot point. Population increase may have absorbed some of the new income. Until fairly recently, however, there was still enough spare irrigation water available for new rice fields to be constructed, so that there was not necessarily any decline in the size of holdings as the number of houses grew. At some time in the Tokugawa period younger sons from Shinohata started two branch hamlets down the hill closer to the Isokawa river, one of which still bears the name New Rice Field.

The new wealth, such as it was, was far from being equally distributed, however. Some were rich and some were poor. Some, once rich, became rapidly poor. Some, once poor, became slowly rich. The rise and fall of families is still a frequent topic of Shinohata conversation.

> Nakanobu's a fine worker, and so's his wife. They've brought up eight children; fine children, too. He left her with six of them, all young, when he was called up for the war. We all helped out a bit, but I don't know how she managed. But bit by bit he's built it up, and now they're fairly comfortable. His oldest son's come back from Tokyo, too. He deserves his good luck, seeing how poor they were. And they used to be rich, too. A lot of land, a big house. But the old man, his father, gobbled it all up. – Gambling, mostly. And drinking. And gambling when he was drunk.

Or, again:

> The old girl – my mother-in-law – had had a hard life. Father – my husband – always used to say: she had her faults but one had to remember she had a hard life.

She came from a big big house in Daibo. They had
once been very rich – I tell you, it had six ten-mat
rooms, and you couldn't get your arms around the
main stem pillar. But her family had fallen on hard
times. And then she fell on hard times again here. Her
husband – father's old man, that is – died when father
was four. Well, actually he disappeared. Nobody knows
where he is buried. As a matter of fact he ran away
from his debts. We'd been running the shop, such as it
was, for generations – nothing much but salt, saké,
sugar, tea and such-like – and he got badly into debt.
He wasn't a bad worker; worked hard in fact, and he
wasn't a spendthrift. He just was too fond of public
office, of doing things for the village, serving on com-
mittees, being chief of this and vice-chief of that. He
was just too good-natured; gave too much of his time
and money to it. He was the one who organized the
work to make that emergency reservoir up below the
shrine – the War-camp Pond, we call it, though I don't
know who ever had his fort there. He put a lot of time
into that. And money. And so he piled up debts. They
had to sell off nearly all their rice fields – and the house;
it was all taken to pieces and sold to someone in Makizawa. Two of the rice fields at the top of the village
went to Kikutarō. Mother-in-law said she remembered
making those fields; carrying the earth up there in
great hods. We let Kikutarō have them cheap, she said,
on the promise that when better times came he would
sell them back. But you know how it is. When the time
came, he denied that he'd got them particularly cheap.
In the end we got the smaller one of the two.

It's partly luck. Mother-in-law was always telling us
what bad luck she had. They used to have a fine horse.
One of the best and strongest in the village. Mother-in-
law took him up into the woods to cut grass, loaded
him up with four great bundles and was leading him
back. Just as they were crossing the bridge, he missed
his footing and fell in. There he was; the load had
turned him over on his back and the stream pinned him
against the footings of the bridge. There he was; the

feet in the air. She couldn't do anything. Rushed back
to the village for help, but by the time they got there it
was too late. A horse is finished as soon as it gets water
in its ears.

As a matter of fact, she was a bit of a bore at times
was mother-in-law with her stories of her hard luck. If
ever we were going that way she used to tell us: just
you go and look at that house in Makizawa that we
sold. Take a look at the main stem pillar. See the size
of it. You'll see, too, it's got a little room in the corner
of the verandah where they put a big pot underneath
that you can take out from outside so that you can pee
indoors without going out into the rain. I never did go
and see it with the famous indoor toilet. I couldn't see
the point.

Or another widowed lady, Hisayō, who clearly looked like
someone who had been to a pre-war girls' high school and
managed somehow to seem gracious even when she was hoeing
her soya beans.

It was the land reform that finished us off, but we
were already pretty much down on our luck by that
time. I was born in this house, I didn't come here as a
bride, and as long as I can remember we had about
seventy bales [over four tons] of rice a year in rent. But
we worked like mad with an acre and a bit under mul-

1835

berry – that was a lot of silkworms, though it was still possible to hire daily help pretty cheaply then. Once, though, we had the headship of the village – before it moved to Gontarō's family. We had as much as Gontarō and the other big landlord, Hachizaemon, put together. I'll show you: we've still got the plans of the house that was built in 1835.

You see, it had two small sitting rooms and two bedrooms, and the formal master's room with the attached attendant's room just like a samurai house, and the big living room just up off the earth-floored kitchen-workspace. And in addition in the grounds of the house there was a small rice-husking mill with a water-wheel, and two big store-houses with thick mud walls and an 'old people's annex' – where the old people withdrew after the father had passed on the headship of the house to his son. But somehow they went downhill after that. Some time in the 1880s great-grandfather lent a lot of money to a family that his sister had married into. They were trying to start some business, but it failed and the debt had to be written off and some of our land mortgaged. Then the house burned down. It was rebuilt with wood from our own land, but on a reduced scale, you see.

1888

It was some time before they managed to get rid of the mortgage by hard work and economy. Grandfather and father were determined not to lose the family's position as a landlord with seventy bales. I remember when we had the roof re-done with tiles to replace the thatch. Father could easily have sold a field or two and had it done at once, but he was too proud. So we had it done a strip at a time over the years.

'Parents work hard (shimbō), children easy life, grandchildren poor (bimbō)' is the Japanese proverbial equivalent of 'shirtsleeves to shirtsleeves in three generations'. The ups and downs were indeed considerable. In Shinohata one can trace some measure of the well-being of some forty-one households through about three generations from 1901 to 1975. The 1901 family registers record the number of horses, store-houses and barns, and the house-plot size of each household, and there is a 1910 list of contributions to the local shrine which is a not implausible measure of current income. For 1938 there are records of the land tax and of the hamlet association contributions which were assessed on the basis of income; for 1954 and 1974 of property-tax and village-tax payments. If the houses of each period are divided into four ranks roughly equal in size, then only five of the forty-one households remained in the same category throughout – four in the top, one in the bottom category. The majority moved both up and down over that span of years, eight between only two adjacent categories, ten across the range of three, two over four. Of those who moved in one direction only, twelve moved up (seven by only one category and one through the whole range) and four moved down – two of them all the way from top to bottom.

But despite the variety of these patterns of family fortunes, it is striking how much more frequent are stories of houses now of modest means having once been impressively rich, than of houses in recent times well off having once been very poor. Perhaps that is because the process of decline was generally more spectacular, sudden and dramatic than the process of accumulation. Perhaps it is because a certain stigma attached, not just to a history of poverty, but to the actual process of becoming rich. For by and large, the opportunity to accumulate land came only through other people's misfortunes. A man in good health, in his working prime, with a hard-working wife and two or three teenage working children, could manage to save a little, but it was only when a neighbour – not necessarily a drunkard or a gambler; perhaps a farmer with several children too young to work whose wife had fallen sick, or whose fields had been badly hit by the rice rust – only when a neighbour fell on hard times and needed rice to see him through to the next harvest that a man with savings could turn those savings into real estate. He might simply buy a tract of woodland or a rice field from the man who needed money and take over ownership rights. Or there might be a mortgage agreement which amounted to a low-price sale with a possible buy-back option, perhaps a loan against the security of a piece of land, followed by transfer of the land as the interest payments sub-sequently mounted and repayment became impossible. The purchaser, when he had accumulated as much land as he wanted to farm himself, would usually leave the seller to cultivate the land as his tenant, paying the new owner a large share of the annual produce from what had once been his, the tenant's, own ancestral land.

During the Tokugawa period the samurai government periodically reiterated its edicts declaring all land sales and mortgages to be illegal. Apart from the principle of the thing (how dare they behave as if they owned the land which has merely been allotted to them to perform their heaven-sent duty to cultivate!), land concentration – and the impoverishment of those who lost land in the process – threatened the stability of the villages and the working capacity of the tax-paying labour force. But the government edicts were unenforceable – the more so because the village self-government system left super-vision of these matters to the headman, and the headmen, com-ing as they did from the upper stratum of villagers, were the main beneficiaries of free land movement.

For it was always easier for the rich to become richer than for the poor to acquire a modest competence. For one thing, apart from illness, most of the disasters that forced a man to borrow were natural disasters which hit everybody alike: a drought, a sudden spell of cold weather in August just when the rice should flower, an outbreak of the imochi virus, a plague of the stalk-borer insect. Only the rich had stores from which to lend. Moreover, the rich were, most of them, *in the business* of provid-ing benevolent protection; prepared, perhaps, to forgo an extra 2 or 3 per cent interest for the sake of gratitude and loyalty and the 'hold' they might have on a man's future service; a poorer man making his way up copper coin by copper coin, tiny field by tiny field, was less likely to spoil a hard bargain in order to buy a little prestige, less likely, therefore, to be able to create the indebtedness which led to the accumulation of wealth.

The development of new products for the market – the paper from the mulberry trees and from the specially grown kōzo rush, saké rice wine, timber, charcoal, etc. – and the increase in rice yields, leaving some surplus to be marketed even after the tax was paid, provided new opportunities for the rich to get richer. They had the capital to act as middle men. They had more leisure to travel and investigate markets. They tended to get their wives from further afield (they had to if they were to marry within their status group, since they were thinner on the ground) and so had more widely scattered kin groups and better sources of news. They were more likely to be able to read and write. They had the status and the confidence and the *savoir-faire* to deal with samurai officials.

And yet there were hazards in being rich. Sometimes the poor were driven to desperation. The best-documented local rising took place in 1836. It started in the silk-weaving areas at the other end of the province, where rice land was scarce, and where many farm families had to buy rice in normal times from the proceeds of their weaving. The harvest of 1833 had been a disaster. The following year and then the following one again were not much better. The price of rice rose. So too – for the weather affected the mulberry also – did the price of cocoons and raw silk which the weavers bought. By the summer of 1836 people were dying of starvation. 'We have not a single grain of any rice or wheat or millet. We have dug up every edible root in the mountains, eaten every edible grass. The people come to us village officials weeping in desperation, clinging to us for help, but we have tried every conceivable measure; we are at our wits' end,' wrote the 'three officials' of one village explaining why they could not fulfil their feudal obligation to take their horses for official duty at the post station. Meanwhile the merchants were believed to be holding rice in their granaries, speculating on a further rise in price. On 20 August, a group of 300 men organized a procession to the house of a merchant. It was said afterwards that their intention was to demand a loan of rice to be repaid later, but by the time they got there their numbers had swollen; the crowd was uncontrollable; the merchant's house was destroyed; his granaries looted. The mob moved on. Within two days they had overwhelmed the small garrison in Sano, the castle town. The news spread; peasants rose all over the province. They were joined by the floating population of porters and day labourers and unemployed who eked out a rough tough bachelor existence in Sano and at the post-stations along the trunk roads. In five days of anarchy, altogether 305 houses were known to have been looted and many burned down.

No one in Shinohata suffered this fate, but the rich of neighbouring villages were not so lucky. An account written some years later, doubtless already somewhat embroidered in the telling, has this description of the rebels' passage through Kakizaka, now the centre of the township to which Shinohata belongs:

First they ravaged the house of the paper dealer Ichibei, then they moved on to Akatsuka's. He had hastily got together a group of hunters with rifles to protect him, but when they saw the size of the attacking mob they dared not shoot. Akatsuka's house was also ravaged and the battle cries of the attackers rang through the hills with a fearsomeness which beggars comparison. The saké brewer Ibei sought to escape by getting neighbours to go to treat with the mob. He offered to feast the whole company, to provide saké and anything they wanted, provided only that they did not destroy his house. There was a clever scoundrel in the advance party who saw an opportunity to enrich himself, and he agreed provided that Ibei undertook to do whatever he was told. So Ibei's household set about preparing the feast. When the rest of the mob arrived they demanded to know why Ibei's house had not been broken into, but they were told of the deal and agreed to await the feast. Then their leader arrived, dressed in the bearskin outer jacket, and set his terms. Two hundred bales of rice and an equal amount of money. Ibei had no option but to agree and the feast was set out.

Then the leader said: further, I want you to make over the rice and the money properly with a bond – declaring your gift, with your signature and the signatures of the 'three officers' of the village as witnesses.

At this Ibei was greatly embarrassed. 'I'll give you the two hundred bales, but as for the bond, please spare me that.' [Presumably it would have laid him open to subsequent prosecution for aiding the rebels.] 'You don't understand,' said the leader. 'We don't want to take the rice to the peasants in Ito-gun [the silk-weaving district where the revolt started]. We intend to distribute it to the poor in this village. That's why we need the bond and the headman's signature.' 'If that's it,' said Ibei, 'then I can promise you I will undertake to do it myself. I will check the family registers from the temple and distribute it fairly, so much per person. I promise you.'

But the leader would not take promises, and so Ibei said he would consult the three officials and see what he could do. Meanwhile the feast had been prepared, and in the interval the scoundrel aforementioned went to Ibei secretly and made him a proposition. 'Give me a hundred gold pieces and I will fix it for you. I know your relatives and the three officials wouldn't agree, but a hundred gold pieces is better than having your house looted; that would cost you more than a hundred gold pieces.'

Eventually Ibei agreed and gave him the money, and when, later, the mob began crowding in and raising their battle cry, the scoundrel rushed out into the garden and jumped up on top of a six-foot barrel which was drying in the yard. 'Wait, wait. Stop it. He's agreed to our demands. There's no need to loot,' he shouted. But nobody took any notice. So then he drew out two swords and started cutting furiously at the air. That attracted attention, whereupon he threw down his swords, raised his arms in the air. 'I've got the bond,' he shouted, beating his breast, and rubbing his hands together. 'Stop! Stop!' And then he pulled out from his kimono a paper handkerchief he happened to

have there and waved it in the air. 'Here it is – and
with the signatures of the head man and the other two
officers.'

And thus with a blank paper bond he pocketed a
hundred pieces of gold and the mob moved on to the
next village.

That, doubtless, is a very garbled account of what actually
took place, but the insistence on legality even in the midst of
revolt, the belief that if the bond was signed no one could take
the rice away from the poor again, has the ring of truth. The
written word carried authority in the Tokugawa village. Although most tenancy agreements, for example, were not written, but simply verbal arrangements, there was a good deal of
account-keeping and bond-writing. One of the houses in the
hamlet established as a branch colony of Shinohata has a set of
ledgers kept by an ancestor who made a journey to Edo in 1760,
apparently on some official village business. One ledger records
all their hotel expenditures, certified by each hotel keeper; another their expenditure on post-horses; another all their purchases, apparently on commission for other villagers. There is
also a bond which they signed, witnessed by seven village
elders, declaring that if there should be any loss of the money
which they were to deliver, not only they but the whole village
would accept responsibility.

The Tokugawa government also relied a good deal – and
increasingly – on the authority of the written word. Instructions
were frequently sent to the headmen on how the villagers
should conduct their affairs. They were required to make two
copies of these instructions, append a paragraph humbly
declaring their full understanding and appreciation of the message and send one copy back, sometimes with the signatures of
every householder, sometimes just those of the three officers,
sometimes, additionally, the signatures of the heads of each
group of eight or ten houses into which the village was divided.
The abandoned 1880-vintage school-house in Shinohata which
was still used in 1955 as a village meeting place had a wooden
box with a number of file copies of such documents. One
probably dates from the last of the great reform attempts in the
Tokugawa administration in 1843. It was obviously addressed

originally to the samurai officials from Edo and sent by them to the villages unchanged.

> The common people are the foundation of the country. Samurai Intendants should be ever sensitive to the sufferings of the people, and make sure that they are not assailed by hunger and by cold.
>
> When the land is prosperous, the common people lapse into luxury. When they lapse into luxury, they are liable to neglect their work. Make sure that they do not become luxurious in their clothing, their food or their dwellings.
>
> There is a wide gulf between the common people and the government. And the government tends to put a wide gulf between it and the common people. You should always have care that such a gulf does not exist.
>
> Take the greatest care of the dikes, river banks, roads and bridges. Report all damages and immediately repair them to forestall a greater disaster. Similarly when there are disputes among the peasants they should both be reported and settled straight away without favour or partiality so that greater troubles do not arise.
>
> To create new rice fields is an excellent thing, but it should be done where it does not cause harm. Sometimes new rice fields take water from older rice fields or use up dry fields or grazing grounds, but this should not be allowed.
>
> It has always been understood that farmers should wear rough clothes and use straw to tie up their hair, yet in recent years they have imperceptibly grown luxurious and forgotten their station. Some wear inappropriate clothes and have their hair done up in oil by a barber, and whereas it was the custom for farmers simply to wear wide-brimmed straw hats and straw shoulder-coverings in rain, now some have umbrellas and water-proofs. This increases their cash expenditure and the villages change character. Some leave the village for other work, and when one farmer leaves the village and does not pay his taxes, the burden falls on the others so that all suffer. The Intendants and their

clerks should set an example in this matter by dressing simply, and what applies to the clerks applies even more so to the farmers. They should be reminded of their long-standing traditions. Barber shops in the villages, farmers engaging in petty commerce in their spare time, are abuses to be corrected. Henceforth they should eschew these luxurious ways, live simply and devote themselves diligently to farming.

The attempt to turn the clock back was, of course, doomed to failure. The very growth of literacy which made such edicts plausible instruments of government was a product of a slowly rising level of living. Schools increased in number and more families came to be able to afford paper and ink and the presents with which teachers were requited for their services. More families could look beyond mere survival as their life objective and aspire to status and respectability – to the family pride expressed in gravestones, to having a son who knew his letters. Towards the end of the Tokugawa period the Shinohata headman ran a reading and writing school for village children as part of his performance of his benevolent duties. When he died in the 1890s a stone was erected in his memory in one corner of the village. It was subscribed for by his former pupils – by the 'foolish children he trained to the brush' as they describe themselves in the inscription in a flowery Chinese phrase.

Probably, however, the Tokugawa government could have gone on for a good deal longer alternately pushing against the tide of history or trying somehow to capture for itself a better share of the new wealth that the peasants and merchant producers were creating. But they could not cope both with these problems and with the foreign threat too. The seclusion of the country was now a hallowed tradition, as well as the only reliable guarantee of internal stability. Unable, in the face of foreign battleships, to fulfil its promise to maintain that seclusion, to stand firm against the foreigners' demand that the country be opened to trade, the government lost legitimacy, confidence and authority. The alliance which overthrew its power and established a new central government was dominated by younger samurai who knew something about the international society into which Japan was being dragged. The

'Meiji Restoration' was indeed in some senses a restoration. The new government claimed to be re-establishing the centralized government system of the pre-feudal age. The Emperor Meiji was both to reign and to rule as none of his ancestors had actually done for the eight centuries of their ritual seclusion in Kyoto. But their more important goal was to make Japan strong, economically and militarily; at first simply to stave off the threat of colonization by the predatory Western powers, later to gain for Japan the position of equality in international society of which the 'unequal treaties' – the treaties which gave foreigners consular jurisdiction over their own nationals in Japanese ports – symbolized the denial.

The pace of change quickened in Shinohata. Farmers were declared owners of the land they tilled – or the land that tenants tilled for them. They were declared free to sell it, free to change their occupation at will. They were given the right to have surnames and to ride horses. Bowler hats and soap and pocket watches and the habit of eating beef; beer, lemonade, steel pens, glass bottles and leather saddles; hops and tomatoes that were called 'send-you-mad aubergines'; green peppers and grapes and Irish potatoes – the new world was full of all kinds of curious new objects to buy and new crops to try. Farmers were exhorted to grow more mulberry; the market for silk exports to America was expanding. They were exhorted to plant their rice in straight rows so that they could weed the fields with simple rotary weeding machines; to make long narrow seed-beds so that they could reach to pick the insects off them every day; to try new rice varieties; to select their seed; to try new fertilizers. And if they could make money in some trading adventure, or some new cottage industry, that was no longer in any way a reprehensible failure to observe the duties of their proper station. That was now called 'productive enterprise' and being a 'success'.

The old feudal tax in kind was replaced by a land tax fixed in money terms, and farmers were now exposed to the vagaries of the market. They had to sell their rice to the merchant and pay their tax from the proceeds, which was fine when the price of rice rose because the taxes were fixed, but less advantageous when the price fell again. Those were the years, the low-price years, when the poorer farmer might be forced to sell a field and become the tenant of the landlord who bought it, or send a daughter to one of the silk-reeling factories in the next prefecture, counting on the advance against her wages to see the family through to the next harvest.

The people of Shinohata had never been much aware of being Japanese because no other kind of people had much impinged on their consciousness, but now things were different. Young men were summoned to serve in the Emperor's army; it was now the conscription medical exam, not any traditional ritual, which marked the accession to manhood. Shinohata and three neighbouring hamlets were merged into a new village unit one of whose first tasks was to establish a state primary school, where the children learned to read and write, to revere the Emperor, to play their part in the national task of making Japan strong and 'civilized', to sing patriotic songs celebrating the victory of Japanese arms against the Chinese and the Russians. The village office became more insistent on the proper registration of births and deaths. (One old lady, still alive, was born in 1892 to one of the last of the Shinohata families to be lackadaisical about such things. Her parents took five years before they got round to registering her birth – a fact which she had cause to regret when the old-age pension scheme was started ten years ago.) Newspapers began to appear in the village, and, after the establishment of elected district councils and then, in 1890, of a national Diet, so did political parties – though at first property qualifications confined the vote to landlords and richer farmers. A regular horse bus already ran up the valley's main road by the turn of the century – and the rough jagged clinker with which the workmen constantly made up the road surface played havoc with the straw sandals of the lesser mortals who still had to walk. In 1904, on the eve of the Russo–Japanese war, the railway came up the other side of the valley, and the school children were taken on the five-mile trek over the bridge and up the winding road through the break in the cliffs to see their first steam locomotive.

3

Farmers of the Emperor

O-matsu, who was twenty-four in 1922 when the electric light came to Shinohata, remembers the electricians as fearsome strangers. 'If you get into conversation with them and say anything to offend, they might go away and not fix the light in, so better just not to talk to them,' was the advice her mother gave her. For women, especially, the world outside the microcosm of the village was a distant awesome place, but Shinohata was by then very much a part of a larger universe. The bright sons of richer farmers could hope to go to a middle school in Sano, perhaps even to a university. Some would join the urban middle classes and come home only for the annual ancestral festivals. Some would return as school teachers or officials of the village office, the railway or the post office, to lead a comfortable life in the village elite, supplementing their salaries with the rents of a few acres of tenanted land. The younger sons of poorer farmers grew up expecting to leave the village to work in the growing towns, and some of their daughters who went to work in textile factories stayed in the towns to marry. With slowly rising living standards and better public hygiene – though there were still bad dysentery and even cholera epidemics in the late nineteenth century, and tuberculosis remained a common fear until the 1950s – more children survived childhood. Younger sons had less chance of being adopted as son and heir of a childless farm family; only a few stayed in the village and established themselves as independent branch families. The feudal land registers showed ninety-three households in Shinohata and its two branch hamlets in 1803, ninety-one in 1830, ninety-five in 1835. The number had grown only to 135 a century later.

Living standards rose only slowly, however. In 1911, of the nearly 700 young men who appeared for the conscription medical in the county only 261 were declared fully fit for service and another 182 were placed in the 'useful in an emergency' upper and lower division of the second class. Eleven years later this 65 per cent pass rate had improved to 76 per cent (though standards may not have been consistent). In those same eleven years the number of young men reaching the age of twenty-one in the county increased from 700 to 1,000. Children still died, however, of measles and whooping cough and dysentery. A couple now in their seventies count themselves very exceptionally lucky – or, more accurately, count it a matter of considerable pride – that every one of their ten children survived to adulthood.

From a world in which everything depended on the harvest they had moved to a world in which everything depended on the harvest *and* prices. The twenties and the early thirties were lean years. Imports of cheap rice from Korea and Formosa depressed prices at home, and the collapse of the American silk market in the late twenties made things worse. 'Nearly half a day it would take to walk the horse loaded with cocoons up through the cliffs to the cocoon auction, and then to be offered a yen for a kan! Nearly four kilogrammes for one yen, twenty or thirty yen for a whole crop! Some people brought the cocoons back in anger, but there was no way of getting a better price.' Some farmers just gave up and used their mulberry to fertilize their rice fields; others who could not afford such a cavalier reaction tried to produce more cocoons to compensate for the fall in price. The merchant, the auctioneer at the cocoon market, were the powerful ones. Even now an old lady reminiscing about these days, having said 'utta' – 'we sold them for . . .', corrects herself and uses the more deferential phrase 'katte moratta' – 'they were good enough to buy them for . . .'

Wages in the silk-reeling factories, too, went down from nearly a yen a day in the early twenties to about 60 sen a decade later. But still, for those who had to buy it, rice was cheaper too, and a daughter's earnings could make all the difference to a family's livelihood.

Old Tanetoshi was a funny old man. He kept his sense of humour although they were as poor as poor could be. That was his big joke: 'That old clock up there,' he used to say, 'used to go "shak-kin shak-kin" [debts, debts] but since our Suzu went to the machines it started ticking "cho-kin, cho-kin" [savings, savings].' Or: 'Look at our old woman,' he'd say, and she'd be sewing away in the evenings at her dressmaking work for the richer farmers, 'Look at our old woman, crushing lice' – because of the way she'd be going through a hem at a terrific speed, thumbnail to thumbnail.

Farmers adjusted to the situation by learning to do with less money, postponed a marriage or a roof repair, wore their clothes longer, mixed a higher proportion of barley in the daily rice in order to sell more rice in the market, gave up some of the once luxury purchases like soap and sugar that had become part of their daily lives. The one former luxury which had become a necessity was kerosene – the fuel for the tiny lamps which made it possible for the women to sew kimono for a richer neighbour on winter evenings, or for the whole family to thresh rice (or rather 'pull' it through the ear-stripping comb), or to make straw ropes and straw bales and straw sandals to earn a few extra yen – though kerosene was superseded in 1922 when the electric light came and for 50 sen a month a dim 'ten-candle' bulb would come on at dusk, and turn off automatically in the morning, and having two, three or even four bulbs became a new measure of status in the village.

Times were hard, but with better techniques, better varieties, better yields, nobody actually starved, though some got into debt.

O-Sasa had come from a good family, but her husband was no good and she was a hopeless manager. She would come for a pot-full of rice in the evenings time and time again and get things on credit from the shop, and the debt would mount up – 5 yen, 10 yen. I remember grandmother telling us, she'd go round to try and collect and there would be O-Sasa, as cool as could be, gazing up at the stars through the holes in the thatch.

'Take it,' she'd say, 'take what you can find. Take the house, take everything. I don't care.'

There may have been some distress sales of small tracts of woodland at this time, but there was little movement of cropland as there had been in the 1880s when farmers were first badly hit by the fluctuations of the market. For one thing, a good number of the poorer families no longer had any land to sell. The process by which the rich got richer and the poor poorer through the concentration of land had reached a kind of 'steady state'. What would have counted as an ideal holding at about this time would be something like five acres – half in riceland, half in dry fields, mostly mulberry – big enough to bring in a decent income, small enough to be manageable by a man and his wife and a working son with perhaps a certain amount of daily help at peak times. In fact, on the eve of the Second World War, only fourteen out of Shinohata's sixty-four households owned that much. Four of these, with more than twelve acres apiece, constituted the village's upper class. They themselves cultivated little of their land. In every case the eldest son was away: a railway engineer, an insurance office clerk, a medical secretary, an irrigation engineer in Korea. Their parents, all of them now getting on in years, looked after one or two acres themselves, though they hired a lot of help to do it; there was never any dearth of villagers willing to work for 30 or 40 sen a day – the price of about one and a half kilogrammes of rice. The rest they rented to other households in the village, this field to that farmer, that one to another. In this way an energetic tenant might get a full four or five acres to cultivate, but a rent fixed at two bales of rice for a field which sometimes yielded less than three bales and never much more than four left him with little to show for his labours – even if it was accepted that he had a right to plead for some remission of rent in years when the yield was so bad as to leave him with a good deal less than a third of the crop if he paid the two bales in full.

Thirteen of Shinohata's households had no land of their own at all. Most of them had managed to get tenancy of an acre or two – enough to be self-sufficient in rice and beans, the bulwark against starvation and the minimum condition for a position of basic respect in the village. For the rest they got their cash – and for every working day their mid-day meals – from the richer farmers who hired them to work on their fields or about the house. One or two families, lacking the few basic implements to farm, subsisted entirely by such casual labour. One or two others had a skill – as mason, carpenter or plasterer – which enabled them to claim higher wages on the days when they could find work to do. None of them got the very few steady jobs available – at the post office or at the timber merchant's in the village. Those went to the slightly better off who had more land, more status, more influence. Of those who did still own crop land, fifteen had an acre or less and were not in fact much better off than the landless; another twelve had between one and two acres and still needed to rent some land to make a decent living. Then there were about a third of the villagers – the solid, respectable-farmer, core of the village as it were, who had enough land to make what counted as a decent living, some with an acre or two to spare to let out to other farmers. Some, in fact, both rented land from others and rented out some of their own land, either to consolidate their fields closer together or because they had lent a field at a time when they had not much labour in the family – perhaps to a relative from whom it was hard to take it back – and then needed more land when a son left school or got married and added his bride to the family's workforce. Altogether, to use the categories that were used later in the land reform, the households in Shinohata divided like this.

Landlords – renting out more land than they farmed   5
Owner-farmers – owning at least 90 per cent of the land
  they farmed and some of them also renting out an acre
  or two   17
Owner-tenants – owning 50–90 per cent of the land they
  farmed   12
Tenant-owners – owning 10–50 per cent of the land they
  farmed   17
Tenants – owning less than 10 per cent of the land they
  farmed   13

There was a similar inequality in the ownership of wood-land – the reserve capital from which, once in a generation or so, one could sell off trees to pay for a funeral or a wedding, or use them to rebuild the house. Two of the landlord families had nearly fifty acres and another four families had more than twenty-five. About twenty families had none at all, with most of the rest owning between one and ten.

But Shinohata was a place where the division between rich and poor was still accepted as part of the order of nature. Not so in other parts of Japan. In the more commercialized areas to the west, where there were more absentee landlords, more formal, hard-bargain contracts and less cohesive village communities, class warfare began to rear its head. Beginning in the last years of the First World War, tenants had started banding together, bargaining collectively with landlords to demand reductions in rent. At first they asked for more generous remissions in years of bad harvest; later, as success bred greater boldness, permanent reductions in rent rates. In some places tenant unions were formed as continuing organizations, and in 1922 these were linked together, with the help of sympathetic urban intellectuals, in a national tenants' league. Nor was this the only thing to alarm the Japanese establishment – the bureaucracy and the political parties (dominated in these years of limited suffrage by landlords and industrialists) which had been allowed a tentative share of power. The founding of a Communist Party reflected the intellectuals' increasing fascination with the Russian Revolution; scattered trade unions formed a National Congress; strikes became more frequent; young scholars back from their two years' study in Weimar Germany spread an interest in Marxism in the heart of the Imperial Universities.

The poison spread down even to the schools. '20 November 1932!' began the 1933 prize-winning New Year's essay in the local Sano newspaper. 'Not all the glorious half-century history of our prefecture's educational progress will suffice to obliterate the shame of what took place on that day – the day when the gleaming altar of Citizen Education was defiled, the day of disaster when the Bolshevization of the teaching profession became clear, the day the storm struck with the news that six middle-school teachers had been "taken for questioning".'

The other prize essay, though, on the Protection of Motherhood, while also very decorously patriotic, amounted to a firm plea for the legal and sexual equality of women. ('By which, of course, I do not mean that women should have the same sexual freedom as men. Rather that women should have the right to expect the same pure chastity of their husbands as society expects of them.') In some limited respects there was, at least during the twenties and early thirties, a shift in the centre of gravity of opinion towards greater tolerance, greater egalitarianism. Economically, too, the new awakening brought concessions: measures to stabilize rice prices, a conciliation law for the 'fair' settlement of disputes between landlords and tenants (but not, as some of the 'advanced thinkers' in the bureaucracy wanted, a law to legitimize tenant unions and collective bargaining; the point was to damp down conflict and restore harmony, not to bring conflict into the open). There was also a small loan scheme to allow tenants (rather expensively) to buy their land. In 1925 there was universal suffrage which, in formal terms at least, made the poorest tenant as much a first-class citizen as a landlord. The other part of the Establishment's answer was repression: a Peace Preservation Law which permitted draconian punishment for any attack on the principle of private property, and gave the reinforced police wide powers to control meetings and publications, and to ban organizations.

Although the more commercialized central areas of the prefecture were a major centre of tenant unrest, and one of the tenants' leaders who later became a member of the Diet once came up to the next hamlet to organize the tenants of an absentee landlord in a legendary dispute, Shinohata itself felt little of this tension – or at least little of it showed on the surface. This place was too feudal for that, said some of the younger men later. The landlords here were pretty considerate and understanding, said others. Shinohata people are 'round', 'have no corners on them', is another favourite, and more neutral, way of putting it. Certainly the relation between landlord and tenant was not an impersonal contractual one; they were also neighbours, they were also patron and client, and sometimes they were also kin. It's hard to quarrel with people you have to come face to face with every day, they say. Besides which many a tenant depended on a landlord not just for land to cultivate, but for the chance of extra work on his fields in the busy season, for permission to cut fertilizer grass from his woodland, or to make charcoal from his trees, as well as for the benevolence of an emergency loan. Shinohata was not seething with militant antagonism. The Nakatani police station half way up the valley was reinforced with an enlarged detachment of 'Special Duty' police, but it found few 'dangerous thoughts' in Shinohata to investigate.

Elsewhere the more dangerous thinkers went to gaol. The Communist Party was suppressed. The tenant leagues became peasants' leagues, more radical in theory because they attacked the system – spoke against the evils of the capitalist system which kept the price of rice low and of fertilizer high – but less explosive in practice because such high-level issues diverted interest from the immediate struggle of landlord and tenant within the village. The depression of the early thirties increased the tension within Japanese society, but when the major explosions came, the Young Officers who sparked them off with their attempted *coups d'état* and assassinations of Prime Ministers – although they claimed that the 'plight of the villages' was one of their main concerns and did, in fact, prompt some further relief measures – only paved the way for their seniors, the army high command, to gain increasing dominance over the civilian establishment. The Japan of the thirties was increasingly militarized as army pressure shifted the centre of gravity of Japan's foreign policy. The traditional goal of gaining equality of power and prestige with the Western powers remained unchanged; but now it was to be achieved not through peaceful competition, alliances and co-operativeness in maintaining the *status quo* of existing imperialisms, but by conquest and force of arms and the enlargement of Japan's own empire at the Western powers' expense. As the Manchurian Incident was followed by increasing talk of the threat of Russian communism, by increasingly ugly incidents in China and finally by the outbreak of the China War in 1937, leading inexorably on to Pearl Harbor, internal repression gave place to mobilization – and nowhere more effectively than in the villages.

The villages, after all, were effectively organized – vertically, horizontally and in every way. Perhaps only China since the revolution (using the same Confucian-culture box of tricks) has ever perfected to the same extent as Japan in the 1930s the art of the 'voluntary' organization that everyone automatically belongs to. There was, in this hamlet of sixty households, the

Shinohata Youth Organization for those between seventeen and twenty-five, the Voluntary Fire Brigade for the next age group, the Army Reserve Association, the Housewives' Association, the Hygiene Association (created in the nineteenth century to organize preventive measures against epidemic diseases), the School Parents' Association, the Shrine Worshippers' Association, the Cocoon Rearers' Association, the General Agriculture Practice Association – not to mention the general-purpose Shinohata Hamlet Association together with its sub-organs, the five ten-to-twelve-household neighbourhood groups into which the hamlet was divided. All were mobilized to play their full part in a Japan united for Victory – mobilized under the active leadership of the owner farmers and under the patronage of the landlords. The Housewives' Association learned patriotic songs and dances, and new ways of pickling otherwise inedible foods, knitted for the troops, sent them body-belts into which every woman in the village had put at least one prayerful 'come-home-safe-and-victorious' stitch. The Hygiene Association collected money to buy bandages. The Hamlet Association and the Youth Association organized the send-off parties for conscripts; the fire brigade did voluntary labour digging up pine roots in the forest and taking them to the railway for a factory on the coast which extracted from them pitifully small quantities of supposedly useful resin. The school-children were sent into the mountains to collect plants that only the very oldest people knew of as famine foods to be dried and sent to the towns. Most of the younger men went off to the war, and eight of them, from Shinohata's sixty households, did not come back.

I once asked some high-school students what period other than the present they would choose to have lived in. They said: 'The war; we hear so much about it; it would be interesting to know what it was really like.' The war is certainly a frequent subject of reminiscence: partly because it is the most recent period of the old regime, before the world was turned upside down by the post-war reforms. Men seem not to talk very much about their experiences as soldiers, or perhaps there's a certain reticence in talking about it in the presence of somebody who was on the other side; there are no veterans' associations to keep alive nostalgia for war-time camaraderie, and recent nationalist revisionism has not much altered the interpretation of the war which took root in the immediate shock of defeat; it was not just a lost war, and not just a foolish war, but somehow also a guilty war.

'I was called up for the third time eleven days before the end of the war, when they were scraping the barrel. Nobody knew what to do when the end of the war was declared. The officers ordered us to collect all the documents for burning, and then they cancelled the order and set about remaking the stores documents that had been burned. I suppose the reason was that the Japanese army had done bad things in China and we expected the Americans to do the same here. I was in China, too. We used to sit and talk in the evenings. What the hell are we here for, we used to say. But we really believed we were there for China's sake. But the Chinese weren't grateful. And we, well, we all were expecting to die, after all. We were all trained not to expect to come back, so it didn't matter much what you did. We saw all the Chinese as enemies. Of course, after a while, when we began to be able to speak a bit of Chinese, we realized that they were human beings just like us, but then when the fighting got tough you forgot all about that. I did some pretty bad things, too. You were doing it "the other side of death", you see.'

For others, the war was an interesting adventure; a lost interlude in a farming life, still seen in retrospect through farmers' eyes.

'It was interesting enough in China. I thought of coming back to stay there once: there were some civilian traders in the part where I was who were making a lot of money. What a dirty, unhygienic place China is, though, and what poor agriculture! Really low productivity, but an easy leisurely life. They never did any work in the middle of the day. From about 10.30 to 4 they would just be lying around. Two meals a day, they had, one at the beginning and one at the end of the rest period. It was interesting seeing other countries, but I was too worried about how they were managing at home to enjoy it.'

Some, indeed, had cause to be worried.

We had a hard time, then. So many of the men were away; everybody was so busy just keeping up with things. The houses that lost their menfolk had a really hard time. Nakanobu, for instance, his wife was left with a sick mother and four young children and she the only one able to work. We weren't much better off: father wasn't called up but he was so busy with all these organizations, all his public duties. He was the shrine officer and on the temple committee and then the fire brigade committee, but the thing that took up most of his time was when they organized the Younger Mature Men's Branch of the Imperial Rule Assistance Association and he was made president and had to organize all these voluntary activities, like helping war widows with their farms and going for voluntary labour to help clear the sites for war factories. He had to help organize the send-off parties for the people who were called up, too. First there'd be a sort of feast at the house, with everybody bringing their own cakes; then we'd all go off to the shrine to pray for their safe return. A priest would come to say prayers over them properly and then in the end it would be: 'Everyone face towards the Imperial Palace! Deepest bow!' Funny, we hardly think about the Emperor nowadays from one year's end to another, but we did then, that's for sure. We were always bowing to the Emperor for one thing or the other.

I remember one of the saddest things. Yoshisada: he got married early in the war; it was one of the first of the simplified weddings. There was a hamlet decision to cut down expense on weddings and funerals. You only invited close relatives and the five neighbours ['the ones on either side and the three across the road']. Less than half a tiny bottle of saké for each man, and everybody came in work clothes. Well Yoshisada got married and they had a little daughter and soon after his wife died. His parents were both dead so there was only Yoshisada and his little daughter and he looked after her. But then later on he was called up. I still remember his send-off. From the shrine, the man would get on his horse – we always got the finest horse in the village for that – and the whole village would see him off down as far as the temporary bridge over the river, and from there just one or two would go with him up through the cliffs to the station. I remember with Yoshisada, his little girl – she must have been about five at the time – not understanding what it was all about: only that her father was somehow going away – clinging to the leg of the horse shouting 'don't go!'. All the women were in tears.

Father wasn't called up, but our horse was. When the war started in China they needed all the horses they could get and the army requisitioning authorities came round collecting them. Father rode ours down to the barracks at Nakatani. He stayed down there in the barracks for two nights so that he could see him off when he was loaded on to the train to be taken to China. The trouble with our horses was that they weren't trained properly. There were hardly any motor-cars up here, but if once in a while one did come when you were coming back with the horse loaded up with grass you had to look out. As like as not, the horse would rear up and the load would go off into a rice field. So they started special training sessions for the horses every Sunday morning down at the school playground. We lost a fine horse, though. Not like the one I bought once, when father was away for the day. A broker came round and offered me a horse for 70 yen for a quick sale – really worth 80 he said. I don't know what was wrong with him, but he wouldn't eat properly and he had no strength. We were lucky to sell him for 40 yen a few months later. After that father bought an ox. They're slower than horses for ploughing, but they're stronger and at the end of the day you probably get just as much ploughing out of them, because they stick at it. They're not so delicate as horses, either: don't get so many sicknesses. And the army doesn't requisition oxen.

It was hard keeping up with the work, with so many of the men away. We had a hop field and the weeds grew shoulder-high. You almost broke your sickle on the weeds. The school-children were mobilized to help with the weeding and once we got people from the emergency factory down the road – when the factory ran out of supplies or something. We grew sweet potatoes in all the rice fields, then, as a winter crop. You cut them in strips and dried them and that was all we had for snacks. That was when they started compulsory requisitioning of rice and beans, too. You couldn't sell them freely as you used to. Some people were smart, though, and kept some back to sell on the black market, though that was much more after the war. Some people were very smart. There was timber requisitioning, too – at a terribly low price – but some people managed to keep their trees and really made a packet when the prices soared after the war. Some people made money out of the refugees, too. We had an old couple living in our store-house; the daughter was at school with the child of a relative of ours and they asked if we could let them have the barn. Pretty cramped they were, but it was weather-proof enough and they were pleased enough. Better than the fire-bomb raids in Tokyo. We used to laugh, though, to see the old lady going up to the woods to collect firewood with a big furoshiki [wrapping cloths used for small decorous presents]. When we went collecting firewood we'd go with lengths of rope and come home with bundles piled high on a carrying frame on our back: she looked so funny with her little furoshiki-full, as if she'd been out shopping.

The end of the war came as a shock to Shinohata. Few villagers had any connections with the circles in Tokyo where people were reasonably well-informed and could just occasionally trust each other enough to talk freely. When the Emperor broadcast his rescript with the famous phrase about the war situation having turned 'not necessarily to Japan's advantage', and announcing the acceptance of the Potsdam terms, nobody understood the convoluted literary phrases spoken in the Emperor's high-pitched voice.

> I'd just been posted to a newly formed engineers' battalion. We had no equipment and I wondered where it would come from but I never doubted that somehow it would come. Then came 15 August and the broadcast. We just didn't understand what it said. The young officer in charge of us told us categorically that the Emperor had said we were going to go on fighting to the last ditch.

A good number of the men were back in time for the harvest. It was not a good harvest because there was precious little fertilizer to be had by then, but at least the farmers had food, unlike the people who came out from the towns in the slow battered run-down trains and tramped the villages with their rucksacks trying to exchange their family heirlooms and wives' kimonos for food. In a way it was a boom time for the farmers. Even if they didn't make much money – and money was not much use, given the rate of the inflation, which reduced the yen to about a fiftieth of its original value in a couple of years – they did add marginally to their wealth and at least it was very satisfying to have the urban middle class treating them with great deference instead of with their usual lofty condescension.

But if they were boom times, they were uncertain and confused times, too. Was it proper to steal the big drum cans from the army supply dump in the woods south of the village? Some felt that all law and order had in effect broken down. It was fair game. Some openly distributed some of the sunflower oil they had stolen among the neighbours – who got sick when they tried making deep-fried tempura because they were not used to such rich oils. Others were thought to have buried a can secretly in their back yard. Three brothers from the hamlet's notoriously feckless family made themselves seriously ill from drinking methyl alcohol from a stolen drum and one of them permanently damaged his sight and wore dark glasses for the rest of his short life.

But the responsible men of the hamlet, the solid core of thirty or so older men who had already done their year's term as head of the hamlet, refrained from anything much more than a little vigorous black-market enterprise. There was uncertainty and confusion, certainly. The newspapers were full of democracy and freedom, and the abolition of feudalism. The children's history textbooks had a few jingoistic pages snipped out and paragraphs inked over. For a while children learned nothing either about the unique superiority of Japan's ancient traditions or about the glorious twentieth-century pursuit of her national destiny through war. Eventually the new textbooks appeared – not quite the whiggish version intended by the Americans who wrote the guidelines, in terms of the gradual forward march of liberal democracy, but rather (for it was the dormant influences of Weimar Germany in the 1920s which surfaced to become the dominant trend among Japanese historians) a pop-Marxist version in terms of exploitation, class struggle, and the inevitable succession of feudalism, absolutism, capitalism and beyond.

An occasional Civil Affairs Team jeep would come to the village office to check up on the progress of 'grass-roots democracy'. Everyone who had been prominent in the patriotic organizations which had mobilized the wartime citizenry, particularly the Imperial Rule Assistance Association into which all the pre-war political parties had been merged, was 'purged', forbidden indefinitely (in the event until the 'depurgings' of the early 1950s) to hold any public office. It was certainly unsettling. So much had Japan been a unitary state, so much had all morality, all ethics, all organizational rules been part of a social order built up around the Emperor, so much had the needs of an embattled Japan, seeking its rightful place in a part hostile, part grateful world, been made the touchstone of all social arrangements, that defeat seemed to remove the whole underpinning of the social order. Japan seemed no longer to have goals, guiding principles or *raison d'être*. The awesome Emperor was reduced to a puny timid figure in the famous newspaper photograph, a visitor to General MacArthur's office, dressed with formal deference and dwarfed by his enormous genial host wearing an open-necked shirt and sucking a pipe.

But in Shinohata there was a substratum of order which did not depend on the superstructure of the Japanese state into which it had been integrated, but had deeper roots – roots in the part-hierarchical, part-egalitarian solidarity of the traditional self-governing village. It was a testimony to the strength of this cohesion that it survived the stresses of – and substantially modified the operation of – the land reform: the most substantial shake-up the hamlet had received since the famines of the 1830s.

'Doomed to disappear' is what Japanese historians are inclined to say about the tenancy system. It had played its part in the process of primitive accumulation which laid the foundations of Japanese capitalism and, as a remnant of feudalism, was destined to be superseded as that capitalism matured. For once the teleological metaphors seem justified. Certainly, plans for reform had been discussed for a long time within the Japanese bureaucracy. The high level of rents (sustained not only by the market demand for tenancies, but in part by conventional, and in origin feudal, notions of what was acceptable subordination) kept tenants so poor that they were bound to be inefficient producers; and a Japan which intended to fight wars could not afford inefficient producers. The extreme inequality which it entailed might have been acceptable enough in a feudal world in which the different 'orders' of society had different legal privileges and different social functions; it was a source of continuous unrest in a society in which the enactment of universal suffrage had established a basic equality of citizenship. An embattled Japan could not afford such threats to its solidarity.

In any case, as time went on, the landlords had less and less to lose from an enforced redistribution of land rights, especially in those areas where tenant leagues had been most active. One landlord in the same prefecture as Shinohata, historians have found from analysing his diary, spent thirty-six days and the equivalent of 15 per cent of his rent revenues on legal proceedings against his tenants in one year – and ended up with 10 per cent of his rice uncollectable at the end of it. And even landlords like those of Shinohata, who were not involved in disputes to this extent, were obliged to lower rent levels somewhat. What definitely altered the situation, though, were the policies which the Ministry adopted during the war. When compulsory food requisitioning was started in 1942, the rice was collected directly from the tenant grower and the landlord was paid in cash at the standard price for however many bales were due to him. As the war-time inflation proceeded, however, instead of raising the standard price, the Ministry added a grower's incentive payment which by 1945 was a good deal larger than the standard price itself, and went straight into the tenant's pocket. In effect, the landlord was getting his rent in 1942 prices, the tenant was getting 1945 prices for his share of the crop, plus the difference between 1942 and 1945 prices on the landlord's share.

Ministry of Agriculture officials had already drafted a land redistribution measure in the early years of the war. When the war came to an end and the age of democracy and freedom was announced, the only question that remained was how sweeping the land reform would be – how much residual land it would leave with landlords and what would be the scale of compensation paid to them. A first land reform bill presented to the Diet within four months of the defeat would have counted as radical before the war, but (for there was still a substantial representation of landlords, especially in the House of Peers) mild by the standards of what followed. The first draft came a few days before (and was apparently not connected with) a ringing declaration by General MacArthur about liberating farmers from the shackles which had bound them through centuries of feudal oppression. A revised law, passed the following year, was a good deal stiffer.

As it applied locally (acreage limits varied in different parts of the country), the law's main provisions were as follows. Absentee landlords were to lose all their land. Landlords who lived in the same administrative area as their land could keep up to an acre and a half leased out to tenants, but they could not keep more than five acres in total (what they farmed themselves plus what they still leased out) and the rent on their remaining tenanted land was controlled at a level which turned out, when the inflation had run its full course, to amount to a mere 2 or 3 per cent of the yield. They were to receive compensation according to a formula which was not unreasonable when it was devised, but by the time the inflation had reduced the currency to about a fiftieth of its 1945 value came to the price of a few packets of cigarettes per acre. It amounted, in effect, to outright confiscation. The land so 'liberated' (to use what soon came to be the standard word) was to be given to the tenants who were actually cultivating it on the day in October 1945 when news of an impending reform first appeared in the press – providing that they were already cultivating at least an acre, thus creating the presumption that they would be competent farmers. The application of the law was entrusted to a committee formed in each village. The tenants elected five tenants, the owner-farmers three owner-farmers, and the landlords two landlords. The committee chose its chairman from among its members. On the local committee, one of the landlords and one of the tenant representatives was from Shinohata; the others from the other six hamlets which made up the administrative village.

The main job of the committee was to establish who was cultivating what on that crucial day in October, and who was a resident and who was an absentee landlord on that date. If it was only a matter of establishing the truth, that would have posed no problems. But the truth needed to be rearranged somewhat to accord with the local sense of justice. For example, there were two families in Shinohata who were strictly absentee landlords entitled to keep none of the two or three acres apiece which they had left in the hands of tenants when they themselves went to settle as officials in the colonies. Towards the end of 1945 they came back penniless, in one case with nothing better than the converted barn of a relative to live in. It obviously made compassionate sense, when the tenant could be persuaded to agree, to declare them as resident landlords on that date, entitled to keep a couple of fields – enough, at least, to grow their own subsistence rice. Similarly, the fact that Nakanobu's wife, left with two and a half acres and four young children when her husband was called up to fight, had rented two of those acres to neighbours did not seem like a reasonable justification for letting those fields pass into the neighbours' ownership when Nakanobu came back (though, reasonable or not, there were some of those neighbours who said that what the law said was what the law intended and stood on their legal rights).

But the bigger headaches were caused by the real landlords, in Shinohata the four who owned more than twelve acres. They would be entitled to keep up to five acres if they were culti-

vating them directly. But, of course, they were directly cultivating only a fraction of that amount. Were their tenants, used
to being brow-beaten by their landlords, or used to being
dependent on their possibly arbitrary benevolence, going to
refuse to let their landlord (bombed out of Tokyo, job gone)
to take back his land (*his* land, after all) into his own cultivation?
And to claim that he had in fact already done so the season
before? Some of the tenants were indeed prepared to stand on
their rights. Most said that of course they saw the landlord's
point of view, and they were fully conscious of how much they
owed to him for all his consideration in the past, and they
realized what a long past it was, how many generations their
ancestors had been indebted to his ancestors, and so on and so
forth, but he would realize how poor they were and how many
children they had and how much they depended on those fields.
Surely he could ask some of his other tenants who were better
off than they were to give up their land.

The main job of the committee members was to mediate, to
act as go-betweens in such negotiations. In most cases, some
kind of compromise was patched up. None of the landlords
was reduced quite to the tiny holding that a strict application
of the law would have meant for them. Sometimes disputes
were fought out in the committee, with a landlord representative giving one version and a tenant representative giving
another. There were some cases, though, where a tenant from
one hamlet rented land from a landlord in another. In such
cases there was no chance of appeal to the ethic of neighbourly
harmony and hamlet cohesion to ensure that matters were all,
as people said, 'roundly wrapped up' not 'leaving any corners
sticking out'. One or two such cases involving Shinohata
families made it clear that the principle of hamlet solidarity was
a good deal stronger than any burgeoning sense of class consciousness which the reform, building on the dissensions of the
twenties and thirties, might have helped to create. The Shinohata tenant representative and landlord representative both
stood up for the rights of a Shinohata tenant against a landlord
from another hamlet, and for a Shinohata landlord against a
'foreign' tenant. If you live in Shinohata, the 'outside world'
begins three hundred yards down the road, and in any case,
given the fine gradations of wealth and mixtures of tenancy

and ownership, the electoral divisions into tenant, owner-farmer and landlord were somewhat artificial (except for the small number of families at both extremes – those who owned a lot and those who owned nothing) and less meaningful social categories than 'from our hamlet', 'one of our relatives', or 'one of our neighbourhood *kumi*'.

So, too, the changes which the land reform brought were less than revolutionary. Gontarō, the landlord representative on the reform committee, in his role as the village's intellectual and only university graduate, was fond of talking in large rhetorical terms of the new age of democracy and equality and the need to abandon all out-moded feudal ways. The other landlord representative in the next hamlet even became secretary of the local branch of the new Socialist Party. Nobody was violently thrown down from seats of power and privilege, and the richer families still had their larger holdings of woodland which the reform did not affect. But there was a significant shift in the spectrum of wealth. Nearly two-thirds of the families in the village were better off by at least a field or two. Over two-thirds ended up owning and farming between two and six acres.

So, by 1955, when I first lived in Shinohata, it had become a hamlet of owner-farmers; the well-off were those who had a son established in a well-paying salaried job; the poor were the few households of younger sons who had lost their livelihood in the war and come back to a rented barn or a make-shift hut. Not having been tenants and so having no claim to land, they survived by day-labour in the forests and on the construction sites, perhaps growing their own family's rice on a half-acre of land rented from a relative.

Nobody subjectively felt that the world had fundamentally changed either. Their holdings were small, they still had to work hard to make a living. By 1955 average rice yields were improving thanks to more reliable crop strains and better fertilizers and insecticides, but the labour-intensive technology had hardly changed: the careful preparation of a fine tilth in the rice fields, the constant regulation of the water in the seed-beds, the hand transplanting, the frequent weeding; it was still hard work which got good rice yields, and left one with a dozen bales of rice to sell instead of ten – hard work and the careful husbanding of resources: even the banks between the rice fields would be planted with a row of soya beans. In winter they would use the rice fields for a crop of wheat or barley. On their dry fields they grew as much mulberry as their wives could manage to turn into silk cocoons, and for the rest two or three crops a year of beans or maize and vegetables for family consumption with, hopefully, a bag or two left over to sell. Forever in pursuit of illusions of great profits, they tried various other cash crops: peaches, and tomatoes, and konnyaku root and pine seedlings and hops and grapes and persimmons and all kinds of other things that according to the Co-operative were going to prove good ways of making a killing. But somehow there was always a snag somewhere. Still in 1958, according to the census of that year, only seventeen households marketed more than 200,000 yen's worth of agricultural produce a year (about $550 at the time) and perhaps 30 or 40 per cent of that had been spent already on fertilizers and other materials. In the winter and on many days in other seasons, too, when there was no work to do on their fields, they would go off to make money in some other way. Some left at dawn to climb ten kilometres or more up steep paths into the forested mountainside, spent all day cutting wood and stacking it in their kiln and came back in the evening with three eleven-kilogramme bales of charcoal on their backs. Some took their ox out to a logging site and spent a long ten-hour day dragging logs down to the road-head for 450 yen – 250 for them and 200 for the ox – and that meant an hour's extra work for somebody in the family to cut enough extra grass to feed the ox for the heavy work he was expected to do. One old man was glad to be employed for the last six weeks of the rice-growing season to wander round the village for 200 yen a day with a stout bamboo tube, a tin of carbide, a bottle of water and a box of matches making loud bangs to scare the sparrows. He succeeded at least in interrupting their feeding on the rice ears for a few minutes and with luck some of them were scared enough to go off to another hamlet's fields altogether. (Nowadays, people buy neat little machines, painted red for danger, which make louder bangs more cheaply every four minutes.) For the evenings there was the job of making straw ropes, partly for sale but mostly for home use, and there were rice bales to be woven too, again out of straw. (The government paid 20 yen per bale and every year in the Rice

Price Deliberation Commission the co-operative organizations fought tooth and nail against government proposals to move to jute sacks; farmers needed that extra income. Japan was not a place where people had to be persuaded of the virtues of inter-mediate technology.)

Their tools were still simple: most had an ox together with a plough, harrow and simple cart for him to pull; a single hand-pushed rotary weeder and a pedal-operated rope-twisting machine; some had a small petrol or electric engine to drive a rice huller or a small thresher, but beyond that nothing much but a miscellaneous collection of sickles and hoes and mattocks. Most of the energy that went into their farming was human energy, provided by meals which consisted predominantly of large quantities of rice together with soya beans in a variety of forms – boiled, or as soya sauce, or as the fermented paste that made the base of most soups – and a liberal supply of fresh vegetables in summer and pickled vegetables in winter.

They worked hard and lived simply (all, that is, except a few feckless deviants). Shrine festivals and weddings and funerals, and the eating and drinking that went with them – the chance of fresh fish or even meat; the chance to get merry or even drunk on second-class saké or sweet-potato hooch – these were their main forms of relaxation apart from, perhaps once a year, an outing organized by the Co-operative – a charabanc ride over rough mountain roads to a hot spring resort. Their hopes and ambitions were equally modest. When I did a semi-formal interview survey in 1955, I asked people what would be their first priorities if they accumu-lated savings. A number wanted to buy more crop land ('it would be nice to be able to do a bit more farming and have to do less forestry work: it's so much easier'). Some would invest in woodland ('to be able to leave the children a good stand of timber'), a power spray for the dry-land crops, a thresher so as not to have to rely on taking one's turn at the communal one or one of the powered hand-guided tillers which were then just beginning to come on the market. Others put money for their children's education first – 'You can't get anywhere without education these days. Like growing crops: you can't do much without putting on some fertilizer.'

The predominance of such 'investment' replies was striking:

one lady said she would buy gold; the only safe thing. At least three men said that they would use the money to do something useful for the village: 'A new pump for the fire brigade or something; it's nice to be able to do something like that when you can.' Apart from one man who mentioned a television set (this was a year before the first set actually appeared in the village) the only talk of self-indulgent consumption expenditure came from those who spoke of spending money on their house. A re-thatching or repairs to the roof tiles, replacement of a few sagging beams or a study room for the children hardly count as great indulgence, perhaps; and when some of them spoke of rebuilding the kitchen – which indeed a number of families were doing – they were responding to the urgings of the young ladies from the extension service who came to lecture to the Women's Association on the hygienic and time-saving advantages of new types of stoves (with chimneys that took the smoke straight out of the house rather than letting it wander up into the roof-beams) and on time-saving ways of arranging sinks and draining-boards now that (two years before) a piped drinking-water system had been installed and water came out of taps rather than in buckets from the stream. The only real indulgers, perhaps, were those who spoke of rebuilding their bath-hut. The majority by that time *did* have a bath-hut; only a few houses made do with an old army drum-can filled with hot water in the open yard. But for most the bath-hut was still a ramshackle affair in the yard, containing a cauldron heated directly from the fire underneath. The few houses which had built tiled-floor bathrooms actually in the house with a sunken tiled tub and a separate circulating water-heater stoked from outside the house were understandably the envy of the village.

4

Better Off

Perhaps the infrequency of my appearances in Shinohata prompt such reflections more than would otherwise be the case, but Shinohata people seem frequently to reminisce about the past, generally variations on the theme: how poor we were then, how much better off now.

Before the war, you could work and work and work and you never saved money, could never eat delicious food, couldn't eat enough food. Now even without working your guts out you have money left over – well, not that much left over, but enough so that we don't feel in need – and our everyday life is sheer luxury compared with what it used to be. My father did the stone torii archway in front of the village shrine. He took it on for a hundred and some yen. It was a time when you were lucky to get a yen a day for a hard day's work and rice was about 10 yen a bale. That was a really big job. I remember the day he got paid and brought the money home. He laid the 100-yen note on the table and we all crowded round gazing at it. We'd never seen one before, ever.

You can say what you like about these politicians, but they certainly know how to run the country: they must be smart. I don't know how it's done, but at any rate here I am, doing much the same as I was doing twenty years ago; don't get much bigger yield from the rice fields; I have gone into the mushroom business in a small way, true, but that's not much. I do about the same number of days' work on construction sites, but our whole style of living is different; everything's mechanized, we don't have to work nearly as hard and we can afford things we'd never dream of a few years ago.

Masanobu, the second speaker, is the man whose turn had come this year to be village headman. Now nearly fifty, he belongs to the middle generation who reached maturity just after the war at a time when people like Masanobu counted themselves lucky to be eldest sons with the secure prospect of inheriting a house and an acre of land rather than, like their younger brothers, having to face the trials and uncertainties of finding a living in the towns where jobs were so hard to come by. The evening I called we went to sit in the best front sitting-room with its fresh mat floor coverings and doors covered with strikingly designed paper. The whole interior of the house had been remodelled a few years before. He offered to turn on the 24-inch colour TV set.

> A full acre of rice that cost me; about twenty-five bales. The money came into the Co-op account on one side of the ledger and went straight out again on the other. An extravagance, I suppose, but it was just after the Crown Prince's wedding and people said how marvellous it was on colour TV so I thought it would please the old people – my mother and father – to be able to see that sort of thing in colour. It doesn't half eat up the electricity, though. We only use it for special occasions. Ordinarily we use the black and white set in the kitchen.

The change in outward appearances is certainly striking. When I left in 1956 I sold my somewhat decrepit motor-scooter to my host. That made him, apart from two or three young men who commuted to jobs outside the village on motor-bikes, the most mobile farmer in the hamlet. He wrote to say how much easier it was to go bumping down the rough village roads on

the scooter every morning and evening to check the water level
in his rice fields and not have to push a bicycle all the way up
again. Now, nearly every house in the village, except those
where there is only a single old couple left, have a car and either
a small 500-cc truck or a 9–12 horse-power two-wheeled multi-
purpose unit which can be used as a walk-behind tiller for the
rice fields or hitched to a trailer with seats on, and with rubber
wheels changed for the spiked metal ones put into high gear
and driven at twenty miles an hour to take produce to the
Co-operative or to pay a visit to the clinic or the village office.
According to the 1974 registrations for the whole Kakizaka
town district of which Shinohata is now a part, the 1,300 households in its fifteen hamlets have between them over 1,400 four-
wheeled vehicles (double the 1969 figure), over 400 of the two-
wheeled farm multi-purpose units and some 600 miscellaneous
kinds of motor-bikes, scooters and power-assisted bicycles. The
roads are changed out of all recognition, too. The main trunk
road got a metalled surface in 1965, the branch road leading
to the entrance to Shinohata in 1970. Five years later the last
of the lanes within the hamlet was being widened and surfaced
with durable asphalt.

Overhead, the single low-power line of 1955 has given place
to a mass of wires – a new power system on tall concrete posts
to feed the hamlet's profusion of electrical appliances, the wires
of the Co-op telephone system and the hamlet broadcasting
system leading to every house.

The other most strikingly visible change is in the houses. The
standard pattern of a traditional Shinohata house, repeated
throughout the village with little variation except in size, was
much as in the plan on page 31. Houses were invariably oriented
towards – had their broad open side towards – the south. At the
east end of that south side was a double door wide enough for a
cart – with an inset pedestrian door: only in the most pretentious of landlords' houses was there a separate entrance with
elegant formal porch at the other end of the south side through
which honoured guests could be conducted directly to the
'upper' sitting rooms, without passing through the workaday
mess of the open area which lay beyond the double doors. This
open area was called the 'earth (floored) room' to distinguish it
from the raised matted area of the house. To the right, as one

came through the double doors, was the stable in which the ox
– or in the houses of one or two horse-lovers still, in 1955, a
horse – spent most of his days 'treading straw' – turning it and
the grass he was fed into stable manure. Only occasionally
would he be taken to be tethered in one of the small patches of
uncultivated grass on a river bank where grazing was possible.

This earth-floored section was the work area of the house,
usually littered with ropes and bags and bales and treadle
machines for making straw ropes and miscellaneous hand tools
of every kind. At the back, dimly lit by a small window if the
housewife was lucky, was the kitchen – a stove, some shelves, a
chopping board and in many houses in 1955 a sink with a
gleaming tap. The recent arrival of piped water meant that
many housewives now washed their dishes indoors, though
they still took cooking pots to the swiftly flowing irrigation
channel at the back of the yard for the scouring properties of
the fine white sand on the channel floor.

To the left of this earth-floored area, as one came in the
double doors, were the main living quarters, the 'upper' parts
of the house with proper floors two or three feet off the ground.
The two sections of the house were divided by sliding doors
of wood and translucent paper, but for most of the summer, and
in winter at meal times for the constant traffic from kitchen to
living room, they were mostly kept open. That constant traffic,
however, was carefully disciplined traffic; every time one went
'up' from the earth-floored area to the living room one took off
one's shoes or clogs or slippers and left them on the stone lintel
step; every time one went 'down' again one slipped one's feet
back in.

The two parts of the house made possible a graduated scale of
hospitality. Full-scale visitors would be invited up into the
living room. Casual visitors, however – the old-clothes merchant who came to display his wares, the fishmonger, neighbours who were pressingly invited to 'come up' but modestly
insisted that they had only just come to mention so and so and
they were quite all right here thank you – would be set cushions
on the edge of the main living room and sit there for their
inevitable cup of tea, with their feet dangling into the earth-
floored area or resting on the lintel.

This main living room was already by 1955 in most houses a

matted room. 'Straw mats' hardly sounds like a luxury item, but the Japanese tatami, firm but resilient from its two-inch thickness of tightly packed straw, smooth and cool to the touch with its close-woven rush surface, is a sophisticated product which not everybody, then, could afford. In the centre of the main living room would be a foot-high table at which the family took its meals seated on the matted floor or on cushions. In winter this table could be turned into a kotatsu heat chamber with the aid of a charcoal brazier set under the table and a padded quilt overflowing from between the table frame and table top. This made a kind of heat chamber into which those who sat round it could thrust their lower limbs and unoccupied hands – a great boon in Shinohata's chilly winters. But this kotatsu did nothing for one's back, which had to be protected with thick padded clothing. In poorer or more traditional houses this living room still had bare plank floors with the dark dull shine of the sooty patina rubbed into them by the dampened cleaning cloths of generations of obedient daughters-in-law. In the centre, instead of the table/kotatsu, a square open hearth provided warmth, and comfort, and lots of smoke which, if you were lucky, curled up around the kettle and up the chain by which it was hung from the roof, and eventually out through the vents at either end of the roof ridge.

From this room in most Shinohata houses a steep open staircase, almost a ladder, led to an upper half-floor which might contain one or two matted sleeping rooms, but was generally one large open plank-floored room used only in the summer when it was given over entirely to bank after bank of silkworm trays. Downstairs and further into the house there were the sleeping rooms and guest rooms. The sleeping rooms were the smaller ones for warmth and intimacy; sometimes only one room would be used by all sexually inactive or only sporadically active members of the family, boys and girls, parents and grandparents. The rooms could if necessary also be used in the daytime, the thin mattresses on which people slept being rolled up and stored in large built-in cupboards or on dry fine days put out to air. Young couples with their very young children would have separate sleeping rooms – sometimes even the converted upper floor of a barn. Even the smallest houses usually boasted one guest room not normally used by the family. With a formal decorative alcove for a scroll or a flower arrangement the room was usually used to sleep guests, or for weddings and funerals.

On such festal or funereal occasions the whole house would be used. The internal room divisions were also chiefly by sliding doors – though of a more solid and decorative type than the doors of translucent paper which separated off the earth-floored area. These internal doors could be removed, thus turning the whole house into one big reception area. One could also remove both sets of sliding doors which ran along the southern 'open' side of the house – another set of translucent paper doors and a set of solid wooden rain-doors – thus turning the garden too into a free-flowing extension of the reception area for a fine-day funeral. There was little glass except for the kitchen window, though some of the richer houses replaced the paper screen doors of the south front with glass doors which, during the five or six months of the year when it was too chilly to keep the whole south front open, let in rather more light and a little less cold than the translucent paper. These could be pleasant airy houses when they were thrown wide open in summer, and one was glad of the shade of the extended overhanging south-front eaves. They could be gloomy, though, in winter when those same eaves reduced the light available to filter through the paper screens.

Only a handful of such houses remain and even they have been to some degree remodelled. The earth-floor is reduced in size, concreted and turned into an entrance porch, with the kitchen at the back given a raised floor and made into a proper room with Formica cupboards and stainless-steel sinks and strip lighting and gas ranges fed by a bomb. Even the extrava-gant Shigeyasu, whom nobody had any respect for as a farmer, who took the 'non-cultivation subsidy' for nearly all his rice fields and ruined them by simply letting the rush weeds grow unhindered, mincing the subsoil floor to pieces – even Shige-yasu, who goes off with his wife every morning to their labour-ing jobs on construction sites in a GT model Toyota which everybody is certain he must be getting on the never-never, so much has he the reputation of not being able to keep money from one day to the next – even Shigeyasu has remodelled his house. Its external appearance may still confirm his reputation for disorderly living, its garden littered with a clutter of barrels and planks and car tyres and broken rabbit hutches, but his thatch has been replaced by tiles and, fitted into the frame of old weathered timbers, smart new all-glass aluminium-frame sliding doors have replaced the old rain doors all along the southern front. Some families had decamped to a barn for a summer, taken the old house to pieces and built in its place a new two-storey town house with separate rooms for their (rarely more than two) children. Some of them, in addition to the daily living rooms and a large traditional-style Japanese drawing room with an alcove in expensive polished rare woods, had added a Western-style best parlour with a carpet on parquet floor, plastic imitation wood panelling, a radiogram, a suite of stiff, heavy sofas and arm-chairs and blonde dolls in glass cases.

Now as one walks around the village, one can more or less guess the vintage of a house by its porch. The earliest rebuildings have the double sliding glass-and-wooden slat doors which have been standard in the towns for centuries. Newer ones have replaced the glass-and-wooden slats with aluminium-frame sliding glass doors with decorative frosting. Some of the newest have the hinged single metal doors which are now the regular Tokyo apartment-block style. The change in material implies too a change in etiquette and social relations. A visitor now is not expected to slide open the door and shout 'excuse me'. There is a bell to ring – and a name-plate outside: Shinohata people no longer live within a microcosm in which everybody is expected to know who everyone else is.

As for baths, there is not a house which has not had a new bathroom in the last twenty years – even the sharp-tongued, tight-fisted 'Grandmother at Masasada's' whose rule over her household finances is undiminished despite her eighty years and the fact that her adopted son is a mature forty-five and chairman of the hamlet's silkworm breeders' co-operative. In 1970 I recorded this snatch of conversation.

> 'Three years ago it is since I said I was going to give up the silkworms, but I'm still at it. Seventy-five and I'm still at it. I took 35 grammes of eggs this time, maybe 10 or 11 for the autumn. I don't know how much I'll get for it. What I do know is there'll still be debts. Never get out of debts.'

'Get on with you, auntie. You can't take it with you, you know.'

'What do you mean: get on with you? Why that tiller mechanical cart-horse thing cost 300,000.'

'Well, it's a big one.'

'And then what about the bathroom? A bathroom, that's another 200,000 yen. [At the exchange rate current since 1970, 1,000 yen has been worth about £1.50 to £2.00 or $3.50.] We've got all the material, but we're putting it off because we can't afford the carpenter yet. The young ones say: let's go ahead and do it. We'll be the laughing stock of the village, they say; there's only two houses left with a cauldron bath out in the yard, but I tell them; I say, as long as we've got a cauldron bath you have a cauldron bath. Enjoy looking at the stars while you can.'

I have experienced three generations of baths in the Yamamoto household; first, the cauldron bath or Goemon-bath as it was called, after the legendary prince of thieves who was once boiled in oil in one. They required considerable skill to use; since the bottom of the cauldron, directly attacked by the flames, was a good deal hotter than the water one could get a nasty burn. There was a circular base-board floating on the surface, and woe betide the man who failed to centre his tentative foot on it properly when performing the delicate manoeuvre of guiding it to its lodgement at the bottom of the bath. A slight miscalculation of balance and foot would go shooting down to the blistering bottom and board shoot back to the surface to hit a tender spot. Already in the early nineteenth century, two Edo sophisticates, heroes of a picaresque novel, found this strange country bath, encountered on their journey to Kyoto, a subject of great fascination and an opportunity for practical joking. (One removed the base-board and hid it; the other, undaunted, avoided the dangers of a scalded backside by bathing in wooden clogs.)

The second Yamamoto bath was a tiled tub – an indoor bathroom with a separate water-heating arrangement stoked with firewood from outside. That part of the house disappeared in the second rebuilding and now there is a gleaming stainless-steel tub with an oil-fired heater and an electric time-switch control so that one can soak for ever in the hottest water, giving the temperature an occasional five minute boost at the flick of a finger.

Once people spent up to ten days a year in the woods laying in a stock of firewood for the year. Even ten years ago, 'Open-wood Day' on 4 December was almost a festival day when the whole hamlet went off to its collectively owned pine forest, each neighbourhood group in the section it had drawn by lot, to collect a year's supply of pine needles for kindling. Now it is hard to know what to do with the piles of mulberry branches; the number of families that would say thank you for them is rapidly diminishing. The old firewood stove, relegated to an outhouse, is lit only three or four times a year when the occasion arises for cooking red-tinted festival rice in quantities that make it worthwhile digging out the old-fashioned cooking pots of so much ampler proportions than the saucepans designed for the modern small-family age.

The bath, for all its modernity, is still a Japanese bath, a deep square tub in which one sits with knees drawn up and water up to one's chin, a bath in which the whole family can soak in turn (or indeed together, especially grandparents and small grandchildren) since you soap and ladle large quantities of the bath water over you to rinse yourself outside the bath itself – the tiled floor and walls of the draining system making carelessly rapturous splashing possible.

Even the toilet has refinements which give it a Japanese distinctiveness, though it is known as a 'Western toilet' since it is a water-flushed bowl one perches on, not a hole in the ground. The local version, however, has features I have never seen elsewhere: an electric heating element built into the seat, and a little bowl built into the top of the waist-high cistern. The water to fill the cistern comes out of a chromium pipe above the bowl; one can intercept it on its passage into the bowl down into the cistern in order to rinse one's hands. The explanation of both these devices, I suppose, is that Japan has reached the age of universal gadgetry, especially electric gadgetry, before she has reached the age of central heating or constant piped hot water. Most houses have a gas or electric instant water heater at the kitchen sink, but it is frequently unused. Washing-up is usually done in cold water.

Few houses have this kind of Western toilet yet, though a number have tall chimneys with built-in electric extractor fans to remove the smells of earth closets, and sanitary arrangements are certainly not what they were. Gone are the days when one ladled out the deep toilet bowls into buckets and emptied them in cisterns dotted about the fields for the manure to mature into a harmless mixture ready to be put on the fields – and when people told stories about stingy guests who would hurry home when they felt their sphincters tightening so as not to give away valuable fertilizer. Now the cisterns are pumped out by vacuum trucks, and sewage disposal is a perennial problem of local government politics. The current solution is an arrangement whereby large drainage-storage cisterns are dug and used for a year at a time alternately in each of the main areas of the town council's jurisdiction.

This year the cistern is close to Shinohata fields, and sanitary sensitivities are now such that its presence causes resentment. 'They say it's so deep down and so well arranged that the flies can't get in, but it's not true, I saw them crawling out of the top!' The occasion which prompted a middle-aged farmer's wife to make this indignant remark – Tsunashige's wife with her twinkling coal-black eyes and slightly flirtatious grin chiefly gets indignant for the sheer pleasure of regaling her audience with the eloquence of her half-serious, half-playful abuse, making full use of the resources of the local dialect – the occasion for this indignant remark was a discussion of the merits of the Co-operative's proposal to establish, also in the middle of Shinohata's dry-field area, a new plant for processing cow manure into expensive deodorized concentrated fertilizer.

After the first disappearance of the family oxen around 1960 when everyone bought his multi-purpose tiller, the hamlet was almost without livestock for a decade, apart from a few chickens, a goat or two, pet rabbits and pet dogs. (Neither dogs nor rabbits to be eaten, though people tell stories of the war period when both were. The standard sheepish joke was 'let's hold a Prefectural Assembly Meeting' – 'kenkai' being a pun for 'dog party'.) In 1969, under the guidance of the Co-operative, some farmers started raising beef cattle. In small herds of five to ten, the animals never leave the tin sheds built for them well away from the houses, and are fed on imported American feed until fat enough to sell. Why, I asked (having only recently spent £6 for a load of manure on my allotment in England) don't people use the dung directly on their fields?

– It's too concentrated; it burns the plants.
– But that's because the cows are made to sit or stand all day on the bare concrete floor. Why not give them straw bedding which would mix into a good manure?
– Well, people use all their straw to mulch their mulberry fields.
– Surely they must have some left over though?
– Well, I suppose they have, but even if they did as you say, they wouldn't be able to use up all the dung they produce. I suppose really it's just not worth the time and energy; people have got so used to using artificial manure; it's so much less bother, so much cleaner. Who wants to be shovelling that shit all day? The stink gets into your clothes and into your hair – right into your bones. Apparently they can still get some of the vegetable growers over on the plain to take it, but it's getting increasingly hard. That's why they've got this new plan. It's all going to be properly handled; the stuff mechanically loaded into big vinyl bags. There won't be any smell.

'I'll bet!' The indignant Tsunashige's wife was unmollified.

Anyway, we're going to vote against it when it comes up at the hamlet meeting. Tell your old man he should too. They just think they're softies for anything, those people sitting up there in the mountains of Shinohata. They think they can get away with it. Who wants all the cow shit of Kakizaka town coming in trucks through Shinohata – and dumped up there in our fields! There'll be shit-maggots and shit-beetles and shit-booboo – you don't know what shit-booboo are? You know – blue bottles – and they'll come straight off the dung and sit on the mulberry and the wee wormies will turn up their noses at it and refuse to make silk, and when the wind's in the north, all the

flies will get blown over here and start sitting on our
food! And besides that, the stink!

The Professor's wife had joined the conversation halfway
through. The harbingers of things to come, the Professor and
his wife are the vanguard of the Tokyo middle-class weekend-
home seekers – the first and so far the only real outsiders to
build a house in Shinohata since Sadashige fetched up here as
a wandering bachelor woodsman in the 1920s, was taken in as
lodger-helper by one of the better-off families, and eventually
earned enough from forestry work to marry and get a house of
his own. The Professor's wife, having just driven from Tokyo,
was still taking extra deep breaths of Shinohata air. She demanded to know what stank. She was told. How did she find
it? Sanenobu's cow shed was only a hundred yards from her
house. Surely the smell must waft across. 'Oh, but that's a
natural smell,' she said, and went on to describe what happened
to your eyes and nose in Tokyo's photo-chemical smog.

She failed, alas, to convince. Modernized they may be, but
Shinohata villagers have not yet acquired the cult of the natural
smell. They look back with no nostalgia to the days when the
houses were full of the flies which bred in the ox-stall across the
earth-floored area, before the oxen disappeared and a DDT
spraying campaign pretty well eliminated both flies and mos-
quitoes from the village. The old mosquito nets were large
tents in a green hemp muslin which filled most of the room and
which three or four people could sleep inside. It was counted
as an amusing, but in a foreigner pardonable, eccentricity that
when I was writing here in the summer of 1956 I insisted on
keeping the net up in the daytime, and sat all day inside it to
avoid the flies. An even more eccentric innovation was to suggest to the Yamamoto family that we had our meals inside one.
Shinohata was already a place where convention allowed
women (except when there were male guests) to eat with the
men rather than waiting until they had finished and taking the
left-overs. Or at least that was so in winter. In the summer their
job was to sit with a fan, keeping the flies off the food while the
men ate, though no one fanned for them when it was their turn
to eat the fly-spat remains. Why, I suggested, don't we all eat
simultaneously inside a mosquito tent, even if it was two or

three degrees hotter? The idea was accepted, though I gather discontinued after I left and there was no foreigner present to provide a legitimate excuse for such bizarre behaviour.

Clothing has changed less than housing. Working clothes are much the same durable and often patched assemblage of garments as they used to be, and women have for several decades been wearing Western-style blouses and trousers. Only a few women over sixty still wore, in 1955, the old Japanese-style clothes – blue-dyed cotton short kimono with floppy sleeves that one tied up with a sash for work. Men's wardrobes have hardly changed; even twenty years ago most men had a morning coat and black trousers made when they got married which served for weddings and funerals for the rest of their lives. Now a farmer's other best suit is less likely to be the shabby, crumpled, 1930s creation that they mostly wore in 1955, and they are more likely to have one for summer and one for winter, while the younger men who go out to work have a much more dandified selection. Women, too, have a greater variety of best clothes, and now they can begin to afford the extravagance of Japanese kimono. A notice on a lamp standard in 1975 advertised a 'Japanese Dress Study Group' which an enterprising clothing merchant organized one evening in the hamlet hall. 'People say,' ran the advertisement, ' "I can't get dressed by myself in a kimono." "They're so tight and uncomfortable, I hate wearing them." "I don't know how to tie the obi sash." Come and learn how! Learn how to tie the obi so that it looks beautiful but doesn't feel like a straitjacket. Every knot from the casual drum knot to knots for formal ceremonies!' The silk-reeling company invited the silkworm Co-operative members to a wholesale-price preview of their new range of kimono weaves. Even at their cheap prices the total cost of a kimono with dyeing charges added worked out at two to three hundred dollars, with a suitable obi sash another seventy or a hundred extra. What to Westerners are simply symbols of Japaneseness, to Shinohata women are symbols of an expensive middle-class way of life which they can only now begin to afford.

Children's clothing has probably changed most of all. A 1955 photograph of a group of Shinohata urchins clambering over the grocer's three-wheeled truck prompted hilarious exclamations. 'Look at them! They look like Vietnam refugees! Look at the hole in his singlet! That one's shirt is three sizes too small for him!' 'Still,' said a seventy-year-old,

> they've got rubber tennis shoes on. When we were children it was just straw sandals with the thong between the big toe and the next. Most children had tabi socks [also with the divided toes] for winter, but patched and patched and handed on from child to child. Some had the sandals and bare feet all through the winter. I remember my parents bought my brother some rubber shoes for 3 yen a pair. My, he was proud of them. But when he took them off at school somebody stole them. One of the shoes came back. Somebody picked it out of the river. Envy, I suppose, because they were unusual then. And look at the children today. For middle school they all have the dark serge uniforms and track-suits to change into when they get to school. Children are expensive nowadays. The boys all want bicycles to go to school, and nothing less than one of these five-gear models will do. Our Senji's cost nearly 60,000 yen.

(The bike is, one should add, an impressive display of gadgetry, which looks like all of its 200 dollars worth. The gear shift is made to look like a car's; it has disc-brakes and an electric horn.)

Gardens are another form of conspicuous display which come in the same category as kimonos, traditional luxuries which recent affluence has now made possible. Even in 1955 a good many of the houses did, indeed, have rather tasteful if modest gardens, a few large rocks levered and rolled and man-handled out of the local river bed, carefully arranged on a little man-made hill facing the house's south front, and interspersed with various evergreen plants, pines and azaleas, sometimes bought at festival booths, more often brought back from expeditions to the high forests; in the foreground a little pond with carp, though usually of the plain dark variety destined to end up as the centrepiece of some festival meal.

The new gardens are of a different scale and taste. The landscape artists come up from Nakatani with their drawings. Here is a $1,200 garden. This one comes to $1,500. Eventually the workmen arrive in convoy; a rock-bearing truck, a crane truck and a cement-mixer truck. Great-grandfather's moss-covered stones are hauled away; there is nothing 'mezurashii', nothing admirably unusual about the local light-grey rocks. A new concrete pool is made, a new array of rocks from more distant geological formations is embedded in concrete around it – one or two of the centrally featured ones of enormous size and a couple of tons in weight. New trees and bushes are planted and some of the old ones are realigned (and sometimes fail to survive the treatment); a stone lantern or two are added, and the landscapers go away leaving a new modern garden and the offer of an introduction to a carp merchant who will provide expensive gold and red and silver carp to stock the pool at reduced prices.

Eventually such gardens too mellow; the clashing hues of the variety of mezurashii rocks begin to blend as they weather to darker shades, the concrete bedding in which the rocks are placed loses its hard smooth plastic appearance and acquires some moss. The garden actually becomes a pleasurable soothing thing to look at, though to the widowed old lady whose son-in-law (as was, of course, his right as new house-head) arranged these things without consulting her, it is not at all the same thing. A garden used to be a thing of memories as well as something to look at, memories of grandfather's stories of how he came by that rare bush and where he found that interesting rock that they called the frog rock because from some angles it looked like a frog. It is not quite the same when the only proud memory is of how much the operation cost.

Perhaps the clearest demonstration of the change in living habits would be photographs of the village shop in the early fifties and the village shop now. In 1955, its chief sales were of cigarettes, salt, sugar and bags of various kinds of sweet or salty biscuits for munching with mid-morning or mid-afternoon tea. It had given up the wines and spirits licence it had once had when the war-time rationing started, so for their saké and sweet-potato hooch people had to go to the Agricultural Co-operative store in the next hamlet. The wholesaler greengrocer's truck also came from time to time with small stocks of early vegetables available from warmer areas before they were ripe in Shinohata. There was a variety of dried fish for use in soups and also various tinned meats and fish and fruits. The latter were very much luxury articles, however, most of them purchased by grubby children sent hastily down to the shops when an unexpected visitor arrived – as indeed were many of the bags of 'chagashi' – titbits to go with tea. I used to feel somewhat conscience-stricken after spending a morning in house-to-house interviewing to discover that the Yamamotos (who keep the shop) knew exactly which houses I had been to because of a succession of such emergency purchases. For the most part the villagers were self-sufficient; even the titbits for morning and afternoon tea consisted chiefly of fresh or pickled cucumber, aubergine or tomatoes; of squash boiled in sugar, or various kinds of sugared or fermented beans; or fresh roasted corn. Sometimes there would be even more complex confections:

> 'We used to take some wheat, soak it in water for a while, then bury it in a container in the ground. After a while it starts sprouting and putting out roots. Then you take it out and chop it up – you can do it with a grinder, but not grind too fine. Then you steam some rice and mix the chopped wheat into it and then you add hot water and boil it for an hour or so. Then you squeeze out the liquid – it comes out a sweet white sort of juice which you then boil down for four or five hours until it becomes a kind of toffee. Then you mix soya bean flour into that and lay it out on a board to harden, cutting it into strips before it gets too hard. Or another chagashi we used to make was with ground-nuts. You chop them up roughly, then roast them, and then mix them with boiled sugar. And then, of course, there were endless things you could do with sweet potatoes; even the vines of the sweet potatoes we used to make up with salt and soya sauce into a kind of pickle.'

The big domestic operations of the year were the making of the year's supply of soya sauce and miso bean paste which provides the basis for most soups. Again these were time-consuming operations, especially the soya sauce. You started with equal volumes of soya beans boiled enough to be soft, and wheat roughly ground into a very coarse flour – in the average household, about 15 kilogrammes of each. This you entrusted to a specialist in the next hamlet who kept it in a sealed room at the right temperature, injected the right sort of yeast and so 'put flowers on it'. Then, having got it back home, you added equal quantities of salt and water, and miscellaneous other things according to taste – left-over rice, some monosodium glutinate, etc. – stirred vigorously and left it in a shed for a year to let nature take its course, aided by a vigorous stir from any passer-by who happened to think of it; the more frequent and energetic the stirring, the more impressively the mixture would rumble and erupt. When it was thought to be finally ripe you ladled the concoction into especially strong muslin bags and rigged up a screw-jack (locally known as a 'giraffe') above it to squeeze all the liquid out. Finally, to make it go further, you boiled that up with extra water, using a thing like a thermometer which measured salt content, to tell you when you were letting your lust for quantity – your fear that your soya sauce would not last the year and you would be forced to *buy* some – go too far at the expense of quality. Several of the hamlet's neighbourhood groups kept a set of this equipment in common, though that caused occasional problems when someone in the neighbourhood, over-desperately keen to get the last drop from the mixture, would screw the jack too tight and split an expensive bag.

Only four or five Shinohata houses still make their own soya sauce. Two of them that I know best, both among the better-off families, make a nice contrast. For Katsunori's wife, making one's own soya sauce is part of a conscious and explicit Women's Institute sort of life-style; she went to a pre-war middle school and reads women's magazines which extol the *quality* of the home-made as opposed to the factory-made and are full of respect for the simple rustic virtues. For Sanetoshi's wife, by contrast, it is just untutored native carefulness, the product of an upbringing which left one unable to spend money on anything without a guilty sense of self-indulgence, much less on something that it required merely labour, care and determination to produce for oneself. Put like that the contrast between middle-class cultism and peasant carefulness is overdrawn; the two attitudes interfuse; the lady who reads women's magazines was also brought up in habits of parsimony, but there is a difference nevertheless: she has acquired these attitudes partly because of the education she got as a member of an upper-stratum family; the other became an upper-stratum family partly because of the care and parsimony of their daily life, the unremitting energy with which they worked, their success in passing the work ethic on to their children, in giving them the drive to pass their examinations and make themselves successful careers as 'salary men'.

Sanetoshi's has the reputation of being a 'katai uchi' – a 'stiff' household. There is certainly an unusually forbidding sternness about Sanetoshi himself. I remember when I first became aware of it at a Shinohata branch PTA meeting in 1955. The local primary school teachers had come to explain to parents their preparations for the summer holidays – the holiday tasks they were going to set, the 'drives' that they wanted parents' co-operation in (brushing teeth after meals, correcting certain bad habits of speech), the schedule for the weekly 'assembly days' at the school when the teachers would check up on the performance of holiday tasks, and for the two outings that had been arranged – one a hike into the forests behind Shinohata, and one a day trip by charabanc to the sea-side. Most of the parents were interested, grateful, respectful. Not so Sanetoshi. 'May I ask how many teachers are going to be taking vacation courses this summer?' – 'Well, then, if only four out of the nine of you are taking courses, why is it that you have arranged so few events for the children during the holidays?'

Sanetoshi was one of the last Shinohata farmers to give up growing a crop of wheat or barley on his rice fields in winter. Neither God nor his invisible hand ever intended anyone to grow little quarter-acre patches of hand-sown, hand-sickle-cut wheat in competition with the grain that flowed across the Pacific from the inexhaustible prairies, and even the government's policy of subsidizing almost anything that a vote-holding farmer wanted to grow was stretched to the limits of credibility. The Co-operative organizations made valiant efforts to keep the subsidies which made sense in the food-scarce forties and early fifties at the same level into the late fifties and sixties but inevitably the relative price level was gently scaled down. Fewer and fewer farmers bothered. But still Sanetoshi, offended by the thought of leaving those fields idle in winter, persisted until 1968. By then he was almost the last wheat-grower in the district, the only farmer offering the sparrows anything substantial to eat in early June. They came from miles around and gave his fields their full attention. Even he was finally discouraged.

At seventy-six and sixty-eight respectively, he and his wife still work hard. I last saw them coming back from their field with a truck full of old mulberry roots which they had just dug out as part of a replanting operation. Their now ageing multi-purpose tiller engine had stalled on the slope and since the brakes were worn, his wife and I held the truck while Sanetoshi, a wiry gnomic figure, wound the rope around the starting wheel and pulled, wound and pulled again, with the stern patient dignity of a father offended by a wayward child. 'Katai', the word people use to describe their household, implies strictness and rectitude; an acute sense of public duty, as well as hard work and the avoidance of indulgence. Sanetoshi, in 1969, decided to donate a new hut to house the fire pump. The timbers of the old one were rotted to the point where its collapse seemed imminent. The wife of his much richer neighbour suggested one day that he might be the hamlet's benefactor. He accepted the challenge, expecting it to cost him $700 and in the end it ran away with $2,100 (his story: the town newsletter said $2,450). Yet the family diet remains of the simplest, still little more than large quantities of rice, miso soup and vegetables pickled to a degree of saltiness which, now that people work less hard and sweat less, few households still find tolerable.

Most households are a good deal less ascetic. The young housewives who have come back with their husbands to Shinohata after living for some time in the towns have changed Shinohata eating habits. From half past five to half past seven in the evening there is a constant procession to the shop to buy the makings of the evening meal; the young returnees in bright coloured jumpers and skirts with shopping baskets, older farm-working women in their work clothes and head scarves carrying their more modest purchases back in their hands. The shop's frozen food cabinets now contain cheese and butter, confections called 'Press Ham' and traditional fish cakes, as well as a daily supply of fresh meat and fish, including cuts of tuna or bonito to be eaten raw dipped in soya sauce and horse-radish, though such things really are expensive and the shop sells five times as much raw whale meat as the three times more costly raw tuna. (In 1955 a tall handsome one-armed fishmonger would stride up to the hamlet with a basket on his back and usually find a few housewives with whom to spend an hour or so in amiable chat, but he was lucky if he found more than four or five ready to buy fresh fish.)

Out-of-season hot-house vegetables in neat cellophane packaging are available all the year round. There is a profusion of candies and sweet biscuits and savoury biscuits and sweet-ened breads, in packages of varying hues, some with traditional Japanese names redolent of wisteria and brocade and pieces of gold, the names of sumō wrestlers and legendary eccentric priests, some – the sweet ones rather than the savoury ones – with English names in both Japanese and Roman letters sugges-tive of quality and modernity: Butter Flower, Banana Scat, Choco Baby, Golden Toffee, China Marble, Ghana Milk.

(In 1960, soon after the shop got its licence back, one of the first brands of local whisky to be stocked was called '45'. Could the Bonny Prince ever have imagined the global nature of his eventual fame? Perhaps, though, the prize for com-mercial xenophilia should go to the barber in Kakizaka town centre. He sells Coronation Talcum, Jockey Club brilliantine, Pomola pomade and Empire lacquer spray – all with their names spelt out in Roman letters. A certificate says that he has a Bacheroa obu Tonsoriaru Aatsu (in Japanese phonetic script) and the footrest of his (1952 vintage) chair has, moulded into the cast-iron, in English, 'Celebrate Peace Treaty'.)

A good many of these sweet confections are primarily treats for children, but adults buy them too to go with their morning and afternoon tea. Every day during the first two weeks of each silkworm season, when the silkworms are cared for col-lectively in the hamlet hall, one of the eight ladies whose duty turn it is comes down to spend the 800 yen communal kitty on such 'tea-cakes'. She has a hard time choosing, so embarrassing is the choice of riches. There is a variety of soft drinks too. A farmer who came to buy half-a-dozen tins of grape juice from the shop refrigerator to be put cooling in the stream beside his rice field and offered to his rice-planting helpers as elevenses, reminisced about the old days when they took a couple of large empty saké bottles and filled them on the way to the fields at the pool by the Odaijin shrine – and refilled the bottles on their way home to bring back to the house. 'Lovely cool delicious water that was, but I don't suppose we'd think so any more.' The idea of what constitutes a treat has certainly changed. The foods people have always prepared for festive occasions – 'red rice', the special glutinous rice steamed with sweet red beans to give the whole confection an auspicious red colouring, the green mochi – the flour of the same glutinous rice coloured and flavoured with the fragrant yomogi weed and turned into a dumpling filled with sweet bean paste – these traditional festive foods are still made in large quantities at New Year, or for a roof-beam raising for a new house, or when one finishes the rice planting – made in order to be liberally distributed to neighbours and relations. But they no longer count as the delicacies they once were; they usually end up being passed to the dog.

Housewives linger over their purchases, though, partly because they are a gregarious lot and enjoy the opportunity for a gossip, partly because they really are taking time to make up their minds, carefully comparing prices. Their daily expeditions are far from extravagant; much less so than one would guess from the lavish expenditure on houses and gardens and children's bicycles. Masanobu's expensive colour television set which he hesitated to use because it absorbed so much electricity is a not untypical case. It is not just a matter of penny wisdom and pound extravagance. It is partly because the extra money tends to come in large lumps – from the sale of a piece of land or a stand of timber, or more regularly, from the sale of the rice harvest. And a rice harvest – especially after a price rise – may bring in what seems an impressive lump sum. A special circumstance in Shinohata, and a partial explanation of the extra lavishness of some Shinohata houses and gardens, was a windfall of some $7,700 per household which came from a sale of collectively owned Shinohata land to a factory – more than a year's total income for the majority of families. But there is also another element, a preference, to go back to an earlier point, for expenditure on what can be considered an investment rather than on ephemeral pleasure, expenditure on something which *lasts*, which you can pass on to your descendants, and which *shows* – something which does your house honour, helps to raise its standing in the community of the village. Keeping up with the Joneses is one way of putting it, but there is a difference; an extra dimension added by the fact that your ancestors were also neighbours of the Joneses' ancestors, and your descendants can expect to live alongside the Joneses' descendants.

One thing that remains unchanged is the central importance of rice in the diet. I still have trouble explaining to Shinohata people how it is that, if England's shushoku, staple food, is bread rather than rice, we do not consume a loaf or two of bread with each meal. Three times a day the centre of every Shinohata meal is a bowl of rice – several times refilled for hard-working men, not quite so often refilled for hard-working women – to which all the other dishes are side dishes. To be sure, on festive occasions, when saké or beer or (for women) the local wine is served, one eats only the side dishes as long as one drinks – until the host or his wife, perhaps observing that the guests are getting somewhat the worse for wear, says 'shall we have the rice now?' The arrival of the rice signifies the end of drinking and even hearty eaters may by then have consumed so much from the plates of batter-fried vegetables and raw tuna and white cubes of bean curd, and pickled cucumber and sliced pork with bamboo shoots, that they can manage no more than one small bowl of rice. But still rice remains the king-pin of any real meal's architecture, and Shinohata people place considerable store on it being *their* rice. Even the hopeless Shigeyasu, who has ruined most of his rice fields by leaving them fallow and unattended, still takes enough time off from the construction sites to plant two-thirds of an acre, enough to provide for the family. Some households send a couple of bales of rice to their children in Tokyo. In 1960, when we were living in Kyoto and Atsushi came to spend a few days with us, he brought a twenty-pound sack of rice with him. It is not that people claim that their own rice really tastes better than anything they could buy – as they say, for instance, that they still make their own miso bean paste because the preservatives added to commercial pastes ruin the taste. It is rather that the notion of a minimal self-sufficiency in food as a precondition for independence and a standing of basic respectability in the hamlet has deep cultural roots. The days are not, after all, so very distant when to have to beg or borrow rice from others, or even to have to work for others and buy rice from the proceeds, was an unmistakable mark of poverty and low status.

Sometimes that is hard to believe in these days of new gardens and new houses, a car in every garage and a telephone in every home. But older people remember the days when what one earned from a day's casual labouring would buy less than a couple of kilogrammes of rice, not the twenty kilogrammes that the four thousand yen daily wage would buy today – not to count the further fact that rice was then far cheaper relative to other goods. To many of them the sudden prosperity seems too good to last. It can't really be true. It has a hollow ring. It is built on sand. I recorded the following conversation in 1970 when the draper from the village down the road brought a consignment of cotton towels to the secretary of the Women's Association. The Association organizes an old people's party, and the towels were to be distributed as keepsakes for them to take home afterwards. Each towel had a picture of a chubby child under a waterfall and the legend: 'Honour the Aged Party: Sponsored by Kakizaka Town Women's Association'. The draper was a bald-headed sixty-year-old, a forceful talker, clearly used to being respected in some circles as the local intellectual. The secretary of the Women's Association had a hard time keeping up a tentative obbligato to his rapid-fire monologue.

'I'm afraid the towels are more expensive this year. Luckily the dyers still had the plates from last year or the expense would have been terrible. They can't get people to do this kind of thing nowadays. They've even started sending work to Korea to be done. It's terrible the cost of labour nowadays. You can hardly get anybody by the day now. They come along and they want a rate for the job. Carpenters the same. A man comes to repair your roof and he looks it over and he says: that'll be so much, and he does it in two days and walks off with 20,000 yen. Same if they come to weed a field.

The young ones today don't want to be bothered learning a trade properly. They go off and get a simple job in Sano and in no time they're getting fifty, sixty thousand a month. But you know, they all look prosperous, but it's all on the outside. Same with the houses. It's all done on instalments. All on credit.

'They were saying on television the other day how some Americans were doing a study of old Japanese commercial practices, and you know what they said: My! they said, these Japanese must have been really prosperous; they must have had a lot to spare. How did these old Japanese merchants come to have that kind of capital? They let you buy on credit from January to July.'

'That's right. January to July and then July to September . . .'

'January to July, and then they'd start a new account in August to the end of the year. And in the interval where did they get their money from? That's what the Americans couldn't understand. In America, now, you buy something and it's cash on the nail.'

'That's right, cash on the nail. That's the way it should be. You take the goods and you should pay for them.'

'Absolutely. It's a matter of ability to pay. Ability to pay, that's what counts. No good thinking you can just be dependent on the wholesalers the way people used to. But everybody's buying on monthly instalments now.'

'Monthly instalments are no good for farmers. It's not like a salary man with money coming in every month.'

'It's these television ads that do it. They make out that everything's so cheap. And so people get taken in. Living above their means, above their real financial strength. And then they find themselves up to their ears in debt and they sell up their rice fields and they sell up their dry fields . . .'

'There's a limit to what you can do, isn't there?'

'That's right, there's a limit. We'll manage somehow, they think. It's a bad Japanese habit that is – this "we'll manage somehow" business. It's not based on proper calculations. There's no worse way of managing than managing somehow. And now, with money getting tighter . . . They were saying on television there's going to be quite a depression next year. Take Kakihara, for instance. I know it's only a small part of the world, but take it for an example. The last few years they've gone in for grapes in a big way. Everybody's growing grapes. This year, well, it's not gone so badly. The price isn't too bad. But you wait, another one or two years and the price will go down and it will be red figures again. It's a vicious circle.'

'Yes, it's a vicious circle. Take tomatoes. It seems they're no good this year. Bottom dropped out completely.'

'Bottom dropped out. And aubergines. Aubergines used to be a good thing and now they're two-a-penny. And that thing with the big leaves; what do you call it – dekasu or something.'

'Dekasu! Retasu [lettuce] you mean! Dekasu!'

'That's right, dekasu. They're no good either this year, it seems.'

'Who'd be a farmer!'

'They all count their chickens. I'll get so much for that, so much for this. They get out their abacus and they work out the yield per acre and they think: now with the tomatoes I can pay a deposit on a car, and then when the lettuce comes in . . . And all their calculations are miles out.'

'And they can't keep up the payments.'

'Miles out. And in the final reckoning it's all red figures again. But really it's the same with business you know. Soon it will be all big enterprise. It will. Mergers, takeovers. The banks and the big manufacturers; they're getting bigger and bigger all the time. That's the tendency. Take the car industry. It's – you go join up with Toyota; you go in with Nissan. The bankers won't lend to the little man any more. And now the next thing is capital liberalization. There're going to be foreign firms investing in Japan. Since we are now about to face foreign competition, we must develop a firm solid basis to fight it off, they say. All this economic growth, that's it. The growth of the economy has gone so far that the balance of – what do you call it? – the balance of payments has got a big balance in the black – billions of dollars – and that means that the pressure's on Japan internationally speaking. Trade protection won't do any more. We've got to be internationally minded. It's going to be a tough time for us Japanese from now on.'

For some, this sense of the fragility of modern prosperity is underpinned by a certain sense of guilt. It's just not quite *right*. The bean-curd merchant, who supplies the shop with fresh supplies of his soft, milky cubes that look like Turkish delight, expressed it rather well. A leading light in Nakatani Rotary, he too has done well out of the prosperity – a new house, a large concrete tank in his garden, equipped with the very latest temperature control and oxygen-content control devices, to house his impressive collection of carp of fabulous hues and ages and price-tags. Was it, he wondered in 1975, the end of the era of prosperity, or only just the temporary effect of the 'oil shock'? His sales were 30 per cent down, which was unusual. The bean-curd business was traditionally a sound business; not much boosted in boom times, not much depressed when times were bad. But this time it seemed different. But then that was general. Business was bad all round.

But you know, I'm not so sure that it is not a good thing. It will bring people to their senses. It was all too good to be true. We've had it too easy. It wasn't natural. Kids coming out of high school and running around in cars after they'd only been working for a year or two. People have lost a sense of the preciousness of things. We take too much for granted. Especially children. They can waste things without a thought. My children are like that. They don't know how to look after things properly. They waste paper. They lose their pencil and simply expect a new one without looking for the old one first. Yes, we've lost a sense of the preciousness of things.

Among the 'traditional songs' recorded in the county history in 1911 – short couplets to be sung in chorus by the circles of dancers at the mid-summer festival – is one which goes:

> Straw sandal, frayed and useless, treat it with respect.
> The straw, after all, is parent of the rice.

A sense of the preciousness of things is something which many Shinohata people still have, and others feel half guilty about having lost.

5

Work

What, the reader may wonder, underlies this new-found prosperity? It is certainly not to be attributed to spectacular increases in agricultural production. Shinohata's citizens are, rather, the beneficiaries, direct and indirect, of Japan's whirlwind industrial advance – directly as some of the established capitalist enterprises come into the district in search of cheaper building sites and new (and less expensive) sources of labour, and as a few local enterprises grow larger; indirectly as the expansion of tax revenues provides more money for the government to redistribute to the backwaters of the Japanese economy – in expanded welfare services, road-construction schemes, agricultural subsidies and general support of local-government expenditure.

Below are the tax-return figures for Kakizaka township for three recent years. They count only those income-receivers who, after the deduction of (rather liberal) allowances, were still liable to pay tax. (And of course, being tax returns, they show differences in the ability to conceal income – lowest of all for wage and salary earners – as much as in the ability to earn it.)

The incomes of the self-employed are, of course, much less likely to be fully reported (and are net of expenses which are often somewhat elastically conceived), so that one cannot take these figures as an accurate indication of the structure of local incomes. And although only those who derive more than 50

Classification of tax-payers by their *main* source of income	Number of such tax-payers and their average incomes from that and all other sources (thousands yen at 1973 price values)		
		1966	1969	1973
Wage and salary earners	Number	391	441	807
	Average income	728	790	998
Agricultural enterprisers	Number	372	222	133
	Average income	516	498	622
Commercial and industrial enterprisers	Number	82	74	89
	Average income	573	658	932
Professional workers for fees	Number	8	5	6
	Average income	1,050	1,760	1,726
Other income earners (day labourers, commission salesmen, etc.)	Number	14	50	42
	Average income	384	506	566
(Consumer's Price Index used in above		65	75	100)
Total number of tax-payers		867	792	1,077
Total number of households		1,285	1,261	1,290
Total number receiving welfare assistance		82	94	51

per cent of their income from agriculture are included in the agricultural enterprisers category, a good many in other categories also derive a part of their income from farming. Nevertheless, the shift is striking; agriculture counts for less and less in the local scheme of things, becoming more and more a spare-time activity or one which is left to housewives and ageing parents, while the able-bodied men commute daily from the village to work elsewhere. In Shinohata itself, the only non-agricultural establishment ten years ago was the shop; now there are a plant producing animal feeds from the waste products of a large local food factory, a structural steel-fabrication yard, a builder's yard and an electrical repair shop for centrifugal separators used in medical and chemical analysis – with a repair franchise for this and the neighbouring prefecture. Nearly every household has either some such reasonably profit- able self-employment, or someone in a steady wage job. In half a dozen houses the younger-generation wives also have outside jobs: one is a school-teacher, the others work in the knit-wear factory or the plastics factory or one of the drive-ins along the main road. Some men commute the twenty-five miles to Sano every day; one or two work at a greater distance and come home only at the weekends (for example, a school-teacher pro- moted from the local school to a headmastership a good deal further away); but most have found work closer to hand, a good proportion of them in white-collar work in the village office, the clinic or the Agricultural Co-operative (about a hun- dred jobs altogether in this township of 1,300 households and 5,000 people), the rest in various enterprises mostly scattered around the main road – the smaller and somewhat makeshift establishments making knit-wear, cement blocks, plastics or precision engineering components on sub-contract from car and camera and watch makers in the next prefecture, the medium-sized chemical dye firm, and, at the other end of the scale, The Factory.

The Factory is a large, highly capital-intensive establishment recently built by a firm with a famous name in the food industry. Most of the upper ranks of its employees are 'posted' here for a while, to move on later to other branches, and live in company houses in Nakatani town (where the schools are better). A good number of the other workers on the site, engaged in packing and transport and cleaning, are the humble employees of on-site sub-contractors. The small number of direct employees, locally recruited from neighbouring villages, who spend their days shuffling papers and pressing buttons in the highly auto- mated inner sancta of The Factory itself, are the elite of the local working population. They happily wear The Factory's uniform even on off-duty Sundays; when they come to the shop they loyally spurn the products of rival firms, even though The Factory's brand may be out of stock. It is not given to every- one, after all, to work for a firm whose name is a household word throughout the land, a firm which bought up so much land with such un-niggling magnanimity, at prices which until then no one had ever contemplated. Some of the older people,

half-jokingly, but half for real, use the respectful suffix '-sama' when they refer to The Factory – just as in 1960 they spoke of the typhoon as 'Taifū-sama' when the Disaster Relief Fund, and the large riparian construction projects it paid for, brought the first whiff of modern prosperity into the district. One of the reasons an earnest, modern, bright young housewife advanced against the cow-dung processing factory was that it would spoil the 'imeeji' – the image – of Shinohata, now so refulgently established by the proximity of The Factory.

Certainly, The Factory and the village authorities have worked hard on the image. The new copper bell which one rattles to arouse the god at Shinohata's Shinto shrine bears a neat label which declares it to be a gift from The Factory. Discreet advertisements on the local TV and in the national press emphasize how the luxurious quality of The Factory's products simply reflects the lush natural beauty of the environment in which they are made. Various sports and welfare organizations in the township receive generous donations. An extension of The Factory site has been turned into a woodland bird sanctuary liberally scattered every day with bag-fulls of corn – leading, indeed, to a dramatic increase in the number and variety of wild birds, though not entirely to the delight of local farmers when the pheasants and pigeons and exotic long-tails come across to their fields for a change of diet.

No harsh raucous sirens disturb the peace of the countryside. That would hardly consort with The Factory's version of capitalism with a smiling face. Instead loudspeakers mark the beginning and end of each work period with the gentle sounds of the Westminster chimes, preceded, at precisely 8.23 each morning, by five minutes of physical jerk music – rhythmic piano punctuated by the 'Hup' and 'Haaaw' and 'Back' and 'Oooover' of a cheery gym instructor – leaving just two minutes for everyone to get to his work place for a prompt start when the chimes ring out.

The stream which runs down the hill past The Factory to flow into the Isokawa river caused something of an image problem. It was never a very distinguished stream except when it turned into a writhing, raging torrent under the influence of a typhoon. Its name was the Muddy River, which was accurate enough, but a little unfortunate for a river flowing past The

Factory, the waters of which The Factory might be thought to be using. (In fact, The Factory bored its own wells, with, apparently, adverse consequences for one or two springs which a few farmers depended on for flooding their rice fields.) So, the Muddy River had to be renamed. Along with the cloudy mud, the river does, indeed, wash down from the mountains large quantities of pure white, slightly crystalline pebbles. For some decades school-children have spent half a day each year collecting these pebbles to be sent to pave the forecourt of the Meiji Shrine in Tokyo. This thought was doubtless salient in the mayor's mind, local cynics suggest, because it is the mayor, not the school-children, who gets entertained as the distinguished guest at the Shrine's annual festival. At any rate the connection seemed good enough grounds to pass a resolution in the town council. Conscious of the honour which the Meiji Shrine did the town and its river, and in recognition thereof, the river would henceforth bear the new name: Shrine River.

The Factory represents prosperity and security. It is not the sort of enterprise likely to be affected by the recessions of the mild variety which the post-war years have seen, or even by the somewhat more serious setbacks of 1974 and 1975. Some of the smaller enterprises are more vulnerable. The dye-stuffs factory in 1975 had stocks equal to a year's sales and was on short-time working, but still had not sacked anyone. Another Shinohata man counted himself lucky to be employed as a guard by the receiver of his bankrupt engineering factory. But still there were jobs to be had even though wages had ceased to rise.

One major source of this stability is the high level of public expenditure. The budget for Kakizaka town in 1975 worked out at slightly under 500,000 yen (£750 or $1,800) per household. Over a quarter of that amount was to be spent directly on salaries. The other major source of employment is the more than 30 per cent of the total apportioned for construction work let out to sub-contractors. In every part of the township – very carefully so, for the town is still in many ways just a federation of hamlets and the central focus of town politics is the even and fair division of benefits between them – in every part of the township one finds little gangs of men, nowadays with big machines, re-making irrigation ditches, paving old roads, making new ones, pouring concrete on wire mesh over vast steep areas of once crumbling mountainside, building bridges and dams and barriers and enormous concrete channels to make the rivers manageable even in the worst of typhoons.

Very little of this is paid for out of local taxes; only about 15 per cent of the total budget is collected by the township itself. The rest comes from the National or Prefectural treasuries – 40 per cent of the budget in the form of a straight equalization grant, the rest from various specific grants and loans and subsidies, an all-important 10 per cent of the total – the icing on the cake – being owed to the skill of the mayor in getting the township designated a Sparsely Populated Area. This made it eligible for a number of special grants to maintain the level of social services and to carry out various development works to make agriculture and forestry viable and to attract tourists. As one drives up the valley through the heavy traffic on the main road, observing the frequent clusters of houses and the way the fields seem always to be dotted with bobbing heads and parked farm trucks, it is hard for anyone who has been to the Scottish highlands, or spent a day walking across Norfolk farmland without meeting a soul, to conceive of this as a sparsely populated area. But Japan is densely populated and sparseness is a relative concept. And the Sparsely Populated Areas Development Special Measures Act of 1969 was something which a rapidly growing economy with an even more rapidly growing volume of tax revenues could quite easily afford.

One somewhat romantic way of putting it would be to say that all this expenditure is an expression at the national level of the old ethic of filial piety – the tribute which the youthful productive industrial sectors of the economy pay to the ageing populations left in the villages, or, more abstractly, to the ancestral rural homeland, the original source from which the capital to build Japan's industry was accumulated. That is not an irrelevant aspect of the matter, either. The ancient principle of Confucian political economy was summed up in the phrase 'Nōhon-shugi' or 'agriculture-is-the-base-ism', a phrase revived in the twenties and thirties in various guises – as radical anticapitalism interlaced with populist agrarian socialism, as romantic militarist fascism seeking to preserve the sturdy rural virtues and food self-sufficiency necessary for a Japan embarking on military conquest. It still has a vestigial appeal, a rationale to be skilfully used by the Ministries of Agriculture and Construction in pressing their claims to a larger share of the budget.

A more important part of the explanation, however, lies in the pattern of Japanese spoils-sharing 'pork barrel' politics and the crucial role played by special-purpose subsidies in consolidating links between local and central government politicians – a role made all the more crucial by the fact that population movement with only slow, lagging adjustment of electoral boundaries has made one rural vote worth two or three urban votes, and it is support from the rural constituencies which has sustained the Liberal Democratic Party through its twenty years of uninterrupted power.

The money is not always wisely spent. Few people in Shinohata were convinced of the need for the new forestry-tourist road being built above the village. Of impressive width and solidity it will eventually stretch some twenty-five kilometres through uninhabited and precipitous woodland to link two remote and somewhat desolate corners of the township. It is hard to see how it would ever bear much traffic. But still the contractors grow fat, and so do many of the villagers whom they employ: Shigeyasu, for instance, who sets off in his Corona GT with his wife every morning and who reputedly doesn't even bother with packed lunches because he prefers to eat in the drive-ins.

Apart from the Professor in his villa, there is only one other household which has no land: that recently established by a younger son. All the other families still count, according to the census definition, as farming families. Yet, thanks to the appearance of The Factory, to the construction projects and to all the other ways in which the outer ripples of the rising tide of Japan's industrialization have spread into this distant corner of the Prefecture, collectively probably a good deal less than half of their income is derived from agriculture. In this, Shinohata's farms are not untypical. According to the government survey figures, the five million farm families in Japan were reckoned in 1973 to have an average disposable income of 2·4 million yen each, or just over half a million yen per family member, which made them, on a *per capita* basis, 7 per cent better off than the average urban worker's family. But of this income about 70 per cent was derived from other than agricultural pursuits.

6

Modern Farming

It is appropriate enough that the modern farmers of Shinohata should tell the time not by the sun, but by the sound of the Westminster chimes which come wafting across the bird sanctuary wood from The Factory's loudspeakers. It is appropriate enough because Shinohata farmers are very conscious of being modern farmers, farming in a very different way from their ancestors; indeed, in a very different way from the way in which they themselves farmed a couple of decades ago.

Quite the most spectacular change has been in the techniques of rice cultivation. The gradual improvement in yields throughout the nineteenth century was achieved primarily by more intensive labour – more careful weeding and field preparation, heavy fertilization with green manure. The seed beds would be prepared first – as far as possible towards the bottom of the village where the water was warmer. The next task was the preparation of fields. First the piles of dead leaves dumped on the fields in the winter would be evenly spread and the stubble ploughed in with a horse-drawn single-blade plough. Then the field would be flooded and the clods broken up with a spiked harrow. Meanwhile a major task was to gather green grass and miscellaneous weeds and the fresh leaves and branches cut from trees to put into the field as fertilizer, for apart from a few farmers who bought bean or oil-seed pressings and those who used lime it was on green fertilizer that people chiefly relied. The banks of the rice fields and the roadsides provided a certain

amount, but the quantities required for Shinohata's fields had
to come from further away. Those who had their own woodland, or who found favour with a landlord who owned extensive tracts of it, could collect undergrowth and leafshoots in
woods close to the village; others had to go further – to the
state land, with its woods and occasional open patches of grass
at the higher contours beyond the first range of low wooded
hills behind Shinohata.

'People would set off on their horses at three o'clock
in the morning sometimes, or even earlier. I don't
know, now, how they did it. Perhaps folks didn't need
so much sleep then, or they could just sleep sitting on
horseback. And they'd ride way up into the mountains
with a couple of rice balls and a bit of pickle and many
hours later they'd be back leading the horse with a full
load – six bundles that is – of grass on his back. Day
after day they'd do that. You had to go that far because
all the near-by grass would be taken. Grass was precious
then. People would take it from right under your nose.
That was partly, of course, because the boundaries of
the house plots never were too clear. You'd look out of
a morning and you'd see somebody cutting grass on
the edge of your yard, and you'd peep to see if you
could get a glimpse of who it was without their seeing
that you were looking at them. Well, it would be
embarrassing, you see, to come face to face when they
were doing it.'

A thorough harrowing with a disc harrow was the next step,
but this was insufficient to bury the grasses properly in the mud
and to produce the fine silky tilth into which one's feet sink a
foot or eighteen inches to touch the hard crust of the field's
floor. For that, the whole family had to come and stamp.

'After the first day at that you'd come back covered
in mud to your thighs and you'd be so stiff and tender,
your feet rubbed so raw that you could hardly move
about the house, except gingerly on your hands and
knees. But you still had to go the next day and do the
same.'

The next task was to make the banks, to build them up with mud, tamping it down as tightly as possible so that it would neither leak water nor grow weeds, and finally came the levelling: flat boards were dragged across the fields, then bumps were flattened and depressions filled more selectively with the flat edge of a broad wooden rake.

The fields were now ready for planting, but planting rice is not just an agricultural operation; it is an occasion. Even now the Emperor gets on his gum boots and goes to one of the Imperial farms and plants a few symbolic seedlings. His ancestors a thousand years ago used to go in full regalia to certain sacred fields; there would be music, elaborate prayerful ritual, and choral singing by the virgin planters as they worked, the songs and prayers weaving around and about the themes of the tender fresh promise of both seedlings and virgin, the hoped-for swelling of the ears of the one and the bellies of the other, and the mana of the Emperor and his ancestral gods which kept the seasons in their courses and made the renewal of life possible.

In Shinohata, too, women still speak of the rice-planting as 'o-taue', using the respectful/festal prefix to indicate that it is something special. 'Have you finished your o-taue?' is the common form of greeting at that season. The planting used to be done in large groups. There would be special school holidays for the children to take part. Groups of neighbours would pool their labour and do each other's fields in turn, a line of men, women and children moving steadily across the field thrusting little clumps of three or four seedlings into the soft mud with a lightning speed which comes only with long practice. When its fields were finished each household would entertain the whole group to supper. It was generally seen as a pleasant occasion – hard, but not too hard, work, special rice-cakes and pickles to be eaten in the tea breaks, a special spread with saké or sweet-potato hooch for the men in the evenings. Requests to help with the rice-planting were issued almost as invitations to a party, though the inequalities of exchange between those who had a lot and those who had very few fields would be settled eventually in cash.

Weeding the rice fields was the next time-consuming process. By the end of the nineteenth century everyone planted rice in straight rows either by using guide-ropes for every fourth or fifth row or by impressing a grid pattern on the field bed with a special roller. There was even a prefectural bye-law passed around the turn of the century which made it a legal offence not to plant in straight rows. This was the era of what historians, in honour of similar authoritarian attempts to boost agricultural productivity on the part of Frederick the Great, call 'extension by the police-agent's sabre'. The point was that straight-row planting made for quicker – and hence more frequent and efficient – weeding because one could push a simple rotary weeder along between the rows. Even so, that did not eliminate the need to go over the field by hand, pulling the weeds close to and in between the clumps, collecting them into a bundle and stamping them firmly into the field. For the third weeding, when the rice was already two feet high, there were special masks to protect one's face from the sharp points and edges of the leaves. And still, even later, when the rice was waist high, there remained the task of walking through to pull out the most resilient and persistent of all weeds, the hie barnyard millet, which could still compete with rice even after it was established and could soon outstrip the rice if left unhindered.

The fields were allowed to dry out for the final stages of ripening and were firm by harvest time. Reaping was not done with stand-up long scythes (they were tried in the late nineteenth century, but too many ears of grain were lost when the stalks were allowed to fall where they would). Instead, one reaped with bent backs, seizing a clump at a time in one hand and cutting it with a short saw-edged sickle with the other. Several clumps laid gently together made a bundle to be tied and hung to dry, ears down, on racks specially built in the fields – and often built in great haste when a shower of rain threatened to spoil the grain.

Threshing could be done more or less at leisure, though the sheaves could not be left in the fields too long without loss from sparrows and other predators, and storage was less of a problem once the threshing was done. Threshing was not quite the right word for the most common process at the turn of the century – that of stripping the ears from the stalk by pulling them through the teeth of a metal comb-like object whose name is best translated as 'millitooth'. Then, after treading and winnowing with a large hand-operated fan, one had the grain ready for storage. There were still two more processes to go before the rice was ready for the table. The de-husking was once a rather skilled task which only few people in the village could do, but later a simpler machine came in which any householder could use. The de-husking reduced the weight by about 40 per cent so that it was in this form that rice was marketed, though households usually stored their rice in the husk. The final operation was to polish off the thin brown outer integument to produce white rice. Nutrition experts discovered fairly early in the century what a lot of nutrients were lost in this way – nutrients which could prevent such complaints as beri-beri – and during war-time their propaganda was effective in persuading people only to half-mill their rice. But established taste prevailed again as soon as patriotism ceased to reinforce scientific advice in the struggle against entrenched tastes – tastes which had their roots partly in food preferences (for only fully milled rice swells to a fluffy softness), partly in the fact that eating white rice, unmixed with inferior grains, had long been counted a mark of superior social status.

Still, in 1955, some of the efforts being made to improve rice cultivation were in the direction of increasing labour intensity. Land was the factor in short supply. Labour was abundant. Any means by which more rice could be got from a given piece of land merely by the expenditure of a little extra effort seemed worth trying. One keen farmer in Shinohata was using a new double-transplanting method. The seed was first sown on dry land in his yard, carefully watered and protected from frost by vinyl sheets. In this way it could be started earlier, at a time when the water was still too cold for sowing in a normal flooded seed-bed, so that when other farmers were sowing their seeds he could transplant tiny seedlings to the seed-bed, and the overall longer growing season made it possible to use later varieties with higher yields.

But already a number of labour-saving innovations were widely used. Chemical fertilizer was a far more important source of nutrients than green manure, and hardly anyone went to the mountains to cut grass any more. Threshing had been simplified early in the century by simple pedal-operated threshing machines. By 1955 a number of Shinohata houses had bigger and better threshing machines powered by petrol motors, and those who did not have their own made use of a larger powered machine owned collectively by the hamlet – or, more accurately, by the hamlet's Agricultural Practice Association to which everyone belonged. Powered tillers were then coming into use, and a few farmers in neighbouring hamlets who owned them did contract ploughing and field preparation for those who had better ways of using their time than doing it themselves with ox-drawn implements.

In the last twenty years, and especially the last ten, however, the pace of mechanization has been faster than ever before. Every house now has its two-wheeled multi-purpose tiller to do all the operations for field preparation in a quarter of the time it used to take with an ox. Simple reaper-binder machines have taken the back-breaking labour out of harvesting, though experiments with small-scale combine harvesters have not been successful because of the difficulties of drying the grain without lowering quality, and the sheaves still have to be dried on racks and threshed much as they were twenty years ago. Many farmers have a grass cutter like a circular saw powered by a back-pack petrol engine which eliminates the tedium of trimming the grass banks with a sickle. This grass from the banks is still thrown into the fields, but no one bothers to go much further afield for green manure. Concrete edging has eliminated the labour of building impermeable banks. Early weeding of rice fields, groping among the plants with one's fingers, is now an archaic practice, replaced by liberal use of herbicide, though the resilient barnyard millet still has to be pulled by hand. Spraying against insects and diseases is done fairly cheaply by the Co-operatives with powerful sprays, and there is talk of their hiring a helicopter this year. (There is a strong collective interest in making disease control effective on everybody's fields, since pests, once they take hold, can spread.) Bird-scaring is no longer the job of the school-children or old men with carbide guns. Children still enjoy making scarecrows in fantasy shapes and comic clothes, but now there are the automatic scarers and plenty of cheap glittering metal strips to suspend from ropes strung across the fields.

But the most spectacular innovation is the rice-planter. These smart, brightly painted machines are certainly ingenious. They are loaded with a pack of seedlings grown in special trays and move under their own power across the fields, with a couple of high-speed arms snatching three or four seedlings at a time and embedding them at just the right depth in the mud in rows as straight as the guiding hand of the operator can steer the machine. Only half-a-dozen houses in Shinohata have these machines as yet, but many more borrow one, or share in the ownership of one, or get their fields planted by an owner, for cash or in exchange for labour. Some older couples, who plant only an acre or so, still use the hand-planting method, partly because it is a pleasant excuse to get one's children to come back from Tokyo for the weekend to help. Some fields towards the bottom end of the irrigation channels which get their water late in the season still have to be planted by hand because the machine handles only small seedlings and later planting requires somewhat more developed seedlings if the growing season is not to be cut too short.

There is still something of a sense of occasion when the planting is done by hand, especially if sons and daughters come home to take part. There is a traditional way of doing things which is still observed. One tries to get enough people to finish the fields in one day. The end of the first operation, the pulling and bundling of the seedlings, should finish by the mid-morning break, the occasion for a special spread. As one moves in a line across the field, one does so at a uniform steady pace, but half-way across each field a halt is declared for three or four minutes to stretch backs, gaze around and comment on the state of neighbours' fields. There is entertainment again in the evening, and red rice is cooked and distributed to neighbours.

But such scenes will probably become increasingly rare, for the pace of mechanization in the last few years has been particularly rapid. According to the Ministry of Agriculture, the proportion of rice fields planted by machine jumped from 4 per cent to 32 per cent between 1970 and 1973; the proportion reaped by machine from 38 per cent to 71 per cent in the same period. The general result is a spectacular decrease in the amount of time and human effort needed to grow a crop of rice. Seventy years ago an acre of rice absorbed ninety or a hundred days of labour (including all the final processing) and fifteen

(60 kilogramme) bales of rice would have been counted a good harvest. Twenty years ago the input was fifty to sixty days and, thanks to improvements in varieties, fertilizers and pest control, one could count on twenty bales in a normal year. Today, thirty to thirty-five days' work and twenty-five bales is the standard. And the work itself is lighter. One does not have to push and tug and shout at a powered tiller as one did at an ox. There is less crouching and bending. One does not have to pull the sheaves up the hill in a hand-cart. 'My tiller broke down the other day and I had to pull a cart full of mulberry roots up the road. My! it was hard work! It shows how soft we've got. Not so long ago I was doing that sort of thing every day and thought nothing of it.'

There is, though, a rough unloving casualness about some of these modern methods which offends some people. One man who still counts himself as primarily a farmer, but gets a good share of his income from work on construction sites, is very conscious that the opportunity cost of every day spent on his fields is the fourteen dollars he can be earning elsewhere. He was explaining how, now that everything was done quickly with machines, they carefully calculated costs. 'For example it's not worth my while to fill in the space round the edges where the planter can't reach, by planting extra seedlings by hand. It means you have to reap by hand, too, and there's the danger of damaging your machines on the concrete edging. So I leave it empty.' 'You do,' said his wife, 'but I fill it in afterwards. I just can't bear to see good land wasted.'

Nowadays this strong ethical sense of the importance of 'good husbandry' is chiefly confined to the old people, especially the older couples with a salary-earning son who no longer have the main bread-winning responsibility and cultivate a few fields to keep themselves active, to provide the family's rice and to earn themselves the independence of their own pocket money – and among them, especially the women with their more than equal share of the work ethic.

One innovation which totally offends this sense of good husbandry is a new planting method which is still in the experimental stage. It is certainly somewhat bizarre. One buys a large number of special cardboard frames divided into little sections about 2 cm square, each one of which is lined with paper. One

fills the frame with earth, then pushes over it a cheap but ingenious roller device which implants three or four rice seeds
in each little section. As one waters liberally and frequently
(keeping the temperature up with vinyl sheeting) the cardboard
frame disintegrates, but not the inner paper linings, the two ends
of which are gummed together to make a circular ring. Hence
when the seedlings are ready each clump of three or four has its
roots and the earth around them neatly encased in a little paper
wrapper. These one shovels indiscriminately into sacks, takes
to the fields, grabs by the handful and throws as high into the
air as possible. They fall, of course, like a shuttle-cock, root
first, and if one has thrown them high enough they sink a
reasonable depth into the mud. If one is feeling extra con-
scientious one can go round the field afterwards thinning out
the places where seedling bombs have fallen too thickly and
filling in where they are thin on the ground, but Shinohata's
current exponent of this method, an employee of the
Agricultural Co-operative, is insistent that such refinements
are unnecessary; the whole point is to save labour, to plant in
half-an-hour a field which would take two man-days by
ordinary methods. It's just not worth an extra hour for the
fiddling business of evening out the spread. It's a lot of
superstition that denser planting reduces yields. Just put an
extra bit of fertilizer on. Last year, he claimed, the first year
he tried the method, he got a 15 per cent higher yield than
usual.

Tomiyo, who had just spent a day weeding three-quarters of
an acre, turning over the mud with her fingers around each
clump of rice ('the weed-killer is all very well, but you can't use
it too soon or it weakens the rice and the early weeds might be
well established by then'), reported this claim with indignant
snorts of disbelief. 'How can a man who can leave a field in that
sort of higgledy-piggledy mess call himself a farmer!' But most
of the men have few such scruples and are rather taken with the
idea, particularly the younger 'salary men' now mobilized occasionally by their parents for a little Sunday work, but destined,
if they are going to continue to keep their land and go on growing rice, to have eventually to take the chief responsibility. To
begin with, the 'airborne planting' method does not require an
expensive machine. 'Mechanization poverty' is the word one of

them used to describe the way things were going. He had recently come back to the village after ten years in Tokyo to take a job in the village office, and his salary was the chief income of the family: his parents, he and his wife, and their one child. His parents were lively active sixty-year-olds, still planting just over an acre of rice and twice that area of mulberry and fruit trees. They had recently had to buy a new tiller for $1,450; then they had indulged in a rice planter, which with all the extras had come to another $1,350. And yet the gross value of a year's crop from their acre-and-a-half would be only in the region of $1,300 – of which close to $100 would already have been spent on seed and chemicals. 'It is only because we don't really rely on making any money from farming,' he explained, 'that we can afford to buy all these machines so as to make life a bit easier for the old people – and eventually for ourselves.'

Not, in fact, that many of these young men are likely to turn into enthusiastic part-time farmers. They are pleased enough with the thought of inheriting valuable land. They would not like to sell it, and would be happy enough to grow their own rice on part of it, provided they can do so in a reasonably painless way. The traditional method of enjoying the benefits of land ownership – to let it to a tenant – is still just possible. There are a few vigorous farmers in their fifties who are prepared to take on one or two extra fields and give the owner about 25 per cent of the crop. But they are rapidly disappearing. A new alternative is to have one's fields prepared and planted by a contractor; the going price in 1975, as agreed by the township's Agricultural Committee and published in the town's monthly bulletin, was about $230 per acre (with a prospective yield worth about $1,200). The most commonly discussed solution is for the Agricultural Co-operative to do the contracting on a large scale. They have not quite worked out the economics of it yet, but, say the younger men, with bigger and more efficient machines and a well-paid professional workforce it should be possible for the Co-op to do all the mechanizable operations, leaving them only with the job of daily checking the water level, pulling the barnyard millet and threshing, and still charge not more than 40 per cent of the value of the crop.

All that presupposes, of course, that the relation between wage costs and price of rice would remain more or less what it is today. And that is by no means certain. Agricultural price policy has hitherto been yet one more method by which the government has redistributed to the traditional backwaters of the Japanese economy some of the proceeds of the great advances in productivity in the industrial sector. Or, more accurately, rice price policy has played this role, and could do so more effectively because nearly every farm household grows some rice.

Greatly simplified, the story is as follows. When the economy took off towards the end of the 1950s, industry and commerce began to suck out all the young unmarried workers and some of the younger married couples from the countryside. But those men over thirty who were settled as married heads of farm families were not so mobile. Few were prepared to face the housing shortages of the town and a second-rate town job (for the biggest and best firms with their 'life-time employment system' continued to recruit their workers straight from school) at the cost of giving up what was, after all, at least a secure livelihood on their inherited farm – and not everybody was able to find jobs to which they could commute from home. So, although the number of workers engaged in agriculture fell between 1955 and 1974 from 40 per cent to 12 per cent of the workforce, the number of farm families declined only from 5·9 to 5·0 million. The average age of the men who remained primarily engaged in agriculture gradually rose: in 1974 over 30 per cent of them were over sixty.

Since the prospects of increasing their productivity were limited, the chief way in which the level of living of these residual workers could be made to keep up with the rising standards in the towns was by changes in relative prices. And that is what has happened. Prices of agricultural products have risen so much faster than industrial products that by 1970 a basket of farm products was buying 80 per cent more manufactured goods than in 1955. In very large measure this has been the result of deliberate government action. Agricultural price policy was in part a substitute for an old-age pensions policy. And, welfare considerations apart, the electoral interests of the Liberal Democratic Party gave it a strong concern with maintaining agricultural prices.

So, in the 1960s, the price the Japanese government paid

farmers for their rice rose steadily to a point far above international price levels. Better prices encouraged further increases in production (helped also by continuing improvements in fertilizers and rice strains) at a time when consumption of rice was declining with changing food habits – and the government was committed to buying everything produced. The invention of the automatic time-switch-operated electric cooker temporarily halted the decline in consumption; the modern urban housewife who had switched to toast for breakfast could feed her family a rice meal and still have her extra half hour in bed. But by 1970 the Kakizaka Co-operative – the Co-ops act as the government's agent in the rice-purchase scheme – was building extra storage granaries and still had some of the 1967 crop in its existing ones. Ingenious plans were devised to store the rice in large inflatable balloons in the cool depths of Lake Biwa. At this point the government introduced a non-production incentive scheme. Farmers could get $310 for every acre of paddy land on which they abstained from planting rice. In 1974, with the world food shortage, that particular scheme was abandoned. The price was increased by a spectacular 32 per cent. The figure had more to do with maintaining parity with urban wages in that inflation year than it did with the rising international price levels: at $800 per metric tonne, the government was still paying well above even the unprecedented world market prices. The 13,600 yen it paid the farmer for every bale was 3,400 yen more than the price at which it released rice into the distribution system. The difference was a subsidy borne by the taxpayer – as also was an additional 2,900 yen per bale which represented collection, storage and transport costs, and the loss incurred in disposing of the surplus which was still expected to be substantial.

These devices have helped to keep up farm income. Even though agriculture now provides only 30 per cent of the total income of the nation's five million 'farm families', it is an important 30 per cent. Rice remains the favourite crop of the part-time farmers with small holdings, and remains an important source of the income of the million or so families who still derive the majority of their income from agriculture. How far, though, future governments will be prepared to keep up present levels of subsidies when the chief recipients are no longer the older generation of farmers whom the industrial boom passed by, but 'salary men' enjoying a liberal rent on their inherited land for a very modest expenditure of effort, remains to be seen.

7

The Silken Caterpillar

Shinohata has never within recent memory been a society where any strong ethical or magical significance was attached to the division of labour between the sexes. Women never did the tougher forest work, but they were expected to be able to take a horse into the woods and bring it back laden with grass or firewood. Men did the ploughing and indeed most of the operations with horse or oxen, as they do now most of the operations with machines. Masayoshi and his wife are somewhat exceptional. He is the gentlest of Shinohata men. He was always slightly apprehensive about his ox and will have nothing to do with these noisy, frightening machines; his wife is a brisk confident lady who handles both with aplomb. They are considered a subject for good-natured fun, but not as outrageous deviants. Women can be seen frequently driving their tiller and trailer at a brisk pace around the village and a number have got licences to drive the light farm trucks. Women are generally accepted to be the more nimble, rapid and accurate rice planters, and the word still used, though half jokingly, for someone planting rice is a 'rice maiden', reflecting all the fertility ritual associations that a thousand years ago probably did make it exclusively a woman's job. But men suffer no loss of masculinity by working alongside them. Generally roles are interchangeable within the framework of the general assumption that men take the major initiative and responsibility and their wives act chiefly as subordinate helpers.

The one activity in which these roles are reversed is the breeding of silkworms. Out of family loyalty, a woman will, of course, boast about the yield per acre of her family's rice fields, but it is her *personal* pride that is invested in her skill in handling silkworms; the weight of cocoons she manages to get from each gram of 'seed'; the proportion of properly oval as opposed to mis-shapen double cocoons. The o-kaiko are *her* o-kaiko.

Mechanization has affected silkworm breeding a good deal less than rice agriculture, although there are dark rumours of a future in which the whole thing can be done in a factory, the worms fed on synthetic proteins under careful temperature and humidity control, untouched by human hand and in defiance of the seasons. But today the basic pattern of work remains almost as it was a century ago. The mulberry stock is much the same and so is the method of gathering it – cutting young shoots early in the season and whole developed branches at the end; in between stripping the leaves from the branches with neat little cutting blades affixed to rings on each index finger – at a speed which, when one clumsily tries it oneself, seems like a feat of impossible legerdemain. The young worms require the tenderest leaves carefully chopped fine; as they grow older they become less discriminating. The leaves should be as fresh as possible, but they must be dry. That means frequent cutting, and frantic activity at the promise of rain; everyone rushes to the fields and the help of all the family is mobilized to get in a stock before the first drops fall. Skill lies in judging exactly the right amount to feed them, keeping them clean, using the right amount of disinfectant, keeping a check on the temperature and humidity and having the keenness of eye to judge exactly the transparency of skin which indicates that the worm is ready to be put in the frames and settle down to spinning its cocoon – so that it is not put in too soon to waste energy wandering around, nor left too late so that it starts spinning in the feeding frames.

One minor innovation in techniques, now about twenty years old, is a revolving cocoon frame which utilizes the simple fact that the worms seeking a niche to spin their cocoon tend always to climb upwards. The weight of the worms turns the frame so that the vacant niches are always towards the top and the niche-hunting silkworms are sent back to the bottom to try another pass over the vacant holes. The revolving frames, as compared with the old flat straw frames, produce a much smaller proportion of the less valuable 'round cocoons' – the product of two silkworms entangling each other in a promiscuous shared cocoon.

Another simple device which saves transferring the silkworms by hand when one wants to clean their tray is a simple net kept taut in a frame. The net is placed on top of the tray of silkworms and fresh leaves spread over it. When the silkworms have climbed through the net and have gone to work on the fresh leaves the whole thing can then be lifted off and transferred to a new base, and the old one cleaned and disinfected for the next change.

The two biggest innovations, though, have been the 'haus' and the Co-operative early-rearing scheme. A 'house' means primarily a greenhouse but by extension any kind of steel-frame building for animal or plant production. Once, poorer families with smaller houses would give over the entire house, best living-room included, to the silkworms; the family would sleep in odd corners or in the walkways between the banks of trays. More prosperous houses had an upper storey especially for silkworms. Some still do, but most of the families in the hamlet which still rear silkworms now have a 'house' with open sides – or at least an open south side – which can be closed with tarpaulin curtains, and warmed with oil heaters to keep the temperatures at the levels which the Co-operative's guidance chart prescribes for each stage of the silkworm's growth.

Co-operative early rearing was started about fifteen years ago. For the first two weeks during which the silkworms come out of their eggs and go through their first two metamorphoses – while they are still small and require less room – there are considerable economies of scale in keeping them all in one place. A section of the village hall is given over to them; the trays are stacked six high, each stack on a set of castors, so that by rotating the boxes up and down the stacks and rotating the stacks around the room, the difference in temperature at different heights and in different corners of the room can be cancelled out and the worms kept at an even level of development. The extension adviser from the prefectural Silkworm Rearers'

Co-operative Federation calls every day, advises on disinfect-
ants and checks for signs of disease. Six or eight women take
each daily turn of duty. The work is not exhausting, there is
opportunity for endless gossip, a hundred yen each, pooled,
buys a fairly liberal supply of titbits to go with their frequent
cups of tea, and many bring home-made cakes as well. The
night before the distribution there is a final feast with beer and
saké for the adviser and the President of the Shinohata Silkworm
Rearers' Co-operative (who is always a man) and sweet wine for
the women.

That evening the announcement xylophones ring out over
the loudspeakers in every home in the hamlet. 'The distribution
of silkworms will take place at ten-thirty tomorrow morning.
There will be some left-over mulberry to share out too, so
please bring something to carry it in. I will repeat that. Distribution . . .' Said Tomiyo:

> You fix anything for a certain time in this village and
> most people will arrive half-an-hour late. But when it
> comes to the distribution of the silkworms, the women
> are up there half-an-hour early. They're that keen.
> They're on their mettle, too. You can't cheat any more
> with this co-operative rearing. Some women would
> turn in 15 kan of cocoons at the end and claim that they
> got them out of 15 grammes of eggs when in fact they'd
> taken 20. Now everybody knows how much each
> woman has taken. It's all written up on the blackboard.

Their skills and their investment of pride and ego apart, there
is a fascinating mixture of tenderness and matter-of-factness in
the women's attitudes to their silkworms. When they sort them
after the third or fourth 'sleep', separating the ones that are
already 'awake' from the slower ones still immobile with their
heads upraised as if frozen in a momentary gesture of attentive
curiosity, they do so with the same brisk efficiency as the women
in the Co-operative packing station sorting peaches. And yet
there is a loose gentleness in their grip that shows their awareness that they are handling living things. They are not just
kaiko, but o-kaiko, with the respectful prefix – or, more affectionately in the local dialect, o-buku.

Indeed, after a lifetime of rearing silkworms, the women have not entirely lost a sense that there is something rather miraculous about the transformation which takes place four times a year under their guiding hands. In five short weeks a tiny black speck on a piece of cardboard is transformed into a perfectly formed two-inch caterpillar which is nothing more than a living bundle of silken thread waiting to spin itself inside out, then to evolve in a few more days inside its extruded self into a winged moth ready to seek its fellow, to mate and start the whole process over again. Somehow it all seems more mysterious and miraculous than the sprouting of a plant from an ear of grain. What impresses most is the strength of the lifeforce, the sheer ceaseless determination with which the silkworms pursue their fate. 'Just listen to them,' a woman will say, as she takes you into her 'house', and it is indeed surprising that the mere crunching of mulberry leaves in tiny caterpillar jaws, even in the ten thousand caterpillar jaws of an average rearing, should produce such a susurration. Night and day they feed relentlessly on, except during their sleeps. 'You should see them,' one dumpy old lady explained, 'when they come out of their sleep. Suddenly their old mouth drops off and the skin splits across the top of the head; they put their new little feet out through the hole, and then they have to struggle to get out of their old skin. And, my! they do have to struggle. You should see them. It's an amazing sight.'

The cash reward is not insignificant for the budget of the twenty-odd families who still rear silkworms. From an acre of mulberry, well fertilized and weeded and mulched with straw in winter, one should get enough mulberry to take about 65 grammes of eggs, yielding, after a month's intensive work, about 65 to 60 kilogrammes of cocoons for a price of $1,050 to $1,300 in 1974. A few years before the price had been some 40 per cent higher. Growing imports from Korea and China were responsible for the fall. Import restrictions on a 'this-year-only basis' were renewed again in 1975 but the Ministry of Trade will make sure that they are not renewed for ever. 'And one can see the consumer's point of view too,' said one contemplative farmer. 'Of course he wants cheap silk.' Already in 1975 two or three of the hundred acres or so planted to mulberry had been left to grow weeds because their owners were busy elsewhere and no one wanted to rent them.

When, eventually, every reasonable calculation counsels the abandonment of silkworm rearing, many Shinohata women will feel a sense of loss.

8

The Search for the Alchemist's Secret

In June, the 200-acre slope of Shinohata's dry-field area looks like a sea of bright green mulberry leaves, for mulberry is planted on a good proportion of the area. A small part of the rest is the housewife's preserve, used for growing radishes, aubergines, carrots, strawberries, Irish potatoes, squash, cucumbers and a variety of lettuces, cabbages and beans exclusively for home consumption and as stock for the incessant gift exchanges which help to mend fences and to keep the ties of neighbourliness sweet.

How to make effective use of the dry land which remains has been the perennial problem of Shinohata agriculture. Wheat or barley, followed by soya beans, was once the answer. After taking enough wheat to make noodles – a long-established food as an occasional substitute for one or two of the three or four bowls of rice eaten at each meal – and enough beans to make one's own soya sauce and bean paste for soups, a few surplus bags could be sold through the Co-operative. Wheat has now disappeared; beans are still grown on a reduced scale for home consumption only. The price of neither makes it worthwhile growing more for sale. Just after the war a beer company organized a hop-growers' co-operative, and tall poles with wires strung across them sprang up in little quarter-acre patches all over the slope. But with fewer children to help in the picking, more expensive labour, and a price that was kept low by cheaper imports, the hop growers gave up one by one.

Then, for a while, tobacco was grown, but as the mulberry came back after the war that had to stop: tobacco grown any-where near mulberry transfers some of its nicotine and spoils the mulberry leaf and in the Shinohata dry-field area, with the tiny plots of different owners lying side by side, the rules of good-neighbourliness meant that it had to be one or the other.

In 1955 there was an enthusiastic response when the Co-operative arranged, or believed itself to have arranged, a con-tract with a cannery to take large quantities of canning peaches. The returns per acre were expected to be fabulous. But by the time the peaches were nearly ready, three years later, it became clear that the cannery had made no firm promises; it had too many alternative sources for a good bargain to be struck, and the trees were chopped down before they had borne fruit.

Since then plums, tomatoes, konnyaku (the slow-growing root which, harvested after three years and powdered, makes the translucent, rubbery, almost tasteless but curiously much prized ingredient of sukiyaki and other stew-like dishes), pine seedlings, azalea seedlings, peaches, chestnuts, paulownia trees (a quick-growing timber used for the best wooden clogs), table grapes, beef cattle, mushrooms, and oak-mushrooms have all at one time been 'in'. One of the extension workers in the Co-operative will persuade one or two friends to try something with encouraging results. Market prospects will be found to be promising. The Co-operative will then organize a tomato group or a peach group, a chairman will be elected and some way will be found of organizing a subsidy or a loan, under one of the many government schemes for encouraging the diversification and modernization of agriculture. After a few years the high hopes of the first season are disappointed, and only a few growers who are satisfied with more modest returns stick it out.

Sometimes the problem will be that the cooler temperatures of Shinohata have not been properly taken into account; more often it will be unexpected price changes – though not *all* that unexpected, because it is precisely the crops which seem to offer the glittering rewards that attract other farmers besides those of Shinohata. In any case, with rarely much more than an acre or two of dry fields, only a part of which they devote to a new venture, Shinohata farmers can hardly expect to get economies of scale or produce enough to make small profit-margins add up to a reasonable return.

> 'A vicious circle sets in. You are disappointed with the first results and so you lose your enthusiasm: you don't bother with that extra spraying; where you could have weeded three times you only do it twice. And so you get a worse crop, and you are even less enthusiastic, and so it goes on.'

So far the least disappointing perishables have been peaches, dessert grapes and tomatoes, the sorting, packing and sale of which the Co-operative organizes on a fairly large scale – though the bulk of the produce comes from the southern, lower and warmer parts of the township. Tomatoes in particular, though risky, have sometimes turned out to offer a fair return. With a price varying between 100 and 800 yen per box, it requires nerve. The price usually falls some time around the end of August, and at that point men with no staying power will neglect the necessary spraying and fertilizing. But if they can hold out, Shinohata, with its cooler climate and later maturing, comes into its own and the price stays fairly high until the hothouse tomatoes from the Pacific coast come in in mid-October. But a good saleable crop requires constant attention.

So is it with the peaches and grapes. Each peach, as soon as the thinning has been done by hand, is enclosed in its own little paper bag (old telephone directories cut, pasted and provided with a little metal fastener by some ingenious back-room entrepreneur). This is a more effective way of producing a good presentable bloom on the fruit than mere spraying, but still the trees are sprayed several times a season. Grapes too have to be carefully pruned after the blossom has formed, and each cluster is dipped in a goblet of a chemical called jiberurin to make them seedless. The trick with grapes is to produce big bunches. The size of the bunch is the basis of the grading system and the price range for a two-kilogramme box can be as wide as 320 to 900 yen. And yet the taste is no different, say Shinohata farmers, contemptuous of, but prepared to pander to, the follies of the urban consumer.

But enthusiasm for new ventures is rapidly dwindling with

the growth of other sources of income. Shinohata's dry-field slope in the early summer of 1975 did not have quite the same neat garden-like appearance as it had ten, or even five, years ago. In a plot given over to azalea seedlings, a few blossoms are visible through a mass of yomogi weed and grasses. Some of the vineyards, after the bad harvest of the previous year, were growing wild, the weeds reaching up to a few meagre bunches of green grapes suspended from the wire frames. Other fields, say their owners, were being cultivated only because it is bad manners to grow weeds which spread to neighbouring fields. Other families, the family income assured by a son's or husband's earnings, have assimilated these once counted-on commercial crops into the category of garden crops to be eaten at home and given as neighbourly gifts.

> 'The year father died he decided we were getting too old to be climbing all over the peach trees putting little bags on each fruit, and it wasn't worth the money, so he cut down all except three for our own use. And then he died. So I planted chestnuts: thirty-five trees. Three years for peach and chestnuts, eight for persimmon, they say. You don't want to have to wait too long when you get to my age, and chestnuts don't need much attention . . . And you can pick them up off the ground and not have to climb all over the tree. All you have to do is spray them and keep the orchard weeded. I thought I'd make some money out of them, but by the time I've given away a bucket of them to everybody around, and then to visitors who popped in, there is not much left to sell, so I just send a few more buckets down to the relatives in the next village and that's it.'

A few years ago there was never any cause to leave a field fallow. One could usually find someone in the village to rent it if only at a nominal rent. There were still enough men in the village whom one could count as ambitious farmers; men who were farmers first and foremost, keen, if they could, to find some way of getting extra land and finding new profitable crops to make a living out of farming without resort to day labour at construction sites. Their number has declined as more have graduated into the older age bracket. Even at seventy, Naka-nobu, the hamlet's prize tomato grower, still comes in the ambitious farmer category, but most of his contemporaries show signs of declining energy and ambition, and are content to potter on with rice and mulberry on modest acreages. ('There's only me and the old woman, after all. We don't spend all that much.' 'With Takaro earning well, it's really a matter of grandpa and grandma earning their pocket money.')

And the remaining ambitious farmers, especially the few in their forties and one or two in their fifties, have recently, at least, found something that works, something that makes money, is not too strenuous and does not require buying or renting dry-field farmland. The new magic crop is 'shiitake', or 'oak mushrooms', a slightly rubbery fungus which grows in the rotting wood of a number of deciduous trees and has a delicate mushroomy aroma. Ways have been devised to induce their growth artificially. The logs are bought from contractors; holes are drilled in them with an electric drill and a plug of sawdust containing the spore is inserted. The logs are left to mature, stacked in shady woods for eighteen months and then soaked in water. A few days later they begin to sprout. The shiitake can be dried or sold fresh, the latter fetching the better price.

Shinohata's three pioneers of shiitake culture have come a long way since they started seven or eight years ago. They have perfected the art of producing fresh mushrooms – traditionally only a summer crop – throughout the winter in heated green-houses. They have rationalized and partly mechanized their handling system; great piles of logs are moved in metal frames from truck to dousing tank and back again by electric overhead lifters running on steel girders. They now have forty to fifty thousand logs each, send a car load of mushrooms to the market every day and make profits of $14,000 to $19,000 a year. One has cut the umbilical cord with tradition; he buys his rice and rents out his rice fields. The others still grow their acre of rice and have planted those of their dry fields which they have not rented out with non-time-consuming chestnuts. They already have a number of imitators, though none as yet on a similar scale.

In all of these developments, the abortive ones and the suc-cessful ones, the Agriculture Co-operative or the township's

Agricultural Committee, or, in the case of the mushrooms, the Forest Products Development Board, have played a crucial role. Japan's mini-farmers never have been independent entrepreneurs in the way that the capitalist farmers of the West, living in isolated houses surrounded by their own broad acres, used to be. The settlement pattern in clustered villages, the crucial dependence on rice agriculture with its shared irrigation systems involving collective village control of water and who could use it, the juxtaposition around each village of tiny plots whose use or misuse could affect the plots of a neighbour, the intricate patterns of labour exchange between households – all created a pattern in which the use of land was a right and a responsibility shared between the individual household and the village community. It was on these foundations that nineteenth-century governments built agriculture associations as a means of diffusing new seeds and channelling new methods, interlaced with appropriate moral exhortation, to the villagers. At first, like the villagers themselves, the associations tended to be dominated by landlords. State paternalism and the paternalism of the village interfused in a relation of mutual support. But in the twenties, new kinds of more democratically controlled co-operatives emerged; their functions were widened to include credit operations and marketing on a wider scale. During the war they came into their own as the channel through which agricultural materials were rationed and agricultural produce compulsorily requisitioned. These functions they retained for many years of shortage after the war, though in structure they were revamped (but again under state initiative, by close legislative prescription) as democratic organizations.

By the fifties they had grown into a formidable structure. The virtual monopoly over rice marketing which they retained even after the loosening of government controls was a major source of their strength, but so also was the integrated multipurpose nature of their operations. They would supply fertilizer on credit, market the crops, pay the proceeds into the farmer's savings account and debit that account for all his purchases of the wide range of goods on sale in the Co-operative shop without his ever having to handle cash. The local co-operatives were further strengthened by their links with superstructural organizations – prefectural and national federations with specialized functions, culminating in a National Marketing Federation, a Consumer Supply Federation and a National Co-operative Bank (which by the late fifties had deposits in the immediate post-harvest months of such magnitude that it had a predominant effect on short-call interest rates).

The structure was a democratic one. Officers at each level were elected from the next lower level: power flowed up from the bottom, from the mass membership. Or at least that was the case in theory. In practice, quite apart from the iron law of oligarchy (immensely strengthened in a co-operative, as compared with a political party, by the genuinely arcane nature of the business expertise which higher-level officers acquire), a crucial determinant of the locus of power was the fact that the money flowed from the top down. As greater affluence made more funds available, the co-operatives were increasingly used as a channel through which a paternalistic bureaucracy delivered a wide variety of loans and subsidies to encourage what they considered to be desirable initiatives most likely to lead to the development of a viable agriculture. As the sixties wore on and the cash available increased, the subsidies and loans policy acquired a slightly broader function: the co-operatives became, along with state finance for local government and a high rice price, the third arm of the government's policy of redistributing to rural areas part of the wealth created by industrial growth. Counting only those loans channelled through the co-operatives the total amount outstanding at the end of 1973 was equal to 1,330,000 yen (roughly $4,750 or £2,050) for each of Japan's five million farm families – over two-and-a-half times the total amount of new fixed investment and 4 per cent more than the total value of agricultural production during that year.

Some of the loan funds remain earmarked for special purposes, their varying interest rates (still, in 1974, mostly between $5\frac{1}{2}$ and $6\frac{1}{2}$ per cent) and length of grace period being a measure of the worthiness of that purpose in the eyes of the makers of policy. There are the Farm Implement Modernization Fund; the Repair and Improvement of Farm Roads Fund; the Owner-Farmer Establishment Fund (to finance the purchase of land by energetic full-time farmers) and the Farm Successors' Fund (to provide cash to modernize the operations of farms they were taking over from their parents).

A number of other loan schemes have had as their purpose to help make village life more attractive and thereby keep the boys down on the farm, or persuade them to come back to it. There is a House Improvement Loan Scheme and a Daily Life Improvement Loan Scheme (chiefly to reconstruct and equip kitchens), and even a Car Purchase Loan Scheme, though this last bears a higher 9 per cent interest rate – deemed a little hard to swallow, perhaps, as part of an agricultural policy worthy of a high level of subsidization. Kitchens are fine; the emancipation of women by lightening the domestic load was a slogan of post-war democracy, and hence partook of proper seriousness of purpose, but a car still counts as something of a self-indulgent luxury.

All of these schemes were part of a general agricultural policy proclaimed with enthusiasm in the early sixties and still not entirely abandoned in spite of a decade of disappointment. Part-time farming – *unserious* farming, and hence *poor* farming – was to be thoroughly discouraged. The flow of labour out of farming with the industrial boom was to lead, instead, to a reduction of the number of farm families, the brisk sale of land and a corresponding increase in the acreage of the remaining farmers who would, it was hoped, be vigorous and progressive entrepreneurs capable of making a good living from farming without excessive subsidization.

So far these hopes have been disappointed. In spite of all these loans and subsidies and exhortations, instead of a million full-time farmers, Japan still has more than five million, mostly part-time, farm households. The security of a steady job on the one hand, and both the investment security and the opportunities of extra income provided by the retention of farmland on the other, have proved too attractive a combination, though each year's Agricultural White Paper continues to make meticulous analyses of land sales and purchases, and of the numbers in the younger age groups returning to farming, manfully seeking some glimmer of evidence that the hopes of those officials who care about *real* farming may one day be fulfilled.

Meanwhile, Shinohata's farmers, both the few enterprisers who fulfil the Ministry's specification as full-time farmers, and also the bulk of part-time or would-be part-time farmers, have benefited considerably from these special-purpose schemes, and even more from the other (and in volume more substantial) general purpose schemes of more flexible application – those for working capital and for 'farm management improvement'. A good many of their machines have been bought with Co-operative loans. The mushroom growers were able to finance all their initial investment with loans, half from the Forest Products Development Board and half from the Co-operative, contributing a notional 20 per cent of the total themselves in the form of the labour they provided in erecting steel-frame 'houses' and preparing the ground.

The Co-operative shares risks too. In 1969 it organized a group of farmers to keep beef cattle. The cattle sheds, the calves and the feed were all provided by the Co-operative and given to the farmer on credit. The Co-operative also arranged the sale of the beef. The final profit was paid into the farmer's personal Co-operative account without his ever having had to lay out a yen of capital. In 1970 the Shinohata farmers who had joined the scheme were sure they were on to a good thing. The calculations seemed promising:

Cost of calf	80,000	
feed	100,000	
interest	10,000	
Total cost	190,000	
Slaughterhouse price	240,000	Profit 50,000

Five years later I found a group of Co-operative officials earnestly discussing how to deal with a very different situation. Calves had been scarce and extremely costly in 1973. The price of feed had soared the following year. Now the figures were:

Cost of calf	450,000	
feed	250,000	
interest	30,000	
Total cost	730,000	
Slaughterhouse price	650,000	Loss 80,000

In theory, instead of paying money into the breeder's accounts they would have to demand a payment from them of 80,000 yen for every cow sold. How could they offer such a

reward for two years' hard work? Eventually some means was found of rolling the loans forward so that, it was hoped, time – and inflation – would take care of the matter.

The Co-operative not only plays an essential entrepreneurial role and shares a good part of the risk-bearing function; it also offers general technical guidance on a day-to-day basis, through the efforts of five technical advisers whose salaries are largely subsidized out of public funds. After the rice expert had been on a tour of inspection in June 1975, for instance, a loudspeaker car was sent round to every hamlet to advise that the seedlings were showing signs of weakness due to the cooler-than-expected weather, and a thorough and early spraying was advisable. Similar advice about specialist crops is diffused through an established person-to-person communications network in each of the special growers' groups. More generally, the monthly news bulletin provides short paragraphs of seasonal advice – on how to plant tomatoes, spray grapes or get a large litter from pigs.

The bulletin is a good reflection of the Co-operative style. There are enthusiastic descriptions of new projects – to take over fallow fields to grow feed stuffs under direct Co-operative management, to install a new machinery repair depot, to open a petrol station, to start a new giro scheme making it possible to send drafts to other Co-operative savings accounts in any part of Japan. There are appeals for members' loyal co-operation in a scheme to increase the volume of paid-up share capital to balance their increase in fixed assets. There are chunks of turgid bureaucratic prose explaining how the revised inheritance tax law applies to farmland or the scope and purpose of a new loan scheme. There is the odd reader's letter complaining that in elections for council members candidates seem exclusively interested in the honour of being elected rather than in improving the Co-operative. And there is always, at the end, a collection of seventeen-syllable haiku triplets, written to a theme set the previous month: 'Mist', 'Spring Kimono', 'Rice Planting'.

> Bare skin of rock
> setting off the peach blossom
> A misty spring.

A misty field
On a bank quietly
an old man fishing.

Spring Kimono
and the faint aroma
of camphor balls.

Just to see again
Mother's dumpy frame!
Spring Kimono.

The Co-operative is not intended to be just a mutual interest
association but also an aspect of community. Once it was more
genuinely so, when the Co-operatives were smaller, organized
on the basis of the old four- to five-hamlet villages, and every
member knew every Co-operative official by his first name. In
1955, when the roof of the Co-operative store-house was falling
into disrepair, the council all gave a day's voluntary labour to
put it in shape again. But now efficiency demands larger units in
Co-operative as in local government administration. Following
the amalgamations of the old villages into a new township, the
Co-operatives have also been amalgamated to create a new unit
covering the whole of the new town. It is now a large organization with thirty-five employees, assets of a billion-and-a-half
yen, and a turnover of nearly half-a-billion on its consumer
operations and half as much again on its marketing operations.

It was bound in the process to become more impersonal and
bureaucratic, but less so than one might imagine. Although in
formal principle a voluntary association, the option of not
belonging hardly occurs to anyone. If one lives in a hamlet like
Shinohata and has anything to do with agriculture at all, membership is taken for granted as it is in the hamlet association
itself. And, as in the hamlet association, the unit of membership
is the household, not the individual. Indeed, the Co-operative
still operates rather as a federation of constituent hamlets. Each
hamlet has an Agricultural Practice Association – simply the
hamlet in another guise with a different set of officers – which is
an official sub-unit of the Co-operative used for the distribution
of insecticides and herbicides and fertilizer, the monthly
newsletter and the annual questionnaire through which the

Co-operative gathers its members' views on what it should be doing and how well it is doing what it already does. The annual general meetings are no longer meetings of the whole membership but of representatives selected (usually on a Buggin's turn basis) in a ratio of one to every five households. They tend to be tame affairs, however. Somewhat more lively debate takes place in what are called 'kondankai', literally 'intimate talk meetings' – discussions which the President or Vice-President hold in the evenings of the preceding two weeks in each of the fourteen constituent hamlets. There, within the hamlet family, people can be less constrained and speak more freely.

It is this cell-like structure which helps to sustain some sense of loyalty to the Co-operative. There never has been much of an *ideological* loyalty. The 'Rochdale spirit', the principle of co-operation as a morally superior alternative to the individualistic self-seeking of commercial capitalism, has never been of much importance. It was not needed, as it was needed in Anglo-Saxon societies where an already established individualism had to be consciously curbed if co-operation was to succeed; the 'natural' collectivism of the small hamlet community provided an adequate substitute as soon as loyalty to the Co-operative became defined as another aspect of good citizenship, another expression of the individual household's sense of duty to the village community. It was in these terms that people spoke with disapproval several years ago of several farmers who started sending their grapes directly to a merchant.

> They don't get a much better price: they just save the Co-op packing charges by doing the packing themselves. You should see them at the Co-op meetings. When the Chairman talks about the need for all members to support the Co-op and to do all their marketing through it, they nod agreement as cool as can be and never say a word. And then look at what they actually do!

'They've got quite a nerve,' a Co-operative official commented, 'to take all their materials and technical advice from the Co-op and then to sell elsewhere. But fortunately they are exceptions.' Without open and formal confrontation, with no more than the general hints and reiteration of principles at hamlet meetings, they could, he implied, be eventually brought back to the path of virtue.

The greater remoteness of the new Co-operative – the greater physical distance of its offices – does make a difference.

> When the Co-operative was just the one large office room with the shop attached, you soon got to know everybody and when you went to see one you passed the time of day with them all. Now you go on some business and you see the relevant man in his room and that's it. They are all specialized. Once, if the consumer department people were out, even the President would take a hand at serving in the shop; now if the man who deals with the insecticides isn't there, you just have to wait till he comes back.

It is not surprising that people's sense that the Co-op is their Co-op has been diminished. The following tea-break conversation was actually about the Silkworm Rearers' Co-operative, a separate though associated organization without quite such strong moral claims as the general-purpose Co-op. Two Shinohata farmers were said to be by-passing the Co-op, getting their eggs and selling their cocoons to a merchant near Nakatni.

> 'Sounds like a good idea to me.'
>
> 'Yes, it seems like you're better off. You don't have to pay the insurance contribution either. Though someone said the price wasn't as good.'
>
> 'And you get the money in your own little fist.'
>
> 'But, auntie, it's the same thing. Whether you get to look your money in the face or whether it's put into your account in the Co-op. It's there in your name all the same. If it was 100,000 in the hand or 80,000 in the Co-op that would be different, but it's the same really.'
>
> 'Oh no it isn't. Here I am, seventy-five years old and sweating over these silkworms and I never get to see the money. If the old man were to go to the Co-op and come back and say: there was so much for summer rearing and so much for the autumn lot, that would be

all right, it's a simple enough thing to ask: but as it is I just feel like a by-stander, a spare member at the wedding.'

'But, auntie, it's the same for everyone: you don't get the second payment for the summer crop until they do the final accounting in the autumn.'

'And then they get it wrong sometimes. The old man said we got 6,000 for the spring rearing last year and I said but that can't be right and when the guidance expert came round I got hold of him and got him to look it up and sure enough . . .'

Greater bureaucratic remoteness does sometimes lead to grumbles and suspicions of this kind. Perhaps, too, there is a tendency to be slightly less indulgent about all the saké drunk and all the food consumed and all the charabanc-person-miles travelled by the elected councillors on the Co-operative budget – though the total sums under the heading travel, meetings expenses, entertainment and 'educational study tours for staff and council members' (a quick look at a vineyard and a mushroom factory and then a boisterous evening at a hot spring hotel) were, at two-and-a-half-million yen, about the same (4 per cent) proportion of the budget as in 1955. One part of these expenditures is seen as fully justified – that part used in the lavish entertainments of prefectural and central officials who might, if adequately feted, channel a larger loan allocation to the Co-operative or designate the district as a Model Experimental Area for the Stimulation of Livestock Breeding by Improved Methods. That is all part of the system. It is the other half of these expenditures, hard to see as anything but the self-indulgence of the power-holders, which invites criticism.

Paradoxically, though, there is a contrary principle at work. In one way, the more remote, the more immune the organization can become from criticism. Traditionally, the world of the Shinohata villager consisted of 'us' – the village – and 'o-kami', 'the honourable above', the local lord, the Baron-Constable, the Tokugawa government. From o-kami one could *hope* for benevolence and considerateness, but there was no question of having a right to it, of 'holding them responsible'. Japan today is a much more democratic society; the governmental crisis of

1974 – 'Japan's Watergate' that saw the end of the Tanaka government – was the result of mounting public criticism of the failure of national politicians to separate their public responsibilities from their ambitions for personal aggrandizement. Yet something of the old attitudes persist, particularly in rural areas where o-kami remains an important source of discretionary benefits – of government grants for a new village school or a new bridge, or loans for a livestock-breeding enterprise, or subsidies for a packing plant – benefits which the all-powerful interpreters of rules and standards can grant or withhold, and which hence have to be sought as a grace and favour. The image has changed. Rather than the common people deferentially bowing forehead to ground before the raised dais of the lord, the old Roman image of the she-wolf succouring her children might be a better symbol of the modern villager's conception of the polis. The difference is considerable, but still, if less nowadays from awe than from calculation of interest, one is careful about criticizing the wolf or what she eats and drinks. People's perceptions of the Co-operatives, one might say, as they have grown from smaller and local to bigger and more remote organizations, have gone through a paradigm shift. Once they were extensions of the hamlet; 'us' rules applied; their officials were subject to the norms and sanctions of hamlet organizations. The newer more bureaucratic organizations have a greater o-kami element. Their officials are just that much more likely to receive the indulgence accorded to the succouring wolf.

9

Couples

In one of Shinohata's unreconstructed soot-blackened houses with earth-floored entrance and open irori hearth, there lives a solitary old lady. It is not poverty which keeps her house un-modernized. O-Sada's was one of the hamlet's four top families. She still has plenty of woodland. Her sons are doing very well in Tokyo. She keeps it this way because she prefers it this way. As she explains, fussing round the room, pushing the bed-pan back into its paper cover under her modestly small TV set (out-side toilets do have their disadvantages for old ladies), going out into the earth-floored kitchen for dry pine needles and sticks to light the fire under a large black bell-shaped kettle, she likes these high, wide and open old black houses. She likes to see the smoke curling up around the kettle and round the fish-shaped height-adjuster and up the soot-encrusted chain on which they are suspended from the roof beams. So much nicer a way of making tea for guests than boiling water on the gas ring in her kitchen.

Apart from the kitchen, her one concession to modernity, the only change she has made in the house is just to whitewash the plaster between the top of the sliding doors and the rafters. The white, in place of the traditional brown, sets off the blackened beams nicely. (Surbiton Tudor and O-Sada's modern style: the old Katsura Palace and the Elizabethan country house. Who influenced whom, or is there a universality in the appeal of the black-white contrast?) They are good solid beams with a nice curve to some of them. High up on one side of the living-room is a kamidana 'god-shelf', ancient, sooted, dusty; a large dice in front of it hints of the gods' function as the providers of good luck. There is also an old Daruma doll, the kind that pop back up when they are pushed over. It must have been many Januaries ago that it was bought wholly eyeless and the first eye painted in one of the vacant spaces, the other to follow as soon as there was a good harvest to celebrate. Out in the doma, the earth-floored kitchen, above the empty stable is an ancient dusty picture of a healthy horse, set there once as a charm against horse disease. Hung on a nail beside it a battered carrier bag from a cosmetics firm bears the legend, in English, 'Lip Art'. But such intrusions of the modern world are few and inconspicuous. Her own personal tastes apart, O-Sada was enjoined to keep things unchanged by the old lady, her mother-in-law, who died ten years ago at the age of ninety-three. The house and the land around it were handed down to them from generations of ancestors and they should be preserved.

I remember the old lady at the age of eighty-nine; the only woman I have ever met who still had blackened teeth, a curious cosmetic device – or perhaps anti-cosmetic since it was confined to married women – which practically disappeared well before the end of the last century. She also had a spinning wheel in her room above where the stable had once been and had used it in earnest in her youth. She was a shrewd and sharp-tongued old lady, but getting a little paranoid about the impoverished ingratiating plausible rogue, Motonori, who lived in the house next door, and who, she was sure, was after her property. (More of Motonori, the bald-headed general, in Chapter 16.)

The great story of O-Taka's – the old lady's – life was her marriage. Hers being a well-to-do family, they arranged a proper 'miai' – a preliminary meeting for the prospective bride and groom to see each other and decide whether they would follow their parents' wishes or whether it was such a *strong* case of dislike at first sight that one of them was prepared to throw filial piety to the winds and create universal embarrassment by saying no. The suitor's family visited her house. But they did not bring the all-important suitor. He was a very ugly young man. But his younger brother was a good-looking boy. He came instead. O-Taka was much taken with him. Then came the day of the wedding: the bride and her relatives arrived at the groom's house. Her suitor was nowhere to be seen. Instead another man was there, dressed up in wedding clothes. 'I found my husband had been bewitched and transformed,' she used to say. When they were left alone he pleaded with her. He agreed that it was a dirty trick, but with a face like his what could he do? She accepted her fate; what alternative was there when things had gone that far? The handsome young brother whom she had seen in her dreams in those few months between miai and marriage was set up in a 'branch family' far away, and O-Taka settled down. Actually, her husband had a truly gentle nature with a considerateness rare in a man. She could, she always used to conclude, have done much much worse.

Her daughter-in-law, O-Sada, had no such dramatic marriage, though she, too, like her mother-in-law, had come from an 'ancient family' (meaning a well-to-do family, for wealth can always be transmuted into genealogy, though not necessarily vice-versa) in a village on the other side of the prefecture. But by her generation the children of such families were no longer simply villagers. Her husband had been to a normal college in Tokyo and was already a teacher. She too was an educated lady. On the wall, beside her sons' university graduation certificates, is a large elaborate floral design in water colour, each flower identified with a little poem. It was her graduation exercise, the product of many weeks of labour at Atomi Girls' High School. In 1910 not more than one or two girls out of a hundred ever went to a secondary school at all, much less to one like Atomi, which was for the aristocracy and wealthy people and didn't, she says, admit girls from just any old farm family. Of course, some people might say that her family *was* just any old farm family, but at least she had a brother who was a judge; the school very carefully investigated the family's property and lineage before they let anyone in.

Of course, she expected her children to become a success and they have. One is a doctor, another an astronomer. But the only place to be a success is in the big towns. So O-Sada and her ancestors were in danger of having no successors to take over the house and the land in Shinohata. The traditional prescription for such situations is to adopt a son, or – O-Sada's preferred alternative – to adopt a daughter and then find her a husband who would be willing to come and take the family name as an 'adopted son-in-law'. A relative in her native village had a suitable daughter. Just eighteen years old, she had been brought up on a farm and was used to farm work. The adoption was formalized by transferring her to O-Sada's family register, but she did not come to live here until she was ready to be married. The young couple were given separate quarters in the house; not having to share a kitchen removed one potential source of friction. O-Sada made over some of her land to them directly, which was already slightly unusual. The normal procedure would have been to keep the property as family property, only nominally in her name as house-head, to pass to the son-in-law as new house-head after her death.

Relations were none too happy. O-Sada could not bear to see the loose way they brought up their children; rudeness, untidiness, would go unchecked and unadmonished. 'It seems to be the same everywhere these days. All the teachers think about is keeping the children happy. One hesitates to think what the next generation will be like if neither school nor home will treat them strictly.'

O-Sada did what she could. She composed for their benefit the Sakuda Family Precepts and wrote it out in flowing brush calligraphy.

> Every morning pay your reverent respects to the ancestors.
> Bringing up children is to make spiritual savings for your old age; strive daily to do right.

To note, further:

> It is the wont of young children to imitate every word, every gesture of their parents. Be, therefore, a model to them.
> If, perchance, they should develop bad habits [O-Sada's education was a long time ago: she used the wrong Chinese character here] these should be weeded out before they reach school age.

Alas, once when she came back from an extended stay with her children in Tokyo, she found that the list of Precepts had been taken down from the wall. She ordered them to produce it. They did so, rather shamefacedly. It was filthy, but she cleaned it and put it back on the wall.

Eventually the young couple decided that they had had enough. (Neighbours say they hadn't, anyway, enough to live on.) Some years ago, while she was absent in Tokyo, they moved out, sold off the land she had put in their name and went off to live in the next prefecture. 'You wouldn't think they'd have the nerve to show their face here after all that, but she still comes once a year with her children to help clean up the graves.' They had lost one of their children when they were in Shinohata and he is buried in the family grave plot.

So O-Sada consoles herself with her haiku. Properly, waka rather than haiku are her thing – the thirty-one syllable five-line poems rather than the seventeen-syllable three-line ones – but the local culture is a haiku culture and she has recently come to know her way around haiku. Two or three of her compositions which have found favour with the local judges are propped up against a cupboard.

> The world of science
> the moon itself
> becomes a neighbour.

> How strained it seems to bear
> it's weight of morning dew
> the drooping hagi.

O-Sada was recently ill, and it was four days before she swallowed her pride and phoned to a neighbour to come and help her. Not many people in Shinohata face that kind of loneliness. Most of the seven widows living alone in the hamlet lead a much more active neighbourly life, quite apart from the weeks they spend with their children in other parts of the country. O-Sada, with her reputation for stinginess, was rather exceptionally friendless. ('Her husband was a very nice, friendly man. He'd often invite father in for a chat, but O-Sada would never serve anything but tea. The old man would have to go to the shelf himself to see if there were any cakes or crackers to offer.') All the same, solitary widowhood is by traditional standards a very sad state to be in. So is that of the nine other older married couples who are living alone, their children having left the village to make their homes elsewhere.

The traditional household was a self-perpetuating unit. The word 'ie' meant both the family unit and also the physical house it lived in (rather like 'House' in the 'House of Windsor'). The constant piecemeal renewal of rotting timbers in the house-frame symbolized the constant renewal of the family as the older members died and children were born. The rules were basically simple. The eldest son in each generation succeeded his father as head of the household. (It would not be right to say he inherited the property. The property belonged to the family: he inherited the head-ship. Though, under the individualistic property system of modern times, he became the legal owner, socially he was considered to be the trustee.) In the Tokugawa period he gave up his 'youth name' and succeeded also to his father's personal name for the house-head's personal name was also, at the same time, the family's name. Marriage, for the eldest son, meant bringing a bride into his family. Marriage for women was a matter of 'going', of 'being sent'. 'If parents have the promise made, there's nothing for it but to go, young maid,' runs one of the old couplets sung at the Bon dances.

A family which had daughters but no son would 'adopt' a husband for a daughter – usually but not necessarily the oldest. The adopted husband would take his wife's family name and come to live in the house of his wife's parents. If a couple had no children, then they would adopt a son – or alternatively adopt a daughter and find her a husband. Most adoptions took place in late childhood or adolescence, sometimes even later, so that one could judge the character of the couple to whom the future destiny of the 'ie' would be entrusted. On the other hand, destiny of the 'ie' and all that apart, another major reason for adopting children was to make sure that one was affectionately looked after in one's possibly helpless old age. That suggested early adoption, especially of the daughter, on whose goodwill, after all, an old couple's comfort was more likely to depend. Kanetake's wife, adopted at the age of ten months some sixty years ago, was however, a rare exception. Generally it was thought hard to separate a child from its natural parents before it was old enough, as it were, to 'leave home and go out to work'. The analogy is not inapt, because being adopted, for a

younger son, or for a daughter, was a way of getting fixed up with
a livelihood – of getting secure membership in an established
production unit – for the 'ie' was not just a consumption unit,
it was an arrangement for working together as well as for
living together.

One old lady in Shinohata, Hidezō's mother, Tsuneko,
seemed still to bear the scars of her adoption experience, her
lower lip thrust forward in the perpetual pout of an unhappy
child whom life has never given its proper deserts. She had
been born in the village, the younger sister of Gontarō, and was
adopted at the age of twelve into another of Shinohata's four
landlord families somewhat less rich and prestigious than her
own.

> That really was a bad time for me, you know. If they
> are not your own parents, well, you know how it is;
> they don't love you the same. It makes me ashamed to
> think of it now, but I used to go home secretly – in the
> morning before going to school, and then in the even-
> ing when I came home. And my real mother would
> keep special delicacies for me. Anyhow, I lived here, in
> this house, calling them mother and father, though I
> didn't feel like a daughter. And I suppose that went on
> for – yes, the last half-year of compulsory school and
> then two years of higher elementary. And then they
> wanted me to start work, but in the end I didn't: I went
> to a girls' high school in Tokyo. My adopted parents
> didn't want me to go at all. They were farmers after all,
> and they wanted me to be a farmer's wife. My father –
> my adopted father that is – said he wasn't going to have
> me go to high school. It wasn't good for girls to get
> that kind of education: they just got ideas above their
> station and put on airs. But my real father said that that
> was an old-fashioned idea. The world had changed,
> this was no time to be saying that sort of thing. Well, it
> went back and forth and in the end it was decided that
> I should go to Tokyo. My brother was there and I
> boarded with him. He was already married and a stu-
> dent at Waseda. So I lived with them, and used to go
> every day to the high school.

After I'd finished school I came back home for a while. I hated having to do all the weeding in the fields, and I was never physically very strong. I soon went back to Tokyo to live with my elder brother and his wife, to prepare for being a bride – learning flower arrangement and the tea ceremony and sewing and all that. My parents here had given up objecting by then. They knew I wasn't very strong, you see. What with one thing and another I was late getting married. I was twenty-eight. I can tell you I felt really ashamed. All my class-mates were married. But my parents were in no hurry. My father used to say: 'what is the use of getting married early and just making lots of children?' I suppose it was meant as a joke really. But, anyhow, at twenty-eight I got married. My husband was a railway engineer.

No, I never had any friends in Tokyo. The marriage was arranged here. An uncle from the house next to my elder brother's house had set up as a saké merchant in Nagano. He'd really made a success, he had. His house was selected to be the house where the Emperor Meiji rested and it is still preserved now. Anyhow, he said that the son of the post office next door was a fine young man who had been to the university and he would make a good husband, so it was all arranged. He was working on the railway and doing very well, but then we lost everything in the firebomb raids, and we were absolutely without food and the American army was coming and we thought we'd all be killed, so we came back here.

Continuity of the family had a triple importance. Securing a successor had a straightforward bread-and-butter importance for one's old age. It also had a ritual importance. Reverence for the ancestors was an important focus of religious sentiment and practice. It was a part of the duty of filial piety towards one's ancestors not only to perform the proper rituals oneself, but also to ensure that they would be performed in perpetuity. In the Tokugawa period, this was more particularly a concern of the samurai gentry. Village religion had a much larger admixture of magical elements; even within the ancestor cult itself there was somewhat more concern with the propitiatory, laying-of-ghosts aspect of the rituals. But one effect of universal schooling from the end of the nineteenth century onwards was to diffuse these samurai attitudes and values more generally among the population.

There was a third, closely related, social element in the concern for continuity: duty not so much towards the ancestors as to the more abstractly conceived 'house'. One had inherited it as a going concern, a member unit of the village community with an honoured place in that community. It was one's duty to pass on the trust to the next generation, to keep, and if possible raise, the position of the 'ie' in the community.

When I first went over Shinohata's family registers in 1955 I discovered what I took to be a curious and probably scandalous situation. According to the registers a man had been adopted as a husband in one of Shinohata's families. He had three children and then died. His widow then had two more illegitimate children, but then, at the age of sixty-three she was married to a second adopted husband – the elder brother of the first – who acknowledged paternity not only of the two illegitimate children, but also of the earlier three fathered by his younger brother. Six days later he died.

It turned out, that he had, in fact, been living a normal blameless married life with the woman in question for forty years, and there was never any doubt as to the paternity of his children. The whole complex set of false entries in the registers was simply the result of the provision of the Civil Code which – both to embody and to propagate among the Japanese people the principle of the supreme importance of family continuity – had made it illegal for the eldest son of any family, or for a single daughter, to leave his or her family for adoption or marriage. For reasons of personal compatibility his family had decided that their younger son should stay at home and carry on the family while the eldest should be the one adopted out. But to conform to the law, they registered it the other way round. (The village office clerks, of course, knew of the subterfuge, but had no wish to make life difficult for people.) In 1947 when the Civil Code was revised and the whole legal system of 'house' and 'house-head' was swept away (making each marriage the start of a *new* family on the Western pattern) the old rule of course disappeared, and five years later, as the old man's imminent death approached, the family decided to regularize the whole affair and put the records retrospectively in accord with reality.

The best way of ensuring the succession, especially in the days of high rates of infant mortality, was to have a lot of children. Older women speak of the small families common today as 'samishii' – lonely – as compared with the 'nigiyakana' – lively – families of eight or ten children common in their youth. One element in the samishii feeling is anxiety. 'If you've got only one son you can never feel really at ease. You'll always be looking at him anxiously. Whenever he catches a cold, you'll always imagine the worst.' Today's families are certainly smaller. The following figures show pretty clearly just when family planning hit Shinohata.

Number of children ever born to women of different age groups, 1955–70.

	1955	1970
25 – 29	2.5	0.5
30 – 34	2.5	2.0
35 – 39	4.2	2.3
40 – 44	4.5	2.5
45 – 49	5.5	3.2
50+	5.4	4.9

The early fifties was the decisive time. Kanetake's wife's abortion was something of a turning point. I remember her in 1955, not the lusty, rotund happy-go-lucky soul she afterwards turned out to be, but listless, her still discernible sensuality dulled and weakened by constant haemorrhages in the months that followed her near-fatal visit to the abortionist. It was typical, people said, that it should happen to her. A really lackadaisical couple were Kanetake and his wife. She'd been a spoiled only daughter, perhaps that was it. No brothers, so she had to get a muko, adopted husband, who would come into the family and take their name. Her father insisted on a farmer, but she fell for Kanetake. There was quite a to-do. Kanetake was an itinerant seller of sweet bean-cakes which he made in the family backyard. A real love-match. In fact she ran away from home with him and father had to give in.

Impulse-living is Kanetake's wife's style:

> Terrible farmers they are. Their mulberry fields get weeds as high as their mulberry. Doesn't worry them. They go off and cut their meagre branches. All the fields around are so spick and span – not a weed – you'd think they'd feel ashamed. Not them. Late risers, too. Their children were always being late for school. They often had to get their own breakfast. Time and again they've been known to run out of rice and she'd send Kanetake over to borrow from the neighbours. Partly it was the bean-cake trade. Kanetake just couldn't give it up. So much easier than farming: a quicker turnover. They used to go off on a motor-bike selling bean-cakes at construction camps and lumber camps. She'd always be with him. Couldn't trust Kanetake to go off alone. He'd be in the saké shop in no time and end up with nothing to bring home.

It was in 1955 when Kanetake's wife found herself pregnant for the sixth time. Women fifteen years older than her had borne ten children and been proud of it. Now it was different. Some women were beginning to talk of having abortions after they had had only three. With five healthy children all alive she began to think she should feel ashamed of having a sixth. But she dithered; could not make up her mind until the sixth month, and although abortion was perfectly legal by then, the only doctor she could get to take her on at that advanced stage made a botch of it. When she eventually went to another doctor after a couple of months of painful bleeding she found that a portion of the foetus had been left behind. It was more than six months before she was right again and it cost the family a rice field or two in expensive medicines and transfusions.

> But still I did other people good too. I served as a horrible warning. People began to think of other methods and of course the nurses and doctors used to come to the Women's Association and give lecture after

lecture about that time. Now everybody uses condoms. In fact the Agriculture Co-op gives them away free. If you buy a pack of toilet paper you'll find one slipped inside. My classmate who emigrated to Peru was telling me the other day – they've done very well; they own three shops there now – that over there they have them quite openly out on display and sell them by the dozen. They sell them here too at the shop in the next village but they don't quite put them in the open like that. Of course, people don't use so many now. Husbands have got cleverer. They used to use them all the time. Now they know all about the fertile periods and the infertile periods.

(Reticence about these matters is less marked in other parts of Japan. I recall the chemist's shop in Hokkaido whose prominent large advertisement for a particular brand of condoms contained, as a promise of the quality of the product and the swinging modernity of those who used it, a few words in English: 'Fine Condom. French Tickler'!)

Twenty years later Kanetake's wife is glad she had five children. They are a great joy to her. The family had prospered; the motor-bike had been replaced by a small truck. Then she had taken to peddling insurance. Her forward amiable manner, her great command of words, had made her one of the company's best life-insurance salesmen in the prefecture. Recently the husband had taken a steady wage job with a sub-contractor at The Factory. 'Ah, the old man! He's hopeless!' she said without rancour as I found her one day pulling half the seedlings out of a rice field she and her husband had been planting out by hand the Sunday before. 'I told him those seedlings were no good. He took them out of the seed-bed in the morning and left them in the heat of the sun for half a day. On the bank – I ask you! – not even in the water! Now I've got to replant half the field.'

But her children were a great consolation. Her second son, for instance. He had been to high school and now he was learning to be a cook at a big hotel at Tokyo airport. He was all set for a ten years' apprenticeship, saving money assiduously. At the end of it he aimed to have saved three million yen and with

that much of his own money he could ask the firm to set him up
in a branch shop and think about getting married.

He's a real hard worker. Very thoughtful, straightforward, open. And very careful. When he was a child
I used to send him to the shop to get something for
supper and he'd say: 'I'll get something we can cook
up with a lot of vegetables to make it go further.' The
other day when he came home he took out his wallet
and I could see him fingering a wad of notes. He pulled
out ten thousand yen and said: 'Here, Mum. I've
brought you some pocket money.' I wouldn't take it
though. I told him to keep it for his shop. He's like that.
He always wants to share things. When he used to come
home with some sweets he specially liked he'd always
bring me one. Pop it straight into my mouth, he would.

It is a truism among students of the Japanese family that the
strongest tie is often the mother–son tie, that many Japanese
women find relief from the emotional aridity of an arranged
marriage relationship with an insensitive or domineering husband in a passionate fondness for their eldest son. That was one
reason for the notoriously bad relationships between mother-
in-law and daughter-in-law when the son eventually married
and brought his stranger bride into the home. Lucky the mother
who had several sons to diffuse her affections on – and several
daughters, too, with whom intimacy is more easily sustained –
even enhanced – after marriage instead of attenuating as with
sons. O-Mari, in her mid-sixties now, thinks herself lucky at
any rate:

No, I wouldn't have thought jealousy had much to
do with the way mothers-in-law used to treat their
daughters-in-law. I don't look at it like that anyway.
It's like a tree. It begins to go rotten, and you think
about planting a new one, and then the old tree gets too
bad and you cut it down and by then the young one is
flourishing. Life is like that. I don't think you'd find
more than one or two mothers in fifty who think in
terms of losing their hold on their sons when he gets a

bride. And then the grandchildren come along. You know, I think everybody needs to have three or four children at least. Our yome [i.e. my son's bride: yome, the usual word, defines her relation to the family *group* as a whole, not just to her husband] isn't very robust and she's got only the one, and that seems to me a terrible pity. I had six and now, with my husband dead early on, as I begin to get older, I've got the pleasure of going off to visit my sons and daughters to see how they are getting on. But if you've only got one, well, he brings a bride home and that's it. You've no visits to look forward to. No place to go.

Early old age, when one can travel from married son's house to married daughter's house and back again, ever the welcome grandmother, and even grandfather, is a serene time – serene that is, as long as one is fit enough to travel; after that what matters is whether one has a son and congenial daughter-in-law, or daughter and congenial son-in-law, to look after one at home. At that stage it is the one son, not the many, who counts, and 'will our son come back home?' is the kernel of many anxieties, the subject of much family discussion – usually open discussion, but sometimes, in families which are more reticent with each other, only a matter of dropped hints, indirect feelers, studiedly casual inquiries about intentions.

The newspapers were full of 'the problem of the younger sons' when I first went to Shinohata in 1955. The economy had more or less recovered from the war. Industry was growing at what was, for the time, a respectable rate. But the number of school leavers seeking jobs – a number which reflected the birth rates of the 1930s and 40s – was far more than industry could absorb. The eldest sons of farm families were considered lucky. They could stay at home. They had an on-going family enterprise to inherit. It was their younger brothers who were the problem. In a number of Shinohata houses there were younger sons, four or five years out of school, still not fixed up with a town job that had any prospects of permanency; helping out at home at the busy seasons, otherwise continuously underemployed; grateful for a casual day's labour here, or for a temporary three-month construction gang job there. One of the gloomiest passages of my book on the land reform (though one which only reflected the gloom of Japanese economists) was on the debilitating effect of this underemployment which the sheer demographic and economic arithmetic of the situation seemed to make inevitable for a long time to come; a grave shadow over the future.

A few years later I learned a salutary lesson about the fragility of economic predictions. The boom started. Growth rates shot up into the double figures. Suddenly the towns could absorb all the younger sons coming out of the village schools – and more. The older underemployed younger sons who had been kicking their heels at home for some years were soon absorbed too. (Though few of them got jobs in the high-prestige industrial firms; they preferred to recruit their workers straight from school and sent their recruiting officers at the request of solicitous headmasters to 'cream off' each crop of new school-leavers by reference to the school mark sheets and a few simple selection tests.)

Still, as the boom continued, and especially from the middle sixties when the lower birth rates after 1949 brought smaller cohorts of middle-school leavers, the needs of industry remained unsatisfied. *Eldest* sons, too, could easily find jobs, and good jobs at that – wages worth far more than the value of their work on the family fields (which was superfluous anyway for the average Shinohata holding if both parents could still work). It was a chance to get out into the world, and the hours and conditions were infinitely less irksome than their uncles and great-uncles had faced when they set off as youngsters for the towns to 'do service' in a merchant's shop in Sano, or to enter a sixty-hour-a-week job as a factory apprentice. By the late 1960s the vast majority of eldest sons were going to high school anyway. A number were going to a university. They were finding not just jobs, but jobs which were potentially careers, when they left school. 'Just for a few years.' That was the arrangement in theory. Most parents who saw their eldest son off to the towns expected that he would eventually come back. By now there was no question of refusing to let them go as there might have been before the war. 'When I left school I badly wanted to go away from home and work for a while, but my father just wouldn't hear of it – partly, I suppose, he wanted me to learn his stonemason's trade properly and help him out at that.' Some eldest sons did, in fact, leave the village before the war. If opportunity came to an eldest son – and the possibility of remittances that would help to feed his seven or eight younger siblings while they were growing up – then primogeniture rules could be bent. If the eldest son became well established in the towns – or in Brazil in the case of one Shinohata family – then a younger son could stay at home and 'take over the family'.

But that *one* son would take over the family – or that, if there were no sons, one would be adopted or an adopted husband found for a daughter – used to be taken for granted. By the late sixties, however, even that was something that no longer could be taken for granted. That was what had changed. 'It's all a bit worrying,' said Toshitada in 1970.

We're getting on, you see, the missus and me. We manage all right, but we won't be able to do so for ever; I'm getting on for sixty and she's fifty-five. And it's not only that. People think you're old-fashioned if you talk about the ancestors, but after all our house has been in this village for generations. Somebody ought to continue it. I just don't know what will happen. My eldest is a tax accountant in Tokyo. He's got about a hundred clients. Does quite well he does. You can't expect him to come back here.

Well, yes, I suppose, we *could* go to Tokyo. But I wouldn't. Definitely not. We usually go for a week or so at New Year – we go and see the Sumō wrestling and that sort of thing. But – well, anyway, it's so cramped. They live in a rented apartment. A four-mat room and a six-mat. You can't move. I'd rather be here.

Then my second son. He's still an extension officer. He's a specialist in potatoes. He's often going to Gumma Prefecture which is the real centre for potatoes, and he's always giving lectures on the latest developments in potatoes. He's down the other side of Sano. In another three years or so he'll have done twenty years and he'll be entitled to something of a pension if he leaves then. I tell him that we're getting old and we must have somebody to carry on the house. I know it would be hard for him, but would he consider it? It's not much of a prospect though. We've got a couple of acres of rice fields – forty bales. That brings in 320,000, and then we get about 110 kan of cocoons with our couple of acres of mulberry and that's maybe another 440,000. And that's about as good an income as anybody gets from farming in this village. But look what he's getting now: 70,000 a month and bonuses of 110,000 or so twice a year. You can hardly expect him to come back and be a farmer, though maybe he can get a job near by and live here at home.

In the event, five years later, when Toshitada's wife was suffering from what everyone knew must be her last illness, it was the eldest son who returned. Or at least his wife and children came back to the village; his wife to nurse her sick mother-in-law and eventually to look after her widowed father-in-law. The son himself came occasionally at weekends. He was looking without very much hope for a suitable accountant's job in Sano to which he might commute. Are they permanently 'returned'? Will Toshitada die in the knowledge that one of his sons will, indeed, 'carry on the house'? It is doubtful.

'"Don't you worry, dad." That's what my eldest son is always saying,' said Toshitada's neighbour, Sanekichi, again in 1970. 'He'll come and see us often. He'll look after us, and if we should die young, he won't get rid of the land. He'll rent it out and come back to farm it when he's older and ready to retire. I wonder, though.' In fact, five years later he *was* back. He had managed to work out an arrangement with his former employer, a small engineering firm. He had acquired the district franchise for repair of the firm's centrifugal separators used in medical analysis. The farmhouse, outside its new cement-block wall, had a smart new sign: Naito Electrical Works. It was a start; he might expand, he liked the relative freedom; 'farm work these days isn't the hardship it used to be'; it was nice to have *space*; to breathe clean air.

Several other sons had returned in those five years: one to a job in the town office acquired (happy coincidence) during his father's term as town councillor; one to a job in a local lumbering firm; almost all of them only when some prospect of a regular job to which they could commute had been assured. That way the life of a part-time farmer could seem quite attractive.

Well, it was always understood really that I would come back. The only question was when. You can't delay it too long if you're going to get a job. Past forty and it's hard to find an opening. Then, the old lady was getting terrible rheumatism and you can't go on putting the neighbours to trouble and making a nuisance of yourself for ever. Wages are so low around here. Half what they are in Tokyo and prices higher for lots of things. If you've got a house to live in, you're better off in Tokyo – *if*. Squeezed up in a tiny apartment as we were, we were glad to come back in some ways.

Very often it *was* the eldest son who returned. For one thing, they often need to. An eldest son is the most spoilt son. He grows up with an elite consciousness – he is destined to be the head of the household: he has that security. As a young man in the town he's more likely than a younger son to be an easy spender. Younger sons are more likely to scrape and save, conscious that they have to make their own careers, buy a house for their family from their own savings.

Apart from which, there *is* still a premium placed on doing the right thing. There still does attach a privilege and dignity to primogeniture in itself. Akira's was one of only four households in the village with an unmarried son at home who had not left for the town. His fourth and youngest son, a happy hard-working boy, had decided that he liked farming and was going to stay and 'carry on the family'. ('It's his own free will. I've never gone on at him about it like some do – about how hard I've slaved to build it up, and about his duty to see it doesn't go to nothing and so on. None of that sort of thing.') The eldest son was well established in Yokohama and had no intention of coming back. Akira, though, was saving to build that eldest son a house, which he was not doing for the other sons who had left home. 'Well,' he explained not very consequentially, 'what's the use of being the firstborn if you don't get some privileges?'

Altogether, a surprising number of sons *had* come back. The forty-nine households in 1975 could be divided as follows:
In ten the house-head was a man who settled into farming

when town jobs were still scarce, was still in his thirties to fifties, and still had children at school.

In four there was still at least one young unmarried son who had left school and was still at home, three of them commuting to regular jobs, only one working on the farm.

In twenty-one households the house-head had a married son living at home, the majority of them regular wage or salary earners. Seventeen of the twenty-one had at one time left the village for jobs elsewhere and returned.

That left fourteen households which consisted only of old couples or a single old person.

The problem of getting a son to be a farmer is as nothing compared with the problem of getting a girl to be the bride of a farming son. Even in the 1950s it was the *hope* of most girls that they would rate a town husband, though many of them recognized they would be lucky to do so. By the sixties, with all the young men leaving, a salary-man husband came to seem like every girl's birthright.

All three of our daughters married into farms. There, that surprises you doesn't it? But, well, 1960 I suppose it was when the youngest got married. That was just a bit before girls finally took against the farm. She was the last of a generation I suppose. The other thing was that with all three of our girls there was some relative's family that was pressing us to let them have one of our daughters. They all went to cousin families.

Our Machiko was over thirty when she married. Worried us stiff, she did. She was happy enough about it. She had her job in the accountant's office. She was always going off on trips, skiing, mountain-climbing and all the rest of it. But we kept telling her that she couldn't go on like that all her life. We had a number of tries to find her a place and she had a number of offers, but she was never keen to settle down. She was enjoying life happily enough. As she got older it got

more difficult, especially as she refused to have anything
to do with a husband who was younger than herself.

'I don't mind if I never get married,' she used to say,
but in the end it was all settled. It's a second marriage
for her husband but they seem to get on all right. He's
got a good job, but still it is a farm-house where they
do silkworms and from May to September she's really
kept on the hop. It's a big change for her. Stuck at
home, two babies, no money that's really hers, no trips
any more. Still the old man – the father-in-law – does
all the field work so she doesn't have that to contend
with. And the old lady, the mother-in-law, as far as I
can make out, does nothing all day except read the
newspaper and gaze at the telly until midnight – really
easy-going. But since she doesn't do any work herself
she can hardly do any complaining, so they seem to get
on well enough.

There are, of course, urban milieux in Japan where a woman
can opt for spinsterhood, and even combine it with motherhood, all in good conscience. But no Shinohata girl that I heard
of has ever penetrated to those circles. Still, for them, not to
marry would be a mark of failure to make the grade as a person,
an even greater failure than marrying a farming boy. And the
Machiko who married late in the end did better than that – a
salary man living on a farm rather than a farm boy.

Though that has its disadvantages, too.

Farming *is* hard work. The women's part in farming always
was hard work, especially the yome's part in farming because
she had to do all the housework under her vigilant mother-in-
law's eye. Now, softer mothers-in-law (more of that in a
moment), washing machines, automatic electric cookers (no fire-
lighting on freezing winter mornings an hour before the men
stirred from their beds) have made things easier; but on the
other hand, a salary-man husband is not much use if the family
is going to make use of their fields and earn the far from insignificant extra income. 'San-chan agriculture', the Japanese
call it: farming by jii-chan (grandpa), baachan (grandma) and
kaachan (Mum – i.e. the yome) and it is the yome who often has
to do most of the work.

Their wives' reluctance is therefore understandably a major reason for sons' reluctance to come back to the farm. Nevertheless, some do and set about the business of adapting themselves to their new situation with a will.

One of the most poignant photographs I took in 1955 was of Tsurukichi, a vague-looking hunched sixty-five-year-old, his wife with a slightly witch-like air about her (was it the wide bright eyes, or the unnatural smoothness of her skin, or the way her near-toothless mouth set in a slightly sardonic grin?), and their fifteen-month grandchild. The floor of the living-room was bare; they had no tatami. They sat around the open fire on the bare boards. There was not even a radio; nothing to relieve the stark austerity of the room. The child was tied by a sash to one of the house frame-pillars and confined to a few yards' radius. Only thus could the worn old couple cope with its young energies. The child was the product of a broken marriage. People said their eldest son wasn't quite right in the head. It was amazing his yome had in fact consented to come. She was quite a decent and intelligent girl. But she had not been able to bear it long, and she had left the child when she went: old Tsurukichi had claimed the family heir and she had not wanted to worsen her chances of re-marriage anyway. The eldest son, shamed by his bride's defection, had left home for God knows where.

Fifteen years later the house was transformed. The eldest son was still away; had not been heard of for years. The grandchild had grown up and was working a hundred miles off. Tsurukichi had died, but their second son, a truck driver for an electricity company in the next prefecture, had returned with his wife and three children aged two to ten. Within its old timber frame the house had undergone drastic change. Tatami, of course, on the floors and a plentiful supply of comfortable cushions, aluminium-framed sliding doors replaced the tattered paper ones giving on to the verandah. There were even curtains. The open hearth had gone; there was a modern kitchen. Tsurukichi's widow, too, seemed reconstructed. There was nothing eerie about her smile now, for a new set of gleaming white teeth had replaced the two or three blackened remnants which were all she had before. Her eyes were getting bad, alas, but she could still see to thread a needle and for someone who set as much store as she did by her seamstress skills, that was important. She spoke with a survivor's pride of her miraculous recovery from a liver complaint a year before: everyone had been convinced she would die.

She thought she was lucky, lucky in gaining the invigorating presence of her grandchildren, lucky that her son had brought home such an excellent yome. Kumiko, the yome, was indeed an attractive young woman; open, good-hearted, fully at ease. It did not seem at all like putting on airs, or a disparagement of her present circumstances when she apologized for not giving me coffee and pointed to her percolator gathering dust on the shelves. No ground coffee to be had in the local shops. When I said that I personally drank Nescafé all the time, she made me a cup and slipped in a tot of whisky by way of compensation. Town-born and town-bred, she had tackled farming with a will; her rice fields, she boasted – well, her husband *had* helped at the weekends – her rice fields looked just as good as anybody else's, even though it was her first year. It was hard work, but it was satisfying, too; nice to see the results of your own efforts, and to know that you could do strange and unfamiliar things if you set your mind to it.

Five years later, she was innovating. Most of their rice fields had been given over to seedlings; there was an expanding market for ornamental trees and shrubs; they required less attention than rice and you could collect the subsidy granted until 1974 to those who abstained from growing rice. And, after all, the idea that to be self-sufficient in rice was a basic condition of respectability in the village community was not even a dim ancestral memory for her; she had been eating 'bought rice' all her life.

There were other equally well-adjusted three-generation families in the village, though the adjustment was achieved on a different basis: Tsunashige's, for instance. Both Tsunashige and his wife were nearing sixty, both still active and both hard workers, the rather dour solemnity which made him a respected village councillor being counterbalanced by her playful grins and teasing, sometimes sardonic humour. Their first grandson was the new centre of their lives. When Tsunashige came back from picking over his logs with sacks of oak-mushrooms in his trailer, and his wife left the silkworms to chew away in their hut, and they came round to the south side of the house to perch on the verandah in the sun for a rest before their next task, the first thing they would do would be to make a cup of tea from the big new thermos with the hand-pressure pump left there on the verandah to be accessible without removing farm foot-gear. The second would be to shout 'Yuki!' in the direction of the new two-storeyed house built for the young couple some thirty yards down the garden. The yome would emerge, as neat as ever in her town clothes, and Yuki, the adored grandson, would be neatly slipped off the sling at her back and set down a few yards from the grandparents to practise his new toddling skills. At 5.30 in the evening mother and son would be out in the yard again, waiting for a repeat performance when Yuki's father came back from his job at the village office in his beautifully polished Toyota. This time Yuki could practise his meagre vocabulary as well as his toddling: 'Papa!' (one of the first words that Japanese town children, and town-mothered country children, learn these days is English rather than Japanese). Tsunashige's yome's job is child-minding. The division of labour in the household is absolutely clear. Farm work is exclusively for Tsunashige and his wife, though Tsunashige's son might help occasionally at the weekends. The yome's job is motherhood plus a share of the cooking. One rarely sees Tsunashige's wife in anything except her work dungarees, her sweat-scarf around her head; one never sees the yome in anything but her trim blouses and neatly pleated skirts.

Her husband, the village office clerk, was one of two or three young returnees talking together about the village in the future. They had their jobs. As far as farming was concerned, their hope was to become rentiers, doing a little weeding on their rice fields, perhaps, but otherwise having everything done under contract by the Co-op. But anyway, they still wanted to keep their fields as an extra source of income. 'And will your wives work then?' Tsunashige's son grinned sheepishly, as another answered, guardedly: 'Well, in time, I mean as she becomes used to the ways here and gets older, and, I mean, sees she has to, as it were . . . But town ways take a lot of living down. They just don't want to have anything to do with farming, even though in my wife's case she was brought up to it once.' 'Are your wives farmers' daughters too?' I asked the others. 'Not a hope,' said Tsunashige's son. 'She wouldn't know a weed from a rice-plant. Jumps in her skin when she sees an insect. Won't go in the vineyards because something bit her last time . . .'

Wives, Husbands and Mothers

Some of the older women would sometimes look at Tsuna-shige's yome as she wandered down for a gossip at the shop in mid-morning, joggling Yuki on her back, pointing out the birdies and the flopping scarecrow – they would look and they would shake their heads in disbelief. That a yome should lead a life of such pampered idleness would have been inconceivable in the Shinohata of earlier times; even in the Shinohata of the 1950s.

To be sure, by the 1950s, ideas had changed. The law had changed for one thing, even if the social reality and the economic pressures which underlay that social reality were changing much more slowly. 'Feudalism' – as the university professors supplementing their meagre salaries with democratic moral-uplift journalism used to describe any gerontocratic or sexist exercise of authority in personal relations – feudalism was in full retreat. The Civil Code of 1947 had proclaimed the theoretical equality of the sexes. The old concept of a self-perpetuating 'house', ruled by its house-head, disappeared from the statute books; only individuals, not corporate families, had rights and duties. The new civil registration system was still based on family registers, but it was not the old 'house' that was the unit, transferring its daughters 'out' and its brides 'in' at marriage, continuing in perpetuity as a registration unit even though its membership changed with the generations. Each new marriage was now treated as the foundation of a new family: *both* the

partners were transferred from their parents' register to the
new.

The principle implicitly asserted by this change was an important one – that the tie between husband and wife should be
deemed more important than the tie between a man and his
parents.

That was not the way it had traditionally been, certainly not
at the start of a marriage. The young bride was the newcomer,
as much a stranger to her husband as to her mother-in-law –
but equally obligated to both. From the mother-in-law's point
of view, she was the 'new help', an important addition to the
family labour force, someone, at last, to relieve her of all the
chores that had been hers since she herself came into the house
as a newcomer yome a generation before. The grandmother at
Masayoshi's, in her late eighties, was Shinohata's oldest inhabitant, a status which she did not much enjoy. (I met her walking
rather forlornly in the woods one Sunday, back bent almost
double and leaning on a tall stick, looking just like an illustration from a book of children's fairy stories. She was taking
refuge from a house full of visiting grandchildren and great-grandchildren. 'It's useless being old,' she complained, in a
voice still surprisingly full and rich. 'You can't stand all the
bustle. I'm no use to anybody except the cow. Came out to cut
him some grass. Time they took me off to the temple, but you
can't just go like that. Doctor says I'm as healthy as a fifty-year-old. Have you heard about the old lady at Toshitada's? Near
her end, they say, eight years younger than me she is.') The
Russo–Japanese war was being fought when she married. There
had been nothing sentimental about it, as she once explained.

> I came here as a yome at the age of twenty-four. I
> was older than my husband – four years older. It was
> like this, you see. Men used to be called up at twenty-one. There was just him and his mother in the house
> and if he went his mother wouldn't have been able to
> manage the fields all alone, so they wanted him to take
> a yome before he was called up – and they wanted
> someone responsible, so that's why I came though I
> was older than he. And all the same he went to the
> other world before me. Eighteen years ago we took

him up the temple hill, even though he was younger than me. Nothing you can do about these things, is there?

Yome came to work, and work they did.

My, we used to have to work hard. Up early in the morning and take the big rice pot out to the stream and polish it with sand – you knew it would get black again as soon as you put it on the fire, but still mother-in-law said you had to polish it. Then light the stove fire under the rice, and then light the hearth fire under the kettle, and then while it was cooking you had to wipe the floor and the beams and pillars and all the sliding doors until they shone like dried bonito sticks [hard dried fish shaved to make soup stock]. Then it was breakfast and off to the fields and only straw zori sandals on our feet and straw raincoats if it was wet. Nowadays you only see them on scarecrows, now everybody has wellingtons and plastic macs. Still, our old lady wasn't too bad, except when she was in one of her moods. Then she'd start criticizing and telling me I should take a lesson from so-and-so who was a model yome. 'See how early *she* gets up,' she would say. I'd pretend not to hear and then she'd get furious. 'Anné,' she'd say: that's what you called a yome around here – 'Anné, yes it's you I'm talking to.' I must say I didn't *always* get up so early. Sometimes I'd sleep right through the alarm clock at my pillow. Funny how young people can sleep, isn't it? Wish I could now.

I didn't suffer much from my mother-in-law because my husband and I went straight to Tokyo when we married, but we came back for a year in 1935 because the old lady was sick. She was a tough mother-in-law all right. She was a very clever person, but very very strict. No schooling and she couldn't read, but she could remember everything. She was so clever she taught herself dressmaking by taking clothes to pieces and finding how to make them that way. She was known throughout the village for that. She'd lost her husband when she was twenty-seven. She had two children. One died and she took the other one with her and went to be a bride again: Akira's old mother found her the place. She had a daughter there, but somehow it didn't work out so she came back here. I suppose she'd suffered a lot and it was no wonder she was sick. If I ever did anything to upset her, she'd come after me, shake me by the shoulders, catch hold of both ears like this and wag my head back and forth. 'Did you hear what I say?' But if I apologized immediately and took the blame, she'd soon be all right again. So what I always did was to say sorry and immediately make some tea to calm her down. My she was strict – but clever too.

One of the old Bon dance songs found in a 1910 collection goes 'Where are you going, old lady, with your two-gallon saké barrel? Who's the present for? I'm going to our yome's house, going to cuddle my grandson.' It reflects an old custom. When a yome was due to have her first baby she went to have it at her parental home. She was allowed to face that testing experience in the comforting presence of mum, not of probably tyrannous mother-in-law. The custom persists, but as far as tyranny is concerned, many older ladies would say that the boot is very much on the other foot. Partly it is a matter of the confident authority of youth in a rapidly changing society. (They have been to school; they know about the latest; the telly and their women's magazines tell them about nutritious recipes and proper child care; they don't need old wives' tales.) Partly, too, the country mother-in-law suffers a special disadvantage: the yome is doing her a favour by being there at all. As Hidezo's old lady, the lady with the perpetual pout, complained:

It's so different now. Obedience: that's what mothers-in-law expected, and that's what they got. And it meant that you could grow old peacefully. Now old people like us just have to cry into our pillows. If you can't stand it, there's nothing to do but get yourself a rope and hang yourself. An old lady down in Yoshino actually did; she was so persecuted by her yome. However hard she worked she couldn't please the yome, and it's not the sort of thing you can talk to people about . . .

Not, always, can one be sure of sympathy if one *does* talk about it. Takasada's old lady was undoubtedly a persecuted mother-in-law, but some thought she deserved it.

Takasada was the second son. His elder brother, Kosuke, went off to Brazil and really made good. I remember when he came back. He gave a kilo of sugar and a silk furoshiki wrapping cloth to every household in the village, and a money gift to all the relatives and a big stuffed crocodile for the school . . . Then he went back and was caught by the war, but after the war he was always sending money for the parents. Made the family he did, really. Then he came back and Takasada sold off some trees and they built him a house in Tokyo. But soon after that Kosuke went blind. He wanted to come back here and smell the good mountain air in his last few years, but it was Takasada's wife who stopped it. She just wouldn't have it. Eight children of our own, she'd say: that's as much as we can cope with . . . Now she's crippled with rheumatism; can't stand, can't move her arms sometimes, though she eats and talks all right. People say she's being paid back. Not only the rheumatism. Her yome's quite a handful too. The son goes to work in the dye factory and the yome was all for making money and she went off to the underwear factory too, but she's given that up now because of the children. She's always telling the old lady off. Some say she even beats her. And she doesn't *do* anything herself either. She goes out to the fields, but she never accomplishes much. Just like going out for a picnic with her, not work. Their mulberry fields have got weeds so high you can't see a person standing in them. If you keep a mulberry field clean you can always sell the leaves, but not when they're in that state. They just have to give it away.

Yome nowadays really are *tough*. And it isn't really that they *know* anything. They just go off to a factory and bring in a lot of money and they think that they're the cat's whiskers. But they don't actually know how to *do* anything in the way of housework and so on. Why, our girls all did both Japanese sewing and Western dressmaking. Our Sadako could even do an Edo-zuma bride's costume, but a lot of these girls can't do any of the things their mothers-in-law do, but they're still stuck up. One came into the shop the other day: said she'd planted some melon seeds and they wouldn't come up and what should they do. I told her: ask granny, I said; she knows. But they hate to ask their mother-in-law anything. They'd rather go asking other people. They don't work, either. Never stick at things for more than five minutes . . .

The yome was at a double disadvantage. To begin with she was the subordinate newcomer; the stranger who had to get used to sleeping with a strange man, serving a strange older woman, keeping on good terms with the younger brothers and sisters; it was she, the newcomer, not the on-going group, who had to make all the adjustments: she had, as the phrase had it, 'to learn the ways of the family'. And secondly she was a woman. The muko – the younger son who came into a family to take over the succession as the husband of one of its daughters – was equally disadvantaged as a newcomer, but as a member of the superior sex he was better able to cope with it.

Or at least, to some extent that was so. From another point of view, the very contrast between the dominance properly expected of a man and the subordination of his position as a muko made him a deviant among men, raised questions about his masculinity, reflected on his position in society at large, and that in turn made him sensitive about his position at home. Masasada, for instance, a smiling, amiable sixty-seven-year-old with an ascetically cropped head, had a rather shy tentative manner. One was not surprised to learn that he was a muko.

There was a time in this village when a muko hardly had a chance of being made hamlet chief – or at least not unless you were in one of the richest families, or were a specially good person with speeches and that kind of thing. It began to get a bit better that way after the war. I had my turn as head, anyway, though I had to wait until I was forty-eight. It was hard work, too. For instance, on all the work days – when we did a day repairing the bridge or working on the village forest land – it was the custom for the hamlet chief to treat everybody to a glass or two of saké afterwards. But if you were a muko you couldn't get away with just a glass or two. You had to be a good bit more lavish than that if you wanted people to take you seriously.

Mind you, one advantage of being a muko is that you don't have 'dependants'. [The modern Tokyo meaning of the word he used, 'yakkei-mono', is 'nuisances'.] You don't have to sweat and scrape to set younger brothers up for life and find dowries for younger sisters. You have to work hard, though; a muko would be up and out to work before breakfast. Nowadays if you went and did an hour or so's weeding before breakfast people'd laugh at you.

Some muko did, indeed, suffer from a father-in-law problem. There were fathers-in-law who would bawl out a lazy muko, but generally they realized the delicate and potentially fragile nature of the relationship. It was commonly one of avoidance. Hisayo, whose family was one of the village's top four and whose muko husband had indeed become hamlet chief at an early age in his mid-thirties, claimed that it was in fact more difficult to take a muko than to go out as a bride. 'As a bride you know what to expect and you know what's expected of you; you're "going into service". But you never know quite where you are with a muko. A man is a man, after all. He's sensitive about being treated as if he's "in service". You've got to tread carefully.'

One thing that has improved the position of muko is the range of alternative opportunities. 'Don't go to be a muko as long as you've still got three bags of rice bran to your name,' said the old proverb, and livelihoods in recent years have not been so desperately hard to come by that a muko needs to swallow all his pride and respond with a yome's humble patience to any kind of maltreatment his wife and her family choose to give him. Shinohata's most muko-like muko, the downtrodden Masasada, belonged to an earlier generation. When he arrived, just before the First World War, alternatives were not so easy to find. Moreover, what put him in a specially weak position was the fact that it was his second time round. He had already been a muko in another family and had left, or been sent away. He could not afford a second failure. Added to which he had not managed to procreate any children in his present marriage. They had had to adopt.

To which, further, one should add that 'Masasada's old lady' was quite the most sharp-tongued and articulate lady of her generation. There was no doubt who was the dominant partner in their marriage – even if she was still, according to custom, known as Masasada's old lady. (Although in muko families the husband takes the family surname, villagers refer to the house, as they do to all other houses, by the house-head's personal name, and refer to individuals by their position in the family.) I once found her at a neighbour's (unpremeditated) morning tea-party and when the conversation got round to marriages and wives wearing trousers I asked as innocently as I could whether it was true that the wives of muko were always strong characters. There were great gusts of laughter. 'What do you say to that, grandma?' Masasada's old lady was unabashed.

> 'Well, you know. I say to 'em, if you don't like me, if you want to go, OK. Go! I won't have any regrets. You can't drive me out because I've got nowhere to go. Me and the grandchild belong here. We're the only two that were born in this house. But the rest of you: off you go, if you want. I'm not saying go empty-handed. They can take some of the property. My old man's been here longest so he can have the most. Then Yoshisada [adopted son] the next most, and then Mariko [his wife] the next – in the order that they came. I'm not being unreasonable, am I? If you don't like me, I say, you can always go. Whenever you like. If in the end I don't have anybody to look after me, there is always old people's homes to go to.'

> 'That's right, grandma. According to what people say, if you take a load of money, and if you're good and quiet and make no trouble, they'll look after you in those places until you die.'

An Englishman who does not hail from the propertied classes which traditionally made marriage 'settlements' and where the property rights of women have been a matter of some contention is apt to be surprised by the rather formal 'juridical' attitudes which Shinohata villagers often display in talking of family matters. The clarity of role divisions in Tsunashige's family – the yome doing child-care and mother-in-law doing field work – is one example. Japanese families – and the villagers were conscious of the fact – were enterprises and not just groups of people bound by blood and sentiment. The house-head was farm director; a bride was a new member of the labour force to be given assigned tasks; a muko was looking for a livelihood, an ecological niche; looking after the aged was a role assignment like any other. And the rights and duties of family members depended on such factors as whether they were insiders, 'born in the family', or outsiders, and if insiders on their sex and birth order; and if they were outsiders on the contribution they brought in terms of trousseau and prestige connections.

Hence the importance of a go-between who played an essential role in settling the size of these contributions to be made by incoming brides and adopted sons (money gifts, furniture, enough clothes to last their lifetime, but not usually land). He also arranged the details of the ceremonies, the value of the presents to be exchanged and the range of guests to be invited. ('Is that all they're going to invite? Who do they think our daughter is? If they're going to show such mean attitudes . . .') And he played an essential role, again, in arranging the settlement if, as very often happened in traditional Japan, the marriage ended in divorce and the bride was 'sent back' – just as often by the mother-in-law as by her husband. There was never any question of formal appeal to the courts, but the go-between, assisted by various relatives and friends of both families, would work with quasi-judicial formality. If the general consensus was that it was a case of 'unfair dismissal' of a blameless bride or adopted son, victim of the unreasonable demands of parents-in-law or parents-by-adoption, then the payment of 'damages' as a token of apology would be arranged.

None of which, of course, is to say that sentiment played no part in the relations between husband and wife. Far from it.

Kanetake's wife and her romantic attachment to her bean-cake-seller husband was something of a rarity by her generation, but a couple of decades earlier a good number of marriages were love-matches made within the villages – particularly in lower-status families. The poorer you were, the less property counted, the more you could afford to live by impulse. But with universal schooling and a rise in living levels the more formal canons of respectability spread from the upper to the lower strata of villagers and formally arranged 'good matches' became the norm. The old custom of 'night-crawling' – teenage boys creeping into a girl's bedroom at night for silent and, if either party chose to keep it so, anonymous, sex – gradually died out. No one is sure now whether it was often the prelude to a love-match, or whether it was just 'playing around', kept quite separate from the serious business of marital relations. More likely the latter, since it was boys from the richer houses who could most easily risk being caught, and who were least likely to make ill-considered marriages. Several septuagenarians said that it stopped in Shinohata 'just a few years before my time', 'in my elder sister's time not mine'. One added that the police actually began prosecuting for illegal entry and in any case by that time there was a proper brothel in the local Kakizaka market centre to provide an alternative source of sexual experience to prepare the young men for marriage. All that 'night-crawling' brings to mind nowadays are apocryphal stories of the guerrilla skirmishes between the young men and the parental generation intent on frustrating their libidinous desires by locking up their daughters. Most people seemed to know the story of the young man who, before he stole out of the house, tied a rope from the pot-hook chain over the hearth to the halter of the horse in his stable across the kitchen. It both created a suspicious rattle which got the old man out of bed *and* tripped him up as he rushed to grab the culprit – into a carpet of spiky chestnut husks according to one refinement.

Now, in these days of democratic freedom, the love marriage is back in again, but Shinohata people hardly see that as a great liberation. A good number of them still have to exercise themselves to 'find good places' for their less forward and enterprising daughters, or to find brides for their shyer sons – and not many of them feel that they were cheated of the fulfilment of some grand romantic dream by the way their own marriages were arranged. The Bon dance songs, to be sure, were romantic enough, with their punning play on 'kaeru' (the country frog/the going home of a lover in the morning) and on 'a itai' (Oh, it hurts!/I'd love to see him) and their references to love letters and to twin pines with limbs intertwined. But that was for the heady August days of the Bon season, once the saturnalia, later the time of dangerous pre-marital flirtation, today the occasion for the Women's Association to display the dances they have learned from the folk-lore experts. Sanekichi is in his mid-fifties.

> Boys and girls mixed pretty freely when I was young. We had a little village library bought out of the money we earned as a youth group doing a few days' labour service in the spring. Then we did drama; we always put on a play every year, at the end of the labour service week. And there was the O-Bon dancing at the August Moon, too. We'd dance until dawn sometimes – five nights in a row. Still, for most people, marriage and the sort of flirting you did with girls in the village were two separate things. I married a cousin of mine. My father wanted it. I'd seen her once before: she came to see father when he was ill in Sano just before he died. I'd seen her then and, well, it was father's wish and he'd died. I had my eye on a nice girl here but, well . . . She got married into another village. I still see her sometimes. No embarrassment any more, but a nice warm feeling though . . .
>
> Yes, a new bride does seem a real stranger when she first comes, as you say, but, you know, she soon fits in. Of course it's hard at first. There are bound to be difficulties. Can't help it. But one gets past that. There'd be a lot of mother-in-law/daughter-in-law quarrels, of course. I always took the line that it was six to four . . .
>
> No, no; in your wife's favour. Six parts to your wife and four to your mother. After all your wife's the one you've got to live with and work with and grow old with.

Not all Shinohata marriages were as strong as Sanekichi's.

Adulterous philandering was rarely the trouble. The men, it was taken more or less for granted, occasionally had women when they went off on weekend outings with the Co-op or the soft-ball team, but they did not covet their neighbours' wives. The balance between id and super-ego lies decisively with the latter in this sober-sided society, and the duties of good-neighbourliness are too overwhelmingly important a constituent of that super-ego's prescriptions. Even the slightly flirtatious manner of the few women who do have a glint of lively sensuality in their eyes is not really a come-hither flirtatiousness. Men do not jealously lock up their wives. They do not need to. Wives alone at home might offer tea in the entrance-hall, or in the kitchen to men callers without envisaging either the actual possibility, or the accusation, of any impropriety. I was always intrigued about the love life of a particularly buxom war widow, but such affairs as she had seem all to have been conducted outside the village: the breath of scandal never touched her.

Adulterous philandering is not often the trouble, but temperamental incompatibility might be. There was Yoshisada, so gentle and inoffensive, but landed with an absolute bitch of a second wife who was a genuine wicked step-mother to his daughter. So mean was she that she would use money sent to her by her parents to buy herself special treats which she then proceeded to eat, without sharing, in front of husband and child. On top of which she was always pleading migraines as an excuse not to work; a real bad lot. There was Koretada and his wife, not really in the same category but a bit like crab and monkey. Koretada's fussy perfectionism was the trouble, really. They would go out to weed their fields together, a happy-looking pair. Then he would start criticizing the sloppy way she was doing the job, and she would answer back, and then after a quarter of an hour's bickering, she'd take off. The rest of the day they'd work in separate fields.

But these are atypical. For most couples the affection that develops through years of shared experience, shared daily work, shared disappointment, shared successes, shared sorrows and moments of happiness, is a deep and strong one. A man who had been called up just after his marriage, when his wife was still a stranger, remarked that he learned what farm marriages were, curiously enough, when he was out of the village. An army comrade – a factory worker from Kanagawa – had taken him home once on a weekend leave. His comrade's wife had remarked to him on that visit how much she envied farmers' wives. The whole day you can be with your husband, she had said, working with him, having a share in all his life. A town worker's wife, by contrast, was cut off from the most important part of his life. There was so little to share. He had often had occasion in the thirty years that followed to reflect on the truth of her insight.

The affection, though, is not often overtly displayed. The physical expression of affection is generally confined to parents and their pre-teen children. Husbands and wives do not touch and fondle each other, except for purposes of – apparently rather perfunctory – sexual congress, or to give comfort in serious illness. I recall the subject coming up once at Shige-yasu's house. Shigeyasu is perhaps Shinohata's least sober and respected citizen. At fifty-three he still has not been elected headman and is feeling the insult keenly. The last loyal retainer of the old landlord (see Chapter 17) his nervous deference is the object of much derision. He is a lightweight. He is feckless. He does not deserve his competent shrewd hard-working wife who saw to *all* their fields when he was working as attendant at the trout pond, who nowadays earns a man's wages on the con-struction works and whose voice comes loud and clear over the loudspeaker once or twice a week to announce the activities of the women's odori dance group which she runs. But Shigeyasu is close to nature. Amid the clutter of the room (miscellaneous clothes hanging on nails, a plank suspended from the ceiling piled with dusty boxes, the case of a primitive camera, satchels and children's hiking water-bottles) there are a stuffed squirrel and a stuffed owl sitting on a gnarled root on the television set – the root of a rare tree brought from the mountains for its 'interesting' shape, carefully cleaned and polished. Shigeyasu knows where to go for wild bees' nests, and indeed he served some bee embryos cooked in syrup. He breeds suzu-mushi in-sects and explained how they vibrated their wings, showed the difference between male and female, and described their manner of copulation. Just like the pheasants, flapping their wings in a mating dance.

Pity human beings don't dance like that? Yes, you're right. Human beings are different. It's a difficult business. You know, it's something we Japanese are very backward in, this business of showing affection. I always think so when I see foreign films on television. The kissing. To us Japanese it seems just rather unpleasant. But that's because we don't understand how it can be a way of showing deep affection. There are all kinds of ways of doing it, aren't there? On the mouth, on the cheek. They all have different meanings. There's a love kiss and a farewell kiss. But we don't understand that and we don't know about it.

'Mummy did that to me when I was asleep,' said their seven-year-old son. 'That's because you're nice,' said his mother, cuddling him a little self-consciously.

Rarely displayed in any overt fashion, affection, genuine and deep, is a strand in a good many Shinohata marriages. Tolerance, grim loyalty, making the best of it, concealed contempt, resignation, a shared sense of humour, are elements that go to make up a viable accommodation in many others. But most at least are *comfortable* accommodations. The death of one partner – and usually it is the (older) husband who goes first – leaves a yawning gap. Once, for the widow, the son partly filled the gap as he succeeded his father as director of the family enterprise. But many widows now, their sons away from home or uninterested in farming, found themselves at the end of a line, thrown on their own resources, to some degree disconcerted – and to some degree given a chance for surprising self-discovery.

It's a shock at first to be suddenly left alone at sixty-five. But it's amazing what widowhood does for you. Father used to do all the planning. He'd decide roughly how many grams of silkworm eggs we'd buy and we'd just go out into the fields and get as much mulberry as there was and feed them all there was and get what we could. But now left to do it myself, things are different. I had a whole field of mulberry I couldn't use so I had to sell it, and so I went and I looked and I thought, now about ten stalks make one kan, and if there are fifteen on one tree, let's see, that's so many trees in a row and so many rows, and I worked it out that it was about 600 kan. And I sold it for that and they said, 'Old lady, you were just about dead right. You must have second sight.' So I said, 'Don't be silly. I've just got a bit wiser, that's all.' But I was proud of myself. What a clever old lady you've become, I thought. Same with the rice field and working out how much fertilizer to put on it. Up to now I'd just helped father put on whatever he decided. But now I have to look it up and ask people and work it out myself. My, I've become a clever old lady. Pity I don't have a few more years to use my cleverness. But it's amazing what you find you can do when you have to. It keeps me so busy, though.

I wonder how many years I've got left. Ten maybe? Father, you know, I think he had a premonition. He was working hard the few months before his death. He went out in the middle of winter and cut those peach trees out in the field right down. Took a lot of timber off them and instead of leaving it in the fields brought it right back to the house and piled it neatly up. And he bought bags and bags of fertilizer. Can't think what got into his head, but there was plenty to last through this year too and still some left. And then he had a funny way, the last few months, of suddenly becoming tidy with his clothes. Usually he'd just take off a suit and leave me to tidy it up, but he started folding everything neatly and putting it in boxes. It was strange, he was never one to do that before. I don't know what it was: not a premonition, really, I don't think. Some kind of instinct, maybe.

11

Growing-Up

In a community of ageing people there is such frequent talk of children as the providers of comfort and security that one is apt to forget all the other reasons Shinohata people have for wanting children. To be sure, people do not talk about these other reasons very much. Tsunashige's yome, who is allowed to give all her time to looking after her eighteen-month-old, is envied by older generations of women chiefly because she has an easy life, not because she can spend her time playing with her baby in a way that few of them had been able to. Nevertheless there is no mistaking the pleasure adults do take in their young children. They are much loved, much fussed over, much indulged. A trip with mother to the shops carries a prescriptive right to a treat; children are expected to demand a lollipop or a packet of sweets or an ice-cream, and parents are expected to concede. The well-behaved eight-year-old son of the Professor with the country cottage was the subject of much bemused comment. He was too well trained by his German mother to try wheedling sweets out of her when she brought him to the shop. Instead he had his own pocket-money allowance and sometimes bought his own sweets out of that. 'How much more *rational* than our way of doing things,' people said, but wistfully – as if these were customs which could only be admired from a distance, not even possibly transferable to their daily lives.

The indulgence diminishes when children start school – for girls at least. Boys continue to be totally indulged by their mothers and grandmothers. I have seen a twelve-year-old boy come into a room where his grandmother was watching that evening's instalment of her favourite soap-opera, and switch to the teenage gangster serial on another channel without a word of either apology or explanation. Grandmother accepted the change with the resignation that sixty-five years' experience of Japanese men had put at her command. The expensive toys; the bicycles with their ten speeds and electric horns and triple-banked headlights; the stereo-record players – expenditure on child-indulgence has been an important element in Japan's consumer boom and the villagers have not lagged in playing their part. There are 'hard' houses in the village where asceticism is still a matter of principle and where they save money because they cannot tolerate the self-indulgence or the child-indulgence involved in spending it. But for most people the asceticism of the past was the asceticism only of necessity. There is little sense that indulgence might be bad for the character.

The expensive bicycle is followed, for some Shinohata high-school boys, by the expensive motor-bike. One Sunday a group of teenagers got together for my benefit to tell me what they felt about life. One boy was already bored with his motor-bike: he still liked touring, and of course it was useful to go to town for the bowling – which he had done at six o'clock that morning.

Where do you get the money for this sort of thing?

Boy 1: Oh, it comes from somewhere. You know, you can usually get around your parents.

Boy 2: I tell them that the school fees are such and such – adding a bit on.

Girl: But how can you? The fees are fixed. Everybody knows.

Boy 2: Oh, you know, you can say the headmaster says we've got to bring extra money for such and such. There are always ways. For my motor-bike, actually, I earned a bit of it myself. My dad gave me the rest.

Girl: I couldn't do that. I really couldn't. My conscience wouldn't let me – seeing how hard my parents work and the hardship they put up with.

(*Scoffing laughter from the boys.*)

Boy 2: It's true they're hard up at times. It's hard to ask them.

Do you mean you don't ask at those times?

Boy 2: Oh no. We ask; I just mean it's hard to. Still, if you explain they usually give it to you.

In some families indulgence alternates with disciplinary control – or attempts at it – in a somewhat unpredictable way, but in few in quite such a tempestuously unpredictable way as in Akira's.

They're famous for their family quarrels. Sometimes, we've been so afraid they'd harm each other that father's gone across to mediate and calm them down. The wife is the centre of it always. She's so amiable most of the time, so warm, so soft-spoken, she almost cat-licks you, but heavens! What a temper! She'd throw things at the children and knock them about and pull their hair. The eldest used to work hard. There wasn't much gumption in him, but he was a good son and no fool. But they would treat him as if he didn't belong. Sometimes it would be all right. He'd go off on the construction somewhere and bring home some money, and then for a few days it would be Ichiro this and Ichiro that. But soon they'd be back at it again. And she'd be complaining to other people about him all the time too. It's amazing how long he stood it, but last year he eventually left home and got a job in a beer factory. He was thirty-eight by then and they really had never done anything to get him a bride. But I hear he's married now.

It was the same with their daughter, Kazu. She had much the same treatment. Last year she went to the bad and started running around with a man – almost completely left home. Whenever she came back there were quarrels. But the man was killed in an accident. His family looked after Kazu and found her a place and now she's well set up. She brings presents home now and they're all over her. It's our Kazu this, and our Kazu that. Things have been much happier altogether lately, though. Their youngest has turned out to be a fine boy. You would never have thought it. High school's a difficult age and high-school children are really hard to control; but he was a particularly bad case. But last year he had an accident on his motor-bike, knocked over a kindergarten child at a bus stop. The kid was in hospital for a long time. They got a relative to negotiate and paid compensation. It cost them a lot of money. But it's amazing the change in him since then. It's almost as if he'd been born again. He's such a different person. It's almost as if he was washed with money. Akira's wife complained about the expense of the compensation, but I told her, 'You shouldn't complain,' I said, 'you've got a good son out of it. You can't buy good sons with money.'

He was, indeed, an amiable young man; a rare case of a boy who decided he was going to stay at home and be a farmer. He gave me a lift one day in his little farm truck. He had been whistling with gusto to accompany the pop songs coming from the radio he'd had fixed to it. He had a couple of stickers inside the cab. One, in English, said mysteriously, 'Going my way.' The other, in Japanese said, 'Beware of anger, laziness, and pride. Don't anxiously fuss – but neither let things slide.'

Order, discipline, self-control; it is the school rather than the family which is largely responsible for building these elements into the masculine Japanese character. Discipline is a real problem, said the headmaster of the large middle school which serves the whole of Kakizaka township. Parents are too indulgent. Children grow up to be selfish and 'not to know themselves'. They vie with each other in conspicuous consumption and don't appreciate the value of money. One of the chief problems is that parents do not get their children to help at home or work on the farm. They think they should give them all their time to study. He tries in vain to persuade parents that work is the best form of education. Although the prefectural authorities frown on it, his school has a three-day 'farm-work break' at rice-planting and another three days at harvest time, but not all the children actually do any work, by any means.

One certainly does not get the impression of disorderly ill-discipline if one visits the school. Classes stand politely (at the instruction of the 'class president') when teachers or visitors enter the room, and remain respectfully attentive until told to be seated. Boys and girls sit in alternate rows (to prevent any shy gravitation to opposite sides of the room, thus defeating the purpose of co-educational integration), the boys with almost shaven close-cropped heads, the girls in uniform white shirts with black middies. Nor does one get the impression of children who are work-shy. My first visit was late on a Friday afternoon at the weekly thorough-cleaning period (as opposed to the daily briefer ten-minute cleaning periods with which each day begins). The school was buzzing with little groups of children wielding brooms, carrying buckets, swabbing floors. The first group I saw, sweeping the edge of the large playground, contained a teacher who was also wielding a broom, setting an example with great vigour.

The atmosphere was relaxed and friendly. It used not to be so, said the older generation in Shinohata. The village school used to be a distinctly forbidding place. The teachers were outsiders; mostly members of the town middle class lodging in the village centre from Monday to Friday. They carried canes and tapped children imperiously on the head. Parents had little contact with the teachers; only a few upper-stratum fathers attended the annual graduation ceremony, though even the poorest contrived to make sure that their children had a formal hakama skirt to wear for the occasion. By the thirties there was no question of children not going to school, even from the poorest families. 'I stayed away sometimes though. There were days when father would say: "We're very busy with the silkworms today: you'd better stay at home and help."'

The post-war school – particularly the six-year elementary school – is a much more intimate affair. PTA meetings are frequent. Teachers do not behave *vis-à-vis* parents like men self-consciously invested with the dignity and authority of an awesome Imperial Japanese State. They seem concerned about the children; accept it as reasonable that parents should be equally concerned. Each class teacher makes it his business to visit the homes of each of his children at least once during the year. (Less burdensome now for the teachers at the elementary school which serves Shinohata and three other hamlets: depopulation has reduced classes from the post-war fifty to twenty-five or so.) There is an annual Participation Day when the school is thrown open to parents. Now that so many fathers are commuting employees rather than farmers who can take any day off, Sunday is made a school day for the purpose and the holiday shifted to Monday.

Just as the Japanese salary man is not just a 9-to-5 employee, but a man who finds his primary *raison d'être* in his work life, so the school-child is not just a 9-to-5 term-time school-child. If one asks how old a child is the usual answer is rarely in terms of calendar years but in terms of 'a standard-four child'; 'a middle standard-two child'. School is the prime focus of a school-child's identity. He is no less a school-child in the holidays, either. There are regular meeting days when the children gather at the school to talk with their class teacher, so that he or she can give them any motivational stimulation necessary to urge them on to the completion of their holiday tasks. The holiday task book is, indeed, an impressive printed document. It contains stories to read, sums to do, a space to record the air temperature three times a day; some outline arguments for 'problems to think about' (e.g. 'the pros and cons of comic books' – somewhat weighted towards the cons) and at the end 'reflections on my summer holiday'. What, the children are expected to ask themselves, did I try to achieve and fail in? What did I fail to try to achieve?

These work books are standard commercial products, but the Shinohata school had stuck in a special addendum: 'My plans for the summer holiday' to be filled in under the three heads: Study; Work; Health. Swimming was the most common entry in the last category. A teacher was on duty at the school pool every day, but only children who brought their swimmer's card with parent or guardian's authorizing signature seal duly impressed on the space for the relevant date were allowed to swim and thus make a contribution to the fulfilment of their health plans. They were even allowed to enjoy it.

There are just a few signs of 'privatization', though, of a shift to patterns of lesser involvement; of a tendency for teachers to take a narrower definition of their role. A new headmaster at Shinohata has recently introduced a few changes. First, in the march to school. The elementary school is about a mile and a half from Shinohata, a mile and a half through fields, with no house in sight. It had been the practice for all Shinohata children to gather at the centre of the village and march to school collectively under the direction of a standard-six boy, formally elected to his position under the auspices of the school. He always, of course, took his duty very seriously and had a stick to tap on the shoulder any younger ones who got out of line. (People thought the reason to be safety in numbers against, say, kidnappers or child seducers, though no one could think of such a case happening within a hundred miles.) The new headmaster had decided that the practice was unnecessary and had dropped it.

Presumably, too, he did not see much virtue in one obvious function of the practice – the reinforcement of the age-seniority principle. Training in a proper deference to seniors starts in the family, of course, where an older brother is still addressed deferentially as 'O-nii-san' and not by his name. It is perpetuated, too, by school tradition. If one travels on a late-afternoon train with a crowd of children, going home from middle or high school, one is liable to be jolted out of one's seat by the apparent ferocity of the greetings exchanged. A junior who gets off the train ahead of members of a senior class must shout 'I excuse myself ahead of you!', and the greater the vehemence with which he shouts it the more satisfactory his conformity to the school norms is thought to be. When one of the sports clubs of the local middle school goes on outings, it is customary for each 'fresher' to take an extra lunch for his sponsoring senior. Some mothers had eventually wheedled out of their children the meaning of this puzzling request for a double lunch and complained to a teacher. His comment: 'It's rather undesirable, but very difficult to stop these things. The boys say they like doing it, and it's entirely of their own free will . . .'

A second thing the new headmaster has done is to reduce the number of extra-curricular chores the teachers undertake, particularly those involving money. Formerly teachers would collect small sums as savings towards the school outing. Now parents or children must do their saving themselves. Formerly the school acted as intermediary for cheap bulk buying of sports equipment or auxiliary textbooks. Now they just get the traders to come to the school on appointed days to offer their wares direct. The school is less considerate and concerned, parents say.

The other change is more deeply regretted. The school sports day used to be a general village festival. Youth groups, the fire brigades, women's associations and the like all helped to organize it and ran one or two events each – inter-hamlet tugs-of-war and the like. There were plenty of booths and sideshows. Everybody had enormous fun. All this the new head had stopped. The day was properly a school sports day, devoted to the children's sports. It detracted from the occasion to have it mixed with extraneous things. Parents were often so busy with the sideshows that they missed watching their children run their races.

Whether or not this form of 'disengagement' foreshadows the future, this head-teacher is still the exception.

The headmaster of the township middle school, for instance, spent several Sundays taking members of his group of retarded children to see prospective employers in the next prefecture or in Tokyo, hoping to fix them up in a small factory with a family atmosphere where they could be given special consideration. When I first visited the school, during the cleaning period, the headmaster was out of his office on a tour of the school. My guide eventually found him talking with the retarded group who were working the school chrysanthemum bed. It was a group of eight children with measured IO between 50 and 65. Until recently they had just been passengers in the regular (unstreamed) classes but now they were brought together into a special group with their own full-time teacher. Parents had fiercely resisted the segregation of their children at first, but the results, he claimed, had amply justified the system; the children had become brighter, more cheerful, had learned more. The headmaster had taken a particular interest in this departure and had read a paper on it at a teachers' conference.

School remains, for most teachers, not just the place where they earn their bread and butter; it is where they belong, a place where 'joys and sorrows are shared', as the traditional phrase describes the solidarity of intimate groups. Ceremonies are one way of affirming that solidarity; outings, parties and jollifications are another. One does not need much excuse for such an occasion. I was a sufficiently exotic visitor to provide

one, at the township middle school, for instance. On my second
casual visit I took a couple of English classes. Could I please
come back on Friday afternoon and talk to some of the senior
classes? And would I please, said the headmaster, seeing me off
in the Yamamoto's little 350-cc farm truck into which I could
just about squeeze if I held my knee-caps either side of the
steering wheel, could I please not drive when I came on Friday?
They would like to 'have a cup of tea afterwards'. They would
see me home. I was puzzled for a moment until I recalled that
'tea' in such a context is capable of liberal interpretation. He
just meant that he did not want to be responsible for aiding and
abetting drunken driving, nor did he wish that my entering into
the spirit of the occasion should be inhibited by considerations
of prudence.

It was an amiable afternoon. After a slow start the fifteen-
year-olds had gradually warmed up to their interrogation, the
girls shedding their shyness more rapidly than the boys and
becoming quite animated by the end. 'What do you think of the
Japanese junior high-school student?' 'How old will you be next
birthday?' 'Where were you born?' 'How can I best learn to
read and write English?' 'What is your occupation?' 'How
many families have you?' There was some hilarity when I explained just why this was not the best way of asking how many
children I had.

Soon afterwards I found myself sitting at the end of a long
table in the school reception-cum-committee room, a table
loaded with beer bottles and monstrous aluminium kettles containing warm saké, slices of expensive raw tunny, sliced abalone
and ink fish, tomatoes and cucumber; plates of white bean curd
cut into cubes and looking like Turkish delight. All the teachers
were there, apparently, except the music teacher; the occasional
rasp of a trombone from the band practising in a distant classroom indicated where she was, still performing her duty. Pre-
dictably the women teachers were all clustered together at the
'lower' end of the table. The room itself was interesting. One
wall was covered with the gaudy flags which the students parade
around the ground on sports day, each one bearing a bunch of
streamers recording the victors of past years. On another wall
were cases of cups and trophies, group pictures of the teaching
staff, portraits of past headmasters, a bookcase containing row

on row of bound volumes of regulations issued by successive generations of regulation-drunk Ministry of Education bureaucrats. Across on the other side was what looked like a reproduction of an Italian primitive; a family of singularly ugly Caucasian peasants getting in the grape harvest. Beside it was a large poster whose central feature was a Raphaelesque Madonna sitting on a cloud and surrounded by a tumble of chubby *putti*. The characters below proclaimed:

THE CHILD'S CONSTITUTION

The child should be respected as a human being.
The child should be given due importance as a member of society.
The child should grow up in a suitable environment

. . .

Think of another country where a wily, corrupt and authoritarian politician could genuinely believe that by promulgating such vacuity (by way of celebrating Children's Day) he would enhance both his standing as a Minister of Education and his party's ability to win votes from the electorate!

As the bottles emptied and the kettles grew lighter, faces grew pinker, spirits rose. Senior staff increased the assiduous bonhomie with which they moved round the table pouring drinks for their juniors. The headmaster raised the pitch of his voice to include the whole table and begin the formal–informal *conversazione*. 'Are marriages arranged in England?' 'How are school sports and adult sports institutionally integrated in England?' 'How do English children behave towards their parents in the home?' 'Is there the same tendency in England as there is here for the capitalist class to exercise an increasing control over education and expand technical training at the expense of other more important things?'

The party was beginning to approach the inhibition-breaking stage at which people get maudlin or cathartically pugnacious and the cement of spiritual unity begins to seep into the cracks of individual personalities. The headmaster was not entirely at ease by then. One couldn't be sure how far an outsider might accept the conventions and somebody might exceed the limit. He made a few tentative moves to wind up the proceedings, but unsuccessfully; by that time the party had a momentum of its own. One of the gayest of the teachers, an ebullient man in a bright blue shirt who had moved up to sit with the girls at the far end of the table, insisted that it was time for the singing. He began with an old work song about leading horses over rocky mountain paths. Then the most vivacious of the women teachers led in the singing of the 'Cherry Blossom Song'. Then, it was decided, it was time for an English song. 'Home Sweet Home' it was to be. But that was really a classroom song, not a party song, so the music teacher was sent for, dragged away from her band practice to lead us in a slow sentimental rendering. There followed what was clearly the tune of 'Coming through the Rye'. The words, however, as promulgated by Ministry of Education Regulation number umpteen some time in the 1890s ran roughly as follows:

> The evening sky is clear, the autumn breeze blows chill.
> As the moon shadow falls, the bell-beetle chirps alone.
> Far, far away, the autumn skies of home.
> Ah! My mother and my father. Are they in good health?

When I explained the distinct overtones of bucolic lust in Burns' original, it caused a sensation.

Finally we all stood for a rendering of 'The Light of the Firefly', which is none other than 'Auld Lang Syne'. But, as was clear from the teachers' faces, it is not boozy New Year party associations that the song has for them. It is the Japanese graduation song. It conjures up moments in their life of painful rebirth: moments when they themselves were wrenched from the womb of school communities of which they had become loyal and integrated members; moments when they said good-bye to children of whom they had grown genuinely and warmly fond. I went home in a glow of goodwill.

The sheer competence of the Japanese school system in pro-ducing literate and numerate adults is striking. Homework begins for all children in the second or third year; class time is carefully programmed; objectives are clearly set. I got one class in each of the three middle-school years to write essays for me.

The fluency of the writing, its grammatical competence, the children's vocabulary and knowledge of the characters with which to write the words they knew was impressive even among the youngest group of thirteen-year-olds. Japanese schools seem to do a more universally good job of teaching the 2,000 symbols needed for writing reasonably competent Japanese than British schools do of teaching children how mysteriously to combine twenty-six. (Perhaps the fact that it *is* so much more obviously formidable a task induces more consistent and prolonged efforts to accomplish it.)

But if they are careful to follow the conventions of spelling and grammar the children are also very careful to follow the conventions of thought. Their essays were full of high sentiments, but mostly lacking in much individuality. They were given a choice of topic: My life in ten years' time; Our township in ten years' time; My most vivid memory. Most chose to write on the future of their township. They were united in expecting astounding developments, similar as many of them said to the progress in the last decade; ten years ago the district was almost without cars, television sets, washing machines. They were divided as to whether progress would come through more factories or more tourist hotels and summer cottages, but united, again, in foreseeing and deploring the horrors of pollution and environmental destruction.

> There was a wood near my house and it was so quiet in there it sometimes felt spooky and you wouldn't want to walk in it alone at night. But the change in the last ten years has been startling. Many of the trees have been cut down and here and there all kinds of buildings are going up. The sound of construction goes on from early morning to late at night . . . What will it be like in ten years' time? We shall probably be plagued with pollution like the towns and wrapped in a grey sky so that children will grow up thinking that grey is the proper colour of the sky. All the green will disappear, and all the flowers which gladden our hearts will shrivel up . . . But it is no use thinking that Kakizaka will not change, because the whole country is developing, and if the factories come they will need to build houses for

the people who work in them and the houses will all be crowded together and there will be so much rubbish and people won't have any place to throw it away. There will be some people who will throw it in the river and the river will get dirty and we shall never see our clear river again. Or there will be some place to burn the rubbish and the smoke will fill the sky and we shall not see the blue sky any more. That is the kind of thing that makes me think anxiously about the future. However, I am sure there are a lot of things that are going to get better in ten years too. Though I think that more things are going to get worse, but I hope not.

Others see the pollution attacking men's hearts.

If Kakizaka gets industrialized, there will be a lot more interchange with other towns and people's ideas will change. Kakizaka people might become like people in the towns now, thinking only of themselves, and Kakizaka will become a dark place. But I hope this doesn't happen. I hope people's ways of feeling stay the same as they are now, and of course that there do not grow to be differences between rich and poor.

There is a good deal of vague moralizing too:

. . . Everybody must be aware of the dangers of pollution, because it is everybody's responsibility, but the town must give a lead otherwise nobody will do anything about it. Everybody taking responsibility means that we must all recognize other people's position and all co-operate together and join our efforts to make ours a bright and happy town . . .

Others are a little more imaginatively optimistic. One fourteen-year-old girl's idyllic future consisted of:

The little birds still twittering in the trees, everybody smiling and being kind to each other, the mountains unpolluted as they are now, the roads all automated so that there are no traffic accidents, and a lot more shops and the railway running through the town and the river clean and pure and still places where you can stretch out and doze in the grass in open country and hear nothing but the sound of the stream . . . Just twice or three times the present population, but not more, a new school built of concrete and our educational record improving so that the name of Kakizaka becomes known throughout the country, and a tall clock-tower in the centre of the town, rising up like a white dove against the sky, and gardens with fountains and ice-cream sellers, and modern-style swings, though swings that you work by yourself are still better than automated ones.

On the whole the boys are more given to sententious generalities than the girls. The minority who chose to write about themselves rather than about the town in ten years' time were mostly girls. Several were going to be nurses; one was inspired by seeing a war film with a nurse heroine who 'stood out like a wild chrysanthemum amidst the horror'. 'I have not known any suffering or unhappiness in my fourteen years of life. What a dull miserable thing it would be if I went prosaically through my whole life without knowing hardship. What regrets I would have if I led an ordinary life and didn't give pleasure or happiness to anybody. It would hardly be worth being born.'

Another had doubts about her ability to live up to the exacting requirements of a nurse's profession. Supposing she had to make the patients eat food that she didn't like herself, and supposing she made a mistake during an operation and the patient died? There were difficulties, too, about her alternative dream, of becoming an FBI agent and helping to clean up the underworld. That required a quickness of mind and athletic prowess which she wasn't sure she had. So she would settle for marriage to a sea captain with two children and a dog in a modern house with a red roof and white walls and a nice lawn and swings for the children – except that that was a little bit too dull and unexciting. Several distinguished between fantasy ambitions to be sports stars, musicians, ballerinas and novelists, and their expectation of working in an office or a department store. One wanted to be an airline stewardess, one a television announcer, one who explained that she did not have the brains to get into a national university and her parents couldn't afford to send her to a private one would like to be a disc jockey because she was a great chatterbox and it would give her plenty of scope.

There are good reasons why the girls should be more willing to write about themselves than boys. Girls have more secure identities; boys are more uneasily caught between externally offered visions of the possible, external urgings to compete, external expectations of competence and maturity and their own uncertain assessment of their capacities. 'The next ten years' for a fourteen-year-old boy are the anxious years, the years of the Great Sorting Out, the years, in the first place, when one or two of the brightest Kakizaka boys, and in rare years perhaps a girl, will get one of the 6 per cent quota of places which the elite senior high schools in Sano and Nakatani offer to out-of-catchment-area children. Once there – barring some anomalous deviation from normality like losing interest in the rat-race and refusing to cram at the normal frenetic pace – they will be set on the royal road to success, for these high-school entrance examinations are good predictors of performance in the university entrance examinations – those talent-sorting competitions par excellence which decide who shall be admitted to which university. The luckiest, or the most dedicated, of course, are those who are admitted to Tokyo University, which produces three-quarters of the country's top civil servants, judges, businessmen and politicians, or to one of the other top-flight national universities with low fees and high reputations whose graduates have a good chance of being accepted by the top firms.

The bulk of Kakizaka's school-children, however, will go to other high schools as the end of three years of middle school at the age of fifteen brings the compulsory schooling period to an end. The top segment of the ability range will go to the local academic-stream senior high school – a low-fee, public institution. The next segment will go to the public agricultural high school or to the (more expensive) private academic-stream high school. Most of the remainder of the ability range will be acceptable to a near-by private commercial and technical high school or to one of the girls' finishing-school type 'academic' private schools in the city, and some, finally, will go straight to work. In the early seventies just under a quarter of Kakizaka children were ending their education at the end of compulsory schooling – somewhat above the average for the whole country, which was between 10 and 15 per cent.

The microcosmic prestige hierarchy of local high schools is matched on a national scale by the hierarchy of universities. Only the children who have got into the elite hot-house high schools have much real chance of reaching the top-flight national universities, but a good many who go to the local academic-stream high school can reasonably aim at a university lower down the scale. Below the top-flight national universities in the pecking order come the more venerable older private foundations which despite their much higher fees (than national universities) can still be quite selective. Then comes the broad segment of mass-production private universities (the biggest has 6,000 teachers and over 100,000 students) which process law, commerce, social science and engineering students by the tens of thousands for the family firms and small businesses which still provide the bedrock of the Japanese economy. About on the same prestige level (that is, level of entrance examination difficulty) are the lesser prefectural universities with large education departments which function chiefly as four-year teacher-training colleges. And if their entrance examinations are still too difficult there remain two kinds of even less demanding institutions – newer private universities which are trying to reach mass-production status but have not yet sufficiently established themselves, and some rather expensive and exclusive institutions which specialize in purveying a suitably gentlemanly – or rather ladylike, since most of their pupils are girls and some are single-sex universities – culture to the not-so-bright children of the affluent. There are also a large number of two-year colleges which do the same thing for the somewhat less affluent.

The devastating thing about both of these sets of filters – the high-school entrance sort-out and the university entrance sort-out – is that everybody perceives the process, not as a matter of individuals *choosing* their future careers, but of individuals being differentially *chosen* or rejected for opportunities everyone would like to have. The sorting process does not discover who has what kind of individual taste or talent, what sort of career preferences: it discovers who is deemed better or worse than whom by some supposed measure of 'general ability'. Hardly anyone goes to the agricultural high school if he is bright enough to go to the academic-stream high school which leads on to the university – unless his parents are idiosyncratically keen that he should take over the farm. Even if they are too poor or too mean even to contemplate his going to universities, he still does the best thing for his job chances by demonstrating that he is academic-stream material. Similarly at the next level: only the poor performer who cannot get into a high-prestige older private university like Waseda settles for bigger mass-production universities like Nippon or Chūō – and he naturally assumes that everybody knows why he is there.

It is this tendency to see the whole process of education and career choice through the perspective of a superior/inferior, intelligent/not-so-intelligent dimension which gives the torment of adolescence a special twist in Japan. Growing-up is a process of being publicly labelled for intrinsic worth in a way just as explicit as in Britain's 11-plus, but at a more sensitive age and with more refined gradations. The system is a product of several factors absent in Britain and the USA. The first is the life-time employment system. When you are hiring someone for a career, not for a job, it is his general ability, not any specific vocational competence, you are interested in, and if you are hiring him straight from school you have only his school record to judge it by. Secondly, Japan has had a strictly fair meritocratic selection system from the time when its modern universities were founded. Dad may get you into 'his' Oxford college, but not into Tokyo University, however distinguished an alumnus of it he may be. Hence the Tokyo University label has a gilt-edged value in the market – at least in terms of how bright you were at the age of eighteen even if there is not much guarantee offered (or indeed sought) concerning what you might subsequently have learned there. Thirdly, Japan has a much more homogeneous and unicentric culture even than Britain, and a fortiori than the United States. There is a single prestige hierarchy of universities, perceptions of which hardly differ whether one is in Tokyo or in Osaka, upper or lower class. Everybody is in the same race.

The extent to which Shinohata children are engaged in the race is probably a little less than among the Tokyo middle class. One should not exaggerate the homogeneity of Japanese modern culture; aspirations to 'get on' are not quite so intense, nor are expectations. The local boy who makes it into Tokyo University is something of a local hero, a universally recognized exception, not likely to be used for 'why can't you be like him' admonitions by the average Shinohata mother. But the gap between Shinohata and middle-class Tokyo is probably a good deal less than divides the London middle class either from rural Somerset or from working-class Barnsley. Japanese universities have never been, like their British and American counterparts, the traditional preserves of a ruling-class culture, not for the likes of the lower classes. From the beginning they were a means of imparting a new, Western, culture, and transmitting it to 'all the talents'. Perhaps enrolment figures are the best way of measuring the cultural distance, the modest size of the aspiration/expectation gap, between town and country. About 80 per cent of Shinohata children continue their education beyond the compulsory period and perhaps 12–15 per cent go on to university, compared with national figures closer to 90 and 25 per cent.

Those Shinohata figures are enough, at any rate, to transmit a certain competitive anxiety to the whole middle-school years. Thus, the wife of the farmer who reserved the colour television set for Sunday best and used the black and white for week days:

> The boys, of course, have their bikes to go to school on, but it's hard on the girls; it takes so much longer to travel by bus. It especially makes a terribly long day for our Sayoko because she has volley-ball practice before and after school each day, and then all Sunday morning. It tires her out rather, but she says she can't leave now. It would let them down, so she must stay until the prefectural tournament at the end of the second term. But we're a bit worried you see because it's her second year, and next year is the difficult year that leads on to high school. Her class teacher came the other day. He said her arithmetic and Japanese language were all right, but the English and science might be the trouble. English is necessary for everything, so she must get that right. So we're going to send her to English extra classes from the third term, as soon as she's finished with volley-ball. There's a private teacher in Haratsu.

Haratsu is a three-mile bus ride down the road from the school – in the opposite direction to Shinohata. Education is something worth putting yourself out for.

But why, exactly, do parents want to push their children through the educational mill? The Kakizaka Town Newsletter carried an interesting anonymous article one November entitled 'to Work or to High School?', obviously emanating from the Director of Education's office. It depicted, on the one hand, that sturdy minority of children seeking to go out into the world to build themselves their own future by their own skill, and then went on to contrast their brave future with that of children who went reluctantly to high school because their parents insisted. Parents might just think it was the thing to do; or be motivated simply by petty vanity – not wanting it to seem that their child 'couldn't make it'; or just want to give their child every chance that they hadn't had; or just be under the impression that everything depended on educational certificates these days and a child had to finish high school to get anywhere.

And so it used to be, said the anonymous author, but now was so no longer. The world was changing; real ability counted now, not paper qualifications. He could quote no evidence, of course, because there is none. If exhortation could make people believe it was so, it would become so; this kind of prophecy is self-fulfilling, but the forces pushing in the opposite direction are too strong. It becomes increasingly hard for those who leave school at fifteen to get a job with any sort of career prospect at all. Major employers recruit all their shop-floor semi-skilled workers from high school. The extension of compulsory education to cover the high-school period is now widely talked of.

But the anonymous author is probably right in his diagnosis of the consequence of reluctant high-school attendance. Children who go to high school only because their parents want them to are likely, he says, to feel that they are doing their parents a favour. They will consider it their right to demand large sums in pocket money and concentrate on having a good time rather than studying seriously. The likely upshot is that they end up out of their parents' control, lacking in the will to work when they graduate, vain, only interested in spending money, a bad proposition for any employer.

Certainly, in uttering such warnings, the author was speaking of the very real anxieties of many Shinohata parents. On the one hand they are not prepared to buck the universal assumption that education is a good thing. On the other, the prolongation of childhood, the delay in reaching maturity, seem pure loss.

> Well, you know, you're a teacher and you've travelled all over the world and I hesitate to say this to you, but you know it seems to me that people get all this education nowadays and it doesn't do them much good. For example we went to school for eight years. Now it's, let's see, nine year compulsory, then they go on to three years of high school – twelve years altogether. But it seems to me they don't get as good an education as we got in eight years. Their general common-sense and everything. Even characters, for instance: they don't learn as many.
>
> By common-sense I mean, for instance, when we left school at fourteen, well, we could already do a man's work. When we met people on the fields we'd exchange greetings. But high school students now – they just go by without saying a word.

They are still in the privileged limbo of childhood. And privilege prolonged without obvious purpose – as for the children with no university prospects – can lead to dangerous symptoms. There is worried talk of glue-sniffing, of loose girls who would actually go off alone with a boy instead of seeking safety in numbers. (Though hardly on his motor-bike pillion: the high school forbids that absolutely, and although the other rule that girls should wear their school uniforms outside the home at all times and not just when going to and from school is often broken, the pillion rule is said to be religiously respected.) The local private academic high school (average ability and below) had actually witnessed a collective protest by the boy pupils against the school rule that hair should not be allowed to grow long enough to cover the ears (though they are not required, like fifteen-year-old middle-school boys, to keep their heads convict-cropped).

That boys with no prospect of getting to university are bored by the seemingly pointless high-school academic routine, that their central life-interests centre on motor-bikes and pop records, and that they have almost no contact with their parents except at the money wheedling level seems to be not uncommon. The boy whose subterfuges for gaining pocket money were described earlier had his own room built where the stable had been, across the concrete hallway (once the earth-floored workspace) from the family quarters. The walls were plastered with pin-ups of sports cars cut from motor magazines and pop-stars cut from film magazines; there was a record-player with stereo-speakers, piles of pop records and comic books, a large collection of pennants from places he had visited on his motor-bike tours. Talk of his school work failed to elicit enthusiasm for anything. His favourite form of recreation was sleeping.

And yet, it was hard to feel, as his parents sometimes did, that he was already a long way along the road to perdition. For one thing, his pin-ups were *so* demure – one, in particular, a girl singer with a group called the 'Panthers', was the epitome of schoolgirl innocence. And there were other things about the room which hardly suggested decadence – a ten-volume history of modern Japan (he looked at it occasionally, he said, but couldn't say what date 'modern' was supposed to begin). There were some of his own drawings, of hands in different positions, of a tiger with the legend TIGER written below it in English. And there was a plaque, a memento of his school's tenth anniversary, which bore, in elegant but bold characters, the single word 'Effort' and two other similar plaques which he himself had bought: 'Perseverance'; 'Guts'. 'Just decoration, really,' he said. 'But sometimes it comes through to you. You get the point. Stick it out: don't give up – that's the message.'

If *that* is the picture of the incipient juvenile delinquent, one can see why Japan has the lowest crime rates of any industrial country. To an outsider there may seem to be an element of overkill in the efforts which have been mounted by the township authorities to halt any tendencies towards modern decadence which might seem to threaten the harmony of the family and the moral character of the young. A Council for the Promotion of Youth Development has been formed, and one Sunday a month is regularly designated Family Day.

It is all, of course, in a good Confucian tradition. No Confucian has recognized the validity of a distinction between public and private morality. No homes are castles in the sense that one can be allowed to do what one likes within them. All moral conduct is of concern to society. The wise ruler encourages private virtue as much as he admonishes private sin. The 1910 prefectural gazetteer records that a few years earlier the Prefectural Governor had sent a letter of commendation to a young man of the next village to Shinohata who had for seventeen years shown exceptionally exemplary filial piety, establishing his widowed mother in a water-milling business, sharing with her the produce of his fields, attending to her every want night and morn . . . And with the illuminated address went a gift of 2 yen 50 sen.

It is the democratic happy family, not the authoritarian virtues of filial piety, which the town's leaders seek to nurture now. Family Day is the first Sunday in every month, as numerous painted signposts are placed around the township to remind one, with accompanying slogans like 'A happy family is a healthy family', 'The family that talks together stays together'. Every month the township Newsletter designates that month's subject for family discussion:

> Let us keep our promises: parents and children.
> Let us read good books and discuss them together.
> Let parents and children together discuss what TV programmes they wish to watch, and let us decide jointly and amicably.
> Let us divide the housework between us.

Alas, I have never managed to participate in a family discussion. They started in 1966 and by 1970 when I talked to people about them I gathered that most households found it hard to take each other seriously enough. But not all, clearly, as this school essay by an eleven-year-old quoted in the township Newsletter testifies.

> We were supposed to have a Family Discussion yesterday evening, but mother was late home, so I sat down to watch the television. Then she came and we were ready to begin, but by that time I was so immersed in my programme that I couldn't tear myself away until father came over and said: 'That's just what we've got

to talk about today' and switched it off. That put me in a bad temper for a minute, but then I realized it was only my own selfishness and joined in happily. Father was the chairman and my eldest sister was secretary. Father said, 'I declare the Family Discussion to have begun. If you have any opinions please don't hesitate to give them.' 'My! aren't we formal,' somebody said, and we all burst into laughter. 'All right. Fumie, you can start. What programme do you want to watch?' said father, so I said: 'Well, on Sunday there's . . ., and on Monday . . .' Mother said: 'But that's something every night of the week.' Then my elder brother said: 'Two hours at the most each week ought to be enough.' But then it turned out that mother and grandma wanted to watch the dramas and father wanted to see the baseball and the other sports programmes, so I put up my hand. 'Yes, Fumie,' said father, so I said: 'Mummy and grandma don't understand the sports programmes, so I think daddy should watch them when they're not here.' 'But they're always here,' somebody said and we all laughed. Father then wound up the television discussion by saying: 'As far as the television goes, we will carry on as before and if it doesn't go well we will discuss it again on the 20th.' Then elder brother moved us on to the next point by saying that we should all get up earlier. Father suggested 5.30 a.m. . . .

Other homes took the matter seriously too, as a teacher's analysis of his children's reports showed in another Newsletter. On the discussion of keeping promises there had, it appeared, been more requests for turning over a new leaf from parents to children than vice-versa, and this was wrong according to the teacher. Also it appeared that parents were more insistent on their older children helping about the home than younger ones, but it should be the other way round because early habits stick. Some children reported asking their fathers to drink less and come home earlier, and their mothers to nag them less about getting on with their homework.

Family Day was a part of the Bright and Happy Family Promotion Movement, one of the early and major activities of the

1. Yamamoto Tomiyo

2. Norio, the Shinohata MacArthur (see Chapter 16)

3. and 4. Glimpses from the 1955 past. *Left*, old clothes dealer; *right*, Akira's father, the last man who could read the early 19th century hand-writing of the documents in the headman's record box

5. The sunny south side of a traditional house, the upper floor for silkworms. Clothes and bedding get a spring airing

6. The gardener gets his elevenses. The new house which replaced the one above has no verandah corridor. Some rooms are lino-tiled

7. A wayside Shinto altar, annually decorated on the feast day of the god to whom it is dedicated, but otherwise unregarded. Stones to the right commemorate farmers' pilgrimages to distant shrines, 18th and 19th centuries

8. The garden and trees which the gardener spent three days manicuring

9. Preparing a rice field, 1955

10. Shinohata's last-but-one thatched house (the same house
as in the photograph above) just before the family moved out to its new house
behind and sold the old one for its timber, 1977

11. The new mechanical bullocks do all the ploughing and haulage –
in this case of large baskets of mulberry leaves for the co-operative silkworm
raising project operating in the village hall

12. View from the fire tower showing Tsurukichi's new house and the
mulberry and other dry fields in the background. To the right of the pylon
is the grove of trees surrounding Shinohata's ujigami shrine

13. The fire look-out tower with bell and loudspeakers. The rice field is to the left, with the new village hall behind

14. The old village hall, 1955. The fire brigade is making the rhythmic three times three clap to seal the settlement of its quarrel with the headman (see Chapter 16).

15. Tsurukichi's family, 1955. The main living room has an open hearth, bare boards rather than mats. The kitchen, at the back of the 'earth-floored area', is behind. Kettle height is adjusted with fish and chain

16. An altar prepared for the summer 'All Souls' feast for the ancestors. Animal offerings are cucumber, aubergine, toothpicks and noodles. Tablets of ancestors are at the back below scrolls of miscellaneous Buddhist iconography

17. Vehicles were something of a rarity in 1955 – even the wholesale grocer's three-wheeler. This photograph provoked the 1975 comment 'They look like Vietnam refugees'

18. The headmaster and his deputy in the staff room of the local middle school

Council for the Promotion of Youth Development. The latter was an imposing body of some forty-nine members appointed *ex officio* (representatives of a sample of the multiplicity of organizations spawned by the town's 3,000 people) plus a few more co-opted members. Some might consider its aims nebulous:

> To ensure that young men and young women fully and proudly appreciate their responsibilities as the pillars of society in the next generation, and grow up full of hope and determination to build themselves a glittering future by their own efforts.
>
> To ensure that not only parents and those in position of responsibility for the guidance of youth, but any ordinary citizen should show greater interest in the problems of youth, should reflect on and adjust their own attitudes and conduct, improve the environment and generally strive positively for the development of youth.

In practical terms this means organizing outings for schoolchildren in the school holidays (now chiefly for the benefit of the minority of children who have no family car to take them on outings), accompanying the young men's soft-ball teams on away games – and buying them ice-cream – persuading the local booksellers not to stock pornographic comics, persuading the bar owners to dutch-uncle the drunken young off the premises before they did harm to themselves, and generally *being vigilant*. There are some people, as a Shinohata member of the council told me – not many of them, of course – who would object if a neighbour were to reprimand their child for doing something mischievous. 'The idea of our movement is to make clear that this is quite wrong; that the younger generation is *everybody's* responsibility.'

And, indeed, as we shall see in the next chapter, the idea that I am and should be the keeper of my brother and my brother's children is an old and deeply rooted one in Shinohata.

12

Brothers' Keepers

Shinohata people are, indeed, members one unto another in a way that, while normal for Japan, is not very common on a world scale in rural communities of fifty-odd households.

> I suppose I was lucky: I escaped the army. I never really thought I'd pass the medical. I cut my finger in two when I was young: my sister was operating the straw cutter and I was holding the straw. It healed, but it won't bend. Even so, when we got to Test 4 for muscular co-ordination I passed. I'd developed the trick of pulling that finger round with the next one. But when I got into Test 5 the local Youth Club leader was sitting there. He asked me how I'd got on and he was angry as hell at me for not telling them about the finger. If you're called and then sent back home on the first day, *the whole hamlet will be shamed*. So I went back and told the doctor, and this time *he* was angry.

The joys of one are the joys of all: the sorrows of one the sorrows of all, is the traditional way of putting it. And the honour and shame of one is the honour and shame of all too.

Once, over a millennium ago, it is probable that the majority of village settlements in Japan were clan settlements in which everyone had some acknowledged kinship relation with everybody else. That has not been the case for many centuries, but still some of the 'one big family' aspects of the village have persisted. The fact that each village settlement is clustered, surrounded by its own fields and clearly separated from other villages has helped to preserve a certain social cohesion. Cohesion has also been fostered – in fact, probably, from time-to-time re-created – by the actions of government authorities. The Tokugawa system, for example, utilized the principle of collective responsibility in important ways. Each village was held collectively responsible for the payment of taxes. Within each village the smaller neighbourhood groups into which it was divided (so-called five-men groups, though they were more commonly ten-household groups) were held collectively responsible for the good conduct of all their members; for serious crimes (like harbouring Christians or rebellious sentiments) the whole group would be punished. Then, in this century, the hamlet was increasingly used as an informal unit of local government, especially in the mobilization period of the war; together with its sub-divisions, the neighbourhood kumi, it was the channel for all rationing: quotas for rice delivery, savings bond purchase or aluminium saucepan collection were first broken down into kumi quotas and then divided among households; it was the kumi which organized work parties and got people out for ceremonies to the shrines or to give a big send-off to the conscripts.

Apart from these 'top-down' uses of the kumi, they had their own more deep-rooted *raisons d'être* in traditional patterns of mutual help. The people of your own kumi are the people you can especially count on in times of crisis. A death really brings the kumi into its own. The women gather to get the house ready and to prepare all the food (and drink) for the wake and the funeral. The men apportion the tasks of arranging for the coffin, commissioning the priests, informing relatives – and before the coming of the telephones that could mean a day's journey for each one of them. At weddings, too, the women of the kumi would help cook and serve the large quantities of food provided for the relays of guests. And the kumi owned collectively all the bowls and dishes, and the four-legged trays to set them on, which feasts of that size required in such large quantities. They are less necessary now. For one thing, it is much less common to hold weddings at home. Instead, a charabanc or two arrives and all the guests are taken off to a table-and-chair reception at a local drive-in or in more affluent families to a Japanese restaurant or wedding centre in the prefectural town where one can sit on floor mats to a more sumptuous feast in more traditional style. That still leaves wakes and funeral-feasts as occasions for rather lavish entertainment, but more houses can afford a substantial basic set of party dishes of their own – enough for the smaller 'christening' or 'shintoing' feasts after a new baby has been ceremonially presented to the god of the local shrine, or for parties after rice planting, and, supplemented by borrowing from near neighbours or relatives, enough too for a funeral. Two of the Shinohata kumi had failed to keep up replacements of their communally owned set; one at the insistence of an eccentric individualist, another just by default.

There were, indeed, obvious differences in social cohesiveness between different kumi in the village – and the variations seemed difficult to explain except by idiosyncratic personality factors. Some seemed very close, were frequently in and out of each others' houses and always organizing kumi outings – sometimes expensive three-day trips. I heard one woman talk about 'strangers' and took some time to realize that she meant in that context someone from another kumi.

In other kumi, members were more distant and formal with each other. The head of each kumi (the position rotates: no honour attaches to it) collects local taxes on behalf of the township tax office – one of the few ways in which this informal organization is still integrated into the salaried administrative structure proper. There is a commission paid for this amounting to $30 to $40 a year (but paid only when *all* houses in the kumi have completed payment – the collective responsibility principle is still used and accepted). The way kumi use this money is one index of their cohesion. For most, it is added into the fund for the next kumi outing, or used to replace broken crockery or lacquer-ware owned by the kumi. In one or two, it is just distributed back to the kumi members.

The town-bred wife of one of Shinohata's returned sons – Kumiko at Tsurukichi's, who set about rice cultivation with such a will and to such good effect – once said that the most difficult thing to get used to was not the hard work of farming, but having to master all the village tsukiai – all the conventions of social intercourse. Tsukiai sometimes means 'gifts' (even, euphemistically, bribes), so large a part does the exchange of gifts play in these conventions. It takes time and the right kind of personality to be genuinely 'expert at tsukiai'. One needs, first, an unerring sense of the appropriate price and nature of gift, or type of visit, called for on any occasion, given (and this is the important thing that requires a subtle calculating mind) the 'closeness' of the relationship as determined by kinship, physical proximity, common membership of the same kumi or other organization, personal friendships between household members, and the past history of gift transactions between the two households. Secondly, one needs confidence in one's judgement of these things; one needs not to be anxious whether the other person will consider the gift mean or over-lavish, for by and large if you are confident enough you have a good chance of convincing the other person of the appropriateness of your gift. Confident people, too, manage to make the standard polite phrases which should accompany such gifts sound as if they are genuinely meant.

Not everyone, by any means, does have either the judgement or the confidence. In some households the housewife is better at these things; in others the house-head. In yet others both are rather unconfident in such matters and often upset each other with mutual accusations of bad judgement. Tsukiai are a common topic of conversation. The subject of the following conversation was the Shinohata priest, a sad old man who lived to be nearly ninety. He was never exactly revered and respected (for priests hardly rank as spiritual advisers in Japanese villages; they are more like the conjurer you might get for a children's Christmas party – providers of rare and necessary skills to grace certain ritual social occasions). But still, everyone thought it sad that he should have died so isolated and disregarded. Really, everyone agreed, it was all the fault of his second wife who had deservedly predeceased him. She was a loud-mouthed trouble-maker of a woman (on one famous occasion at a particularly acute stage of the Great Timber Quarrel, she had declared, stone sober, of the village's richest landlord and only graduate doctor: 'I piss on Gontarō'). Reputedly, she had been a chambermaid of notoriously loose morals before she ensnared the

priest into marriage. She then set about an asset-stripping operation: selling off the timber on the temple land. She said the land
was hers: the villagers said it belonged to the temple – whatever, in legal form, the registers may have been made to say at
the time of the land reform in order to avoid the possibility of
confiscation. As a consequence of the Great Quarrel, all but a
handful of houses had 'withdrawn their custom' and deposited
their family ancestral records with another temple in a neighbouring hamlet. Only a few remained loyal out of consideration
for the old priest: the rest of the village had little to do with
the couple, and after his wife died he was taken care of by
another priest in a neighbouring village (who later 'inherited'
his remaining 'custom'). However, they had opened up the
Shinohata temple to bring him back for his funeral.

'We didn't even know about the funeral.'

'We did. We heard about it. I said to the old man [her
husband], I said: I wonder if we should give kōden [a
condolence gift; literally, "incense money"]. After all,
despite all the troubles, it wasn't the old priest's fault.
He wasn't responsible for all his wife did. And I asked
Taka over the road and she said, too, she felt we should
all give kōden, but the funeral was over so quickly and
the temple was all shut up again, so we didn't quite
know where to give it. The priest at the Hōsenji [the
successor priest] seems to have taken care of the funeral,
but it's not his family: it didn't seem right to take the
kōden to him; and we heard that the adopted daughter
Masako didn't even come to the funeral: they hadn't
been on speaking terms for years, so we couldn't take
it to her.'

'But still the Hōsenji priest did all the return gifts,
I think. He gave out a kilo of sugar or something to
everybody who came to pay their respects.'

'Yes, so I heard afterwards, but we didn't know at
the time.'

'What my old man said was: I look at it this way; if
we ever had anything from them when we'd had a
funeral . . .'

'Well, we had, you see. It was an uncle of our grandmother – not grandma here – the last one who's dead; that is to say the grandma before the grandma before the grandma here came from the house in Uchigawa – the house that the uncle of the old man at the tobacco shop went to as adopted husband: well, it was that uncle in Uchigawa who brought up the girl who became the priest's first wife who died, you see, so we had that connection: she'd be a kind of grandma-in-law, a sort of cousin.'

A man needs all the friends he can get. Traditionally, the hazards of life were legion. At least a third of Shinohata's families will tell you how – three generations back or five generations back or when so-and-so was in standard two – their house had once been burned down. That was the sort of thing one needed friends for, friends who would rally round, provide gifts to set you on your feet after a fire, provide loans to pay medical bills after a bad illness, provide a delegation of articulate persuasive go-betweens who could argue with a money-lender about to foreclose on a mortgage, turn up at your weddings and funerals *as* your friends and relatives, thereby demonstrating to your neighbours what a large network of connections you had. The more friends you had who could do all these things for you, the better off you were.

But 'friends' is, in fact, quite the wrong word. A man does have personal friends, particularly with the age-mates with whom he was in the same class at school, or his army contemporaries. But these personal ties between individuals account for only a small part of each household's network of 'connections'. Connections are ties between households, for the most part created by marriage alliances stretching back for several generations. Various customs serve to keep these connections fresh. On the first All Ancestors' Day in the year after a woman's death, the head of the household into which she was born must visit the house into which she married and in which she died to present a mourning lantern. The house-head in question may well be her great-nephew, even her great-great-great-nephew's widow, and he or she may have seen little of his ancient relative and care less, but the two *houses* are 'shinrui' – they are relatives and are by that token mutually obligated to each other.

There is, in fact, hardly any formal limit to the range of kin ties which can be allowed to create a mutually obligated relationship. If one side presumes a given tie sufficient to *treat* the other as shinrui, the other is more or less obliged to reciprocate. One pair of houses in Shinohata treated each other as shinrui although the tie hardly seemed a close one. Household A was Household B's aunt-in-law's nephew-in-law (though the connection had been reinforced by a member of Household A acting as partial mediator in the adoption of House-head B).

One of the reasons why large families were thought to be such a grand thing, and the couple who managed to bring ten children to adulthood was so much a matter for envy, was that a large family promised an expanding network of shinrui as the children married or were adopted into other families. There is a snowball effect, too, provided one has got the right sort of 'brokerage personality', that is to say the sort of presence, gravity, trustworthiness, articulacy, 'concern' – a genuine interest in other people's welfare – which makes one a good go-between. The wider one's network of shinrui the more connections through which one can sort out possibly compatible marriages/adoptions, and to 'make' a marriage for another house is a standard way of creating a shinrui tie.

The anxiety which some people feel about making the right gestures or the right judgements about the 'closeness' of a relationship is somewhat mitigated by the formality with which the rituals which reaffirm them are prescribed. Spontaneity is still possible in small things – and prized. A casual gift to neighbours of a bag of peaches when one's back-yard peach tree comes ripe, the 'try some of our strawberries, we've had a good crop this year', are gestures of friendship, or of deference, or sometimes a sign of manipulative intentions – of plans to ask for a favour which the acceptance of the gift will make it difficult to refuse. There *is* a grey area where, in the very nature of everyday contingency, rules cannot be prescribed. If you hear voices raised in apparent altercation in the daytime in Shinohata (before anyone has had time to get drunk, that is) it is as likely as not to be over acceptance or non-acceptance of a gift – as when Tsunashige's wife brought back to her neighbour a half bucket of red beans she had borrowed a month earlier. No, no, we've got plenty: we meant you to have them. But you must take them. No, please don't say that. No, you must let me pay you back, otherwise how can I come borrowing again? Of course you can come any time. I'll just have to leave them . . . And so on and on.

No one at a funeral would similarly argue about accepting the two-thousand-yen notes formally wrapped in the appropriate gift envelope of high-quality paper, overprinted with make-believe black knotted string and the characters 'incense offering', or the five hundred yen in a red-bordered wrapper marked 'congratulations' on the day one of one's children enters primary school, or the three thousand yen when he gets into university. Not even urban middle-class Japan has really approached the age of total spontaneity (or anomie, depending on how you look at it): the mores, the tsukiai, are seen as firmly and objectively established – as much so as they were in polite Victorian society when as a matter of course one consulted books of etiquette to find out what the rules were.

In Shinohata – though some may consult etiquette books when they are setting out to plan a wedding – for most purposes it is the community's collective knowledge that one can draw on. If in doubt, see what a neighbour thinks of it. You may have a funeral and be uncertain which houses in the village you should (given the closeness of the ties between the houses *and* relations with the dead person individually) give a first-order invitation – for both house-head and wife – and which a second-order invitation – for house-head only. The two kumi neighbours who take on the task of going round the village to issue these differentiated invitations verbally will always help you to decide, and three heads are better than one in these matters.

There have, indeed, been times when the rules *have* been formally prescribed – set out in written regulations and 'enacted' by community decision. At least twice – once in the 1850s and for a second time during the war – there have been formal written agreements austerely limiting the numbers of cups of saké to be served per guest at wedding feasts, the number of side dishes, the maximum number of guests, even how expensive a hair-do the bride should have. Both were almost certainly inspired by higher authorities – the first, probably the end-of-the-chain repercussion of the austerity policies decreed after Commodore Perry arrived with his threatening warships. The

204

reckless expenditure on the occasional 'blow-out' by the improvident and indigent poor has always been a matter for concern on the part of the middle classes, but it takes a national crisis for them to try to do anything about it.

Quite a lot of the villagers were probably happy with the regulations too, though. The more prudent ones did not necessarily enjoy providing an obligatory banquet for the rest of the village. Formal regulations freed one from the claims of reciprocal obligation. If Taro was served enough saké to get happily drunk when he went to Jiro's son's wedding, Jiro had a right to be as liberally provided for when he went to the wedding of Taro's son – unless there was the excuse of new – and authoritative – rules to hide behind.

The reciprocity principle is very important indeed. Nothing so burns a little hole of uneasiness in the mind as much as a gift too long left unrequited, or a gesture inadequately reciprocated. That is why, at weddings and funerals, a senior friend of the family sits at a little desk at the entrance to greet guests, receive their offerings, and immediately record the name of the giver and the size of the contribution. The ledger is carefully preserved as a guide to gifts at other people's funerals, until the next senior death in the family provides a more up-to-date reference guide. One house in the next hamlet has an early eighteenth-century ledger which records who gave how many bands of rope, rafter slats, uprights, etc. after the family house had been burned down.

In addition to this long-term reciprocity, there is also the practice of immediate 'return gifts'. Wedding guests take away with them some food, some useful household utensils. When a Shinohata house was rebuilt (with the help, for the erection of the frame, of all the men in the hamlet) the family received large quantities of gifts in cash and in food for the continuous feasting over two days of a workforce seventy-five strong. In return, every guest came away from the final feast with a box of rice cakes, a parcel of tinned food and a shiny new galvanized bucket with a legend in beautiful red characters recording that it commemorated the raising of Nobufumi's roof. Even the primary school when it had completed its new swimming pool made a 'return gift' of a small cotton towel to all who had contributed. Nowadays, in fact, return gifts can run away with a large part of the receipts from a function such as a funeral. Shigeharu had held several minor village offices and was well liked. 350 guests came either to his wake or to his funeral and the total contributions in incense money (which house-heads bring) and 'rice-bale, in lieu of' money (the legend on the money wrapper which housewives bring) came to over twelve hundred dollars (in 1969). When the senior relative finally closed the funeral ledger, $200 had gone to the priests, $250 to payment of doctors' bills, and all the rest to providing four kilogrammes of sugar as a return gift to each guest.

To return to the austerity regulations in the 1850s and the recent war, another reason why many welcomed them was that they not only permitted a scaling down of the 'tariff' for 'basic' gift and entertainment exchange (that is, the normal level, maintenance of which is a prerequisite for respectability and full membership in the village); they also ruled out competitive upping of the ante. Shinohata in the 1970s is a basically egalitarian community (more of that in Chapter 17) where everyone – or almost everyone – enjoys what Tocqueville would call a 'basic equality of condition'. In such communities it is keeping up to the normal tariff which is what counts for most people. But fifty years ago – even twenty years ago – the status hierarchy was much more overt: rich families had *very* different weddings, gave different levels of gifts, from poor families. Family fortunes rose and fell, of course, and the best measure of how far they had fallen or risen – a matter of intense concern to all neighbours – was the level of tsukiai expenditure. Conspicuous display and conspicuous generosity were the ways in which one translated the fruits of hard work, or greed or undeserved luck, into status advancement – or tried to stave off a status decline. Formal austerity rules always in the end foundered on the rapids of status striving.

We were very keen in the youth club on these austerity rules, but I remember when Masao got married. When his bride arrived she had a Takashimada hair-do with all accessories – one of the really expensive ones. I remember Masao looking pretty shame-faced about it. 'I gather the rules have been changed,' he said. That's what he said, anyway.

Nowadays, status striving is more muted. For one thing a not insignificant portion of Shinohata's villagers now have an active work-life outside the village. Their reference groups – the people in whose eyes they discern the reflection of their own worth – are elsewhere. They are not, as was the case sixty years ago for everybody, probably, except the single landlord active in prefectural politics, wholly confined to their village neighbours. And even those who still are wholly in and of the village have absorbed, or at least been affected by, a more sophisticated set of values according to which lavish display in feasting is a somewhat vulgar form of competition.

Public service is a more legitimate field for status striving. Traditionally a man could always make his mark by a handsome donation to the village shrine or temple – perhaps the gift of a gateway or a set of steps that would bear the donor's name. (Even now, when a temple is being re-roofed, huge wooden frames will be built along the avenue leading up to it and hung with wooden slats recording individual donations, carefully ranged from largest to smallest.) Modern Shinohata has managed to turn the appetite for honour to even more useful purpose. Sanetoshi's gift of a new concrete shed for the fire pump was mentioned earlier. Akira had re-built the filtering plant for the Shinohata water supply at even greater expense, a gift recorded for all time on a fine marble stone outside the new concrete building. The God of Water, said the flowing characters, and at the bottom corner, modestly, Akira's name. Hidezō (who did, it must be said, aspire to be a township councillor) gave his patronage to sports: a complete set of uniforms for the Women's Club volley-ball team, and another for the soft-ball team. One of the ways a hamlet headman measures the effectiveness of his exercise of office is by his ability to evoke public-spirited munificence. 'In my year I got a total of twenty-four gifts – $12,000 altogether – ranging from $4,000 for repairs to the meeting house to a couple of hundred for new table-tennis equipment.' Such was Hidezō's proud boast. He was, indeed, persuasive and forceful, but he had been lucky in coming the year after The Factory made its handsome purchase of the village land and put large sums of money into everyone's pocket. Akira's filtering plant – he was not generally given to such demonstrative acts – resulted from similar circumstances.

He had been lucky enough to have some private land as well as his share of village land in The Factory's purchase area, and had been under some considerable pressure to share his good fortune.

The formal organization to which the position of headman belongs is, of course, a key element in providing unity and purpose to the village. It is a formal system of village self-government only in the sense that its functions and procedures are clear and formally agreed, and the obligations it imposes are accepted and fulfilled, but all this is owed to consensus on the part of the villagers, not to the force of government statute. The local government law which regulates the affairs of the township government has not been concerned with these local neighbourhood affairs since the war. In fact very deliberately not concerned: the pre-war system was seen by the American occupiers as a device for totalitarian mobilization: a means of turning the nation into a vast conformist beehive by the leverage of face-to-face pressures. (It was for that reason that the local government electoral system after the war avoided tiny-ward constituencies: a township council is elected by single non-transferable vote from a single central list of candidates.) But the patterns established in the 1930s – only modifications, in any case, of ancient customary patterns – have persisted. In an informal way the township office still uses the village organization for communications purposes, and it plays an important role in electioneering, but the village organization's main function – as it has always been since villages had collective responsibility for law and order and for tax payment in the Tokugawa period – is to regulate the village's internal affairs.

And these affairs can keep a headman busy. Hidezō, for instance, kept a diary for his year and claims that he was able to spend only 130 days on his farm. But he was an exceptionally active headman who was determined to leave his mark and was not content simply to look after the routine affairs of the hamlet. He devoted a good deal of time to trips to the township office to smell out new forms of subsidy the village might benefit from. He spent long hours visiting individual fellow villagers persuading them to agree to road-widening schemes or to make donations. As for the routine activities, perhaps the best way of giving an idea of what they are is to detail the annual budget for 1955, 1970 and 1975.

	1955 (Expenditure)	1970 (Budget)	1975 (Budget)
Meetings (refreshments)			
General meeting	6,560	13,000	40,000
Executive council	100	12,000	15,000
Shrines			
Yakushi festival	550	1,500	6,000
Illuminations		2,000	15,000
Repairs to Hachiman Shrine	2,750		
Repairs to Dōsojin Shrine	360		
Purchase of tablets of Akiba (fire-prevention) Shrine	560		
Remuneration			
Headman	⎫	3,000	3,000
Vice-headman	1,500 ⎬	1,500	1,500
5 kumi leaders	⎭	7,500	7,500
Travel (headman and councillors)	20	2,000	5,000
Stationery	586	3,000	4,000
Repairs to village hall	3,500	3,000	5,000
Heating & lighting village hall			
Charcoal	620		
Electricity (including street lights, 1975)	3,624	50,000	120,000
Subsidies			
Fire brigade	10,000	5,000	5,000
Children's Club	1,000	4,000	4,500
Hygiene Association	1,500		
Youth Club	9,800		
Youth Guidance Society		4,000	
Sports		10,000	70,000
Old Folks' Club		5,000	6,000
Women's Club		5,000	7,000
Ground rents, taxes	10	3,000	5,000
Communal work			
Parties after work	11,318		
Hire labour: 3 man-days	300		
Party after electing PTA officers	123		
Congratulatory gifts to Furuta village on completion of their watch-tower	1,000		
National Community Chest contribution on behalf of Shinohata	1,050		
Saving for new watch-tower	5,000		
Sanitary		3,000	3,500
DDT spraying		14,500	25,000
Maintenance of broadcasting facility		5,000	5,000
Expenses for report to education commission			5,000
Insurance on silkworm hatchery			2,500
Entertainment			10,000
Contingency			10,000
Total	67,639	157,000	380,500
Consumer Price Index	100	196	335
Total in 1955 prices	67,639	80,000	113,500

Over the twenty years, expenditure in real terms has not quite doubled – a rather lower rate of increase than the improvement in household living standards. One would not want to make too much of that, but it does reflect to some degree an increasing 'privatization' of Shinohata life, most certainly in the recreation and entertainment sphere. The Shrine Festivals, the parties after a day's work filling in the ruts and potholes in the hamlet roads, and other opportunities for the men of the hamlet to get lightly drunk together on a communally provided 'cup of strong tea' used to be highly prized in 1955, in the days before the car and the television set. Now only the annual meetings remain such an occasion. Communal work still has to be organized (though much less frequently because the township has metalled most of the hamlet's internal roads), but now at the end of the day everyone goes back home to his solitary saké bottle in front of his own TV set.

Many of the older men much regret the change. The reformist mayor of the Kakizaka township, reflecting on the reasons why, after fifteen years of energetic and progressive rule, he decided that the support which had carried him unopposed through three elections probably would not carry him to a fourth term, spoke of his mistake in ending the booze-ups which had traditionally followed council meetings. After the cars came, it did not seem at all proper for the council to sit there solemnly discussing means of reducing traffic accidents and then set about turning themselves into twenty dangerous drunken drivers. Besides, could one justify that sort of expenditure of public money in the mid-1960s? So he compromised with a single New Year feast with a bottle of saké each – all wrapped up in cellophane to take home and enjoy with their wives. 'But what fun is there drinking with their wives? They can do that any day of the week. They felt that something had gone out of their lives. It really wasn't a very clever move on my part.'

If expenditure on conviviality has diminished, one thing on which expenditure has increased is a range of modern conveniences like street lighting or the hamlet broadcasting system. Once, for his meagre honorarium, the headman had to do all his message carrying on foot. Any announcement that everybody had to know had to be told personally to the five kumi leaders who passed the message on to all their members. Now every house has a loudspeaker and there are others strategically placed in the village and out in the fields. There are microphones in the village hall and (complete with xylophone to summon attention with a simple tune) in the headman's home. The Shinohata day is punctuated by messages and announcements and sometimes admonitions.

A message from the Women's Club. Will all the women who ordered dancing fans and records please bring the money with them tonight.

We're just about to clear the sand out of the topside channel, so we'll be turning the water to the south channel for the rest of the morning.

Suzuki Kitahachi-san. You've got a visitor. Come back home.

A message from the Education Committee. At two-thirty this afternoon on Channel 20 there will be a programme about Minamihara Shinjin, the local poet. The children should watch it: it will be a good opportunity to give them a sense of local patriotism.

The bear appeared again last night and stripped Harunori's peach tree. We're going to keep watch tonight so would everyone keep alert for suspicious noises.

Shinkichi! This is the soft-ball team. You're late. We're going off. Catch us up at the sports ground.

A message from the Health Committee. The doctors will be here at the village hall at 2.30. Everybody is urged to come for a check-up. They will be doing blood pressure and a urine test, so everybody should come.

Somebody has been dumping rubbish behind Nobushige's. I'm sure it's not anybody from Shinohata, but just in case it is, please don't do it.

Today is Respect the Aged Day, and the Old People's Club is going to weed and tidy up the Memorial Stone yard. Will everybody turn up there at 9.30 and the committee members bring a hoe.

Tomorrow is the agreed day for spring-cleaning, so will everybody please do their spring-cleaning. Don't forget to take out your tatami mats and beat them, and the Health Committee reminds you to take particular care with the kitchen, and the fire brigade chief reminds you to take particular care to clear up piles of combustible material that might be a fire hazard.

Katatoshi. Your wife says don't cut any more mulberry. She's got enough.

Being a member of the village is very much like being a member of an organization like a school or a factory. One is 'organized'. The social contract contains quite a lot of fine print. Shinohata did not go so far as some hamlets once did in fixing village holidays when no one was allowed to work, but it did, for instance, continue the tradition of a community sanctioned spring-clean. Part of the headman's job was to go the rounds, visiting each house for an inspection (usually a rather diffidently polite inspection, but in Hidezō's case a *very* polite but officious one), and then posting a little paper sticker on the gate-post (along with the metal tags which showed proof of ownership of a TV licence and dog licence) so that all the world could see that duty had been done.

There was still communal work to be done, even in 1975, too. All the preparatory road-widening work before the Kakizaka town council men came in to asphalt, for example, was done by collective effort and sometimes involved dismantling and re-assembling some very considerable stone walls. The principle was: one able-bodied adult worker per household – or a fine which, at $13 in 1975, was on the high side for a day's wages.

Few chose to pay. Apart from being expensive, one's absence might be interpreted as aloof lack of concern, and few even of the commuter heads of families who spend little time in the village are yet *so* aloof and unconcerned with village affairs that they would not mind giving that impression. Likewise most people turn up to the annual New Year's meeting when the new headman is elected and the budget approved, and to the special meetings called from time to time to discuss particular proposals for widening roads or re-building a shrine. Average attendance in the 1970s was around forty-five house-heads or their representatives out of fifty-five households, with the absentees sending a voting proxy form instead – still a rather higher rate of absenteeism than in the 1950s, and one that distressed some of the older men for whom a public-spirited concern for the village was the touchstone of virtue.

We've increased the budget for the general meeting so that we can offer something of a party afterwards – saké and some beer for the men and port-wine for the women: you can't put the women off with tea these days. We can have a fair party with the budget we've got now, especially if there are donations. When Gontarō was appointed to the Public Safety Commission, for instance, most people took him a bottle or two of saké for congratulations and he gave half of them to the meeting. But still there are some people who don't turn up. They don't seem to realize that we all depend on each other. I suppose it's inevitable with so many people working outside and just using the village as a dormitory. In the end, I suppose, it will come to having a salaried headman; nobody will be interested enough to do the job voluntarily. And I suppose we'll have a paid fire brigade centralized in Kakizaka instead of our own volunteer brigade. It used to be that everybody left the youth group at the age of twenty-five and joined the fire brigade for ten years, but now there are so few men here between twenty-five and thirty-five, and so few of those who live here are ever actually in the village, that you have to stay on into your fifties just to make up the numbers. And it's increasingly hard to get people to turn up for practice.

Those are the prospects. But in 1975 they were still some years ahead. The fire brigade was still functioning, and every night one of its members went up to the look-out fire-spotting tower in the centre of the village (a steel lattice mini-Eiffel tower replaced the wooden structure in the 1960s) to sound the single 9 o'clock stroke on their resonant fire-bell. 'Take care of fire' is the intended message – a somewhat less explicit substitute for the clear fresh voices of the youth group party which in 1955 used to tour the village every night shouting exactly that. It is not only self-preservation that is at stake: a careless man can burn down his neighbour's house as well as his own. The bell remains a nightly reminder of community responsibility, of the virtue of neighbourliness as well as of prudence.

13

Pleasures Shared and Pleasures Solitary

There is a variety of rites and celebrations which help to foster the sense that living in Shinohata is not just a matter of residential location, but of membership in a community. Funerals are one such occasion; a house-building is another. Once, the exchange of labour for house-building was highly functional; the rest of the village came in to help because there was no other way of getting things done: one mobilized the labour for one's rebuilding by the promise of one's own labour – or more likely one's son's or grandson's – when it was needed. Now it is more a sociable honouring of tradition. The labour contributions are less, the cost of suitably requiting them in feasting and return gifts is greater.

Nobufumi was one of the last in his kumi to respond to the new affluence by extensive rebuilding. He saved his money assiduously, determined to do the thing properly and build a whole new house. I recall being in the village when his father died; a shy, gentle, rather low-energy part-time stonemason who, one morning, carefully placed his hammer and chisel on a block he was chipping, laid down beside it, covered his face with the blue-print and quietly breathed his last. Nobufumi was working away at the time, but he came back to nurse his widowed mother through a long and extremely expensive final illness which left the family with considerable debts. For more than a decade, by consistent hard work and thrift Nobufumi had repaid the debts and built up savings. By 1975 he was ready to demonstrate to all the village how far he had 'raised the family'. A house of some eighty square metre floor space was planned, a master-carpenter was commissioned to do it for $360 a square metre, the family moved into a barn and the old house was taken to pieces. For weeks the carpenter and his helpers worked at the basic structure, putting in the concrete footings, cutting and shaping and planing the wood until they could promise that all would be ready the weekend after next.

On the Saturday, for the actual raising of the roof-beam, there was a relatively small group of twenty to twenty-five helpers – relatives inside and outside the village, members of the kumi and other 'close' families were invited to take part. With a few adjustments here and there everything fitted. From the great pile of timber mysteriously marked with black hiero-glyphs (felt-pens, though, not the old Indian ink and brush) the master-carpenter's magic had conjured up a plausible and solid house-frame.

On Sunday every male house-head in the village except one or two who had unavoidable business elsewhere came for the nailing of the roof shingles, and the neighbourhood echoed to the sound of their hammers. By early afternoon the work was done. Word went round that the ceremony was about to begin and the women and children flocked to the scene. The workmen had built on the roof a kind of makeshift altar decorated with symbols vaguely redolent of shrines and gods and general cele-bratiousness. There were two waving young bamboos, two large saké barrels wrapped in straw, rice and vegetables, more saké in bottles, a bow with its arrow pointed north-east to the 'devil corner' to drive off wicked spirits, a tall piece of two-by-two marked off as a carpenter's measuring stick and inscribed with the house-owner's name and the date – the souvenir which the master-craftsman takes home to add to his collection. At the top of this pole two fans were spread to form a circle (fans 'spread at the end' when opened, just as prosperous families multiply through the generations) and below them was attached a big white streamer with, in a knot at the end, a piece of hemp, a bag of rice and some vegetables. 'And what do they sym-bolize?' Everyone seemed to think that was a daft question – tradition is tradition – until Takenobu came along and said authoritatively that they stood for strength and endurance and luck.

The master-carpenter is also master-of-ceremonies. All the workmen, relatives and near-neighbours go up to the low-pitched roof. Prayers are said, saké drunk, cups exchanged, hands clapped (the rhythmic clap used to mark the end of a shrine ceremony or clinch a deal with a horse-broker), salt thrown, saké poured from either end of the roof beam and – the climax – on the head of the proud owner standing in the middle of the floor below. Then comes the scramble. The saké barrels are full of 'mochi' – rice-cakes made out of glutinous rice which are thrown among the crowd. Children vie with each other to see who can get the most and grandmothers abandon their dignity to join in the fun. Once greed, or hunger, or at least appetite would have played a part in the scramble. But few of Nobufumi's mochi are likely to have been eaten. Lumps of glutinous rice-flour have a hard time competing with Choco-Baby and Banana-Scat.

And so, after the men had been home and changed out of their work clothes, there came the final party; the men eating inside the new frame, the women in the family's temporary quarters.

It was a good party. More friendly tonight. People didn't drink quite so much. I think they were a bit remorseful about last night when the quarrelsome ones drank far too much and Kenshichi and Kanashige were shouting at each other for hours with Kenshichi calling Kanashige a black-hearted bastard until he couldn't take it any longer and rushed off home in his bare feet without putting his clogs on.

But tonight it was more friendly. A lot of songs. You could tell Kanashige wanted to sing like mad, but he was one of the three hosts – representing the kumi – so he had to let all the others sing. Funniest of all was the brother-in-law from Niihara village. He did a funny dance, waving his hands all over the place. Then at the end after Nobufumi had said his thank you, the brother-in-law got up and said: 'Well, hum, I suppose I should say a few words as representative of the relatives . . .' and launched into the longest, stumbling, rambling speech you'd ever heard. He'd say something and then clear his throat with a funny little cough, forget where he'd got to and start all over again. And it went on and on. Everybody looked down at the floor in embarrassment and then just as they thought he was finishing they'd look up expectantly – and then he'd give another of his coughs – if it had been an ordinary sort of cough that would have been all right, but it was a funny little high-pitched squeaky cough – and then he'd start up again, and people would look down again, and you could see them shifting their heads from side to side trying to suppress their laughter, until first one and then the other would start spluttering and trying to turn their giggles into a cough. My, it was funny, but the brother-in-law had had so much to drink he just didn't notice. Shigeyasu got as tight as a coot and came inside to where the women were to tell his wife Miyoko that she should come and dance. She had, as a matter of fact, brought her fan and her record-player but she said she wouldn't dance unless Shizuko did too, and Shizuko said she wouldn't because if she did her old man would give her what-for tomorrow, so Shigeyasu got angry and said if Miyoko wouldn't dance then he wasn't going to let her go to any more dance lessons and stormed back to the main party. Afterwards he came back and said he'd danced in her place and he didn't mean what he said and she should go on taking her lessons . . .

Before the recent rash of new houses, a roof-raising ceremony used to be a pretty rare occurrence – most commonly the result of a fire. But the annual calendar contained a good many more occasions for sociable celebration – celebration which combined feasting and drinking with some sense of contact with the numinous, some gesture of attunement with nature and the gods, some attempt to keep the world in balance and the forces of fate on one's side. Shinohata is well endowed with shrines: there are three major ones supported by the hamlet as a whole, through its various associations (see the official subsidy to the Shrine Association in the hamlet budget) either alone or together with neighbouring hamlets, and a couple of smaller ones sustained by neighbourhood groups of devotees. The least regarded shrine is the official ujigami – the shrine which was subsidized through the official State Shinto system before the war as the village's protector deity, the shrine where the frock-coated local gentry – the postmaster, the headmaster and the mayor and councillors – went for the stiffly formal celebration of the Spring Equinoctial Festival of the Imperial Ancestors and other official occasions. It was also the shrine where conscripts went to be officially blessed and impressed with a sense of the solemnity of their mission. All of these official functions were lost when State Shinto was dismantled after the war, and only a vague sense of duty prompts the older villagers on the Shrine Committee to keep it in a minimal state of repair, to hire a Shinto priest to come and perform a short ceremony on the god's annual festival day, and to round off the day by inviting a few friends to empty a few bottles of saké. For the rest of the year the weeds grow high in the forecourt and hardly anyone comes even to trim them down.

The ujigami and his shrine, associated with all the formal stuffiness of the official cult, never did have anything like as much of a hold on Shinohata's affections as one of the other 'ungraded' shrines, the Hachiman-san, and any visitor to Hachiman-san can see why. He (or his shrine: one can never tell from the way people use the word 'kami' whether it means the 'god', as all the dictionaries say, or the shrine he is supposed to inhabit) sits on the top of a wooded spur above Shinohata. One approaches through an avenue of magnificent cryptomerias which gets steeper and steeper until it ends in a vertiginous staircase, two hundred and twenty steps of rough-hewn stone – so steep and with such high rises to many of the steps that one needs the hand-rail set in the centre to haul oneself up. But it is worth it. At the top is a sandy clearing, and set back in a surround of fine gnarled red-barked pine, with the folds of the mountains rising behind them, the shrine with its unpainted carved wood, its simple design and, in 1975, a new shingle roof with copper trimmings, perfectly blends into its setting. Its courtyard is uncluttered; only a few guardian deities (of Buddhist – or more remotely Hindu – origin!) and the tall six-inch shell which Kentarō brought back from manoeuvres in 1921 and had cemented into an inscribed block: his thank-offering for the protection that afforded him safe return from his military service. Was Kentarō mindful, one wonders, of the phallic affinity? The 'god-body' in the inner inner shrine is in fact a single stone pillar about two feet high, with a neat little foreskin bib tied around the top at an appropriate angle. So little is Hachiman-san an object of worship or prayer, or even of curiosity, that most Shinohata villagers have no idea what the inner sanctum contains, and those who do are vague about its origins. One old lady had a long garbled story which clearly goes back to the days before Shinto and Buddhism were disentangled for 'national purity' reasons in the 1870s – the days when the Shinohata Buddhist priest had charge of the Hachiman shrine. It goes as follows. The hundred volumes of the great (Buddhist) Diamond Sutra were being brought up the Kiso road from a great Kyoto temple. But the load slipped over to the left-hand side of the pack-horse's back, so they put a stone on the right-hand side to balance it. But then, when they got near Shinohata, the load miraculously shifted back again so the stone was taken off and thrown away. But then there was a mysterious outbreak of illness. It was a long time before they realized that it must be emanating from the stone, still radiating the mana it derived from its awesome function. The stone was enshrined and worshipped and its once baneful became a beneficent influence.

Hachiman-san has few visitors; one of Shinohata's town migrants, perhaps, bringing his children for a walk on a Sunday visit to grandparents; a couple of widows with time on their hands calling in to pay respects on their way to gather wild ferntips up in the hills for pickling; Wataru the woodman on his way to work at clearing the underbrush on a forest plantation behind the shrine; somebody, once, who was close enough to being a worshipper to leave three oranges by way of an offering. But still enough people in Shinohata have affectionate memories of past festivals for the fire brigade and the Children's Club to be prepared to put in a few days work to keep the steps and courtyard in trim, and for individuals to donate shrubs and bushes and cash to supplement the small income from the shrine's own woodland and so keep up with essential repairs.

The festivals, every April and September, were once very splendid affairs. The pedlars and fortune-tellers and itinerant merchants and the showmen with their freaks and fantasies would come from miles around to set up their stalls and booths. Their carbide lamps would burn on into the night. Lucky children would get pocket-money, and candyfloss was cheap enough to be within the reach of almost everyone. Every house would cook special foods and relatives would flock in from other villages. There would be sumō wrestling 'offered up' to the gods, at the special mini-amphitheatre at the bottom of the steps, and up top in the outer shrine, the men – or at least the important men – would drink to their hearts' content and nod sagely at the news of fights that had broken out among ruffian youths from 'foreign' villages and exchange the stories they had heard about what went on behind the bushes on the more Dionysian festival nights their grandfathers once enjoyed – before the benevolence of an Imperial Government and its schoolmasters brought prudence and decorum to the villagers. They too would gamble a bit for coppers, but their sessions less often ended in the fierce quarrels that marked the gambling sessions of their grandfathers.

Today's festivals are even more decorous affairs, but everybody tries to make the September festival, at least, something of a show. The Children's Club do the weeding on the preceding Sunday, most of those who are farming that week and a few of those who work elsewhere take the day off, and the men who like that sort of thing go up to the shrine to drink saké – straight out of the bottle, the symbolic assertion that the festival day releases one from normal restraints – and a sign also of the absence of women even to perform their normal serving-maid functions. The central attraction is still the sumō wrestling and all its attendant flummery: the umpire dressed in tenth-century costume, the ritual thigh-slapping parades of wrestlers, the crouching and staring and constant false starts before each ten-second bout, and the intermittent throwing of purifying salt. The fire brigade has traditionally organized the sumō. One year in the 1960s, discouraged by the poor attendance, they gave up. In the year that followed there was a good deal of illness in the village. That the kami had been displeased at being thwarted of the spectacle he annually looked forward to was an obvious inference. So they resumed the following year, though reluctantly and with constant grumbling at the small amount the Hamlet Association offered as subsidy for the sumō. So much so that in 1975 Shigeyasu stepped forward and offered to organize it himself and bear any extra cost from his own pocket. His brief moment of glory as impresario (and umpire) might indeed bring him closer to his ambition to become hamlet headman, and in any case Shigeyasu has sumō in his blood. His father was a noted local wrestler and the heavily embroidered and braided velveteen apron, inscribed with his father's sumō name, sits in the Buddhist memorial altar in Shigeyasu's living room. Country sumō used to be enormous fun, he explained, and there were some good local wrestlers, but nobody much appreciated the part-time amateur's efforts these days when they could see the enormous 400-pound professionals on television. Tokyo sumō week is rather like Wimbledon week in Britain in terms of television coverage and the tendency to monopolize conversation.

Shrines, then, play a very much reduced role in the festal, recreational life of Shinohata villagers these days. So do they in their outings. Once the pilgrimage was probably the dominant form of popular travel – certainly the dominant form of recreational travel – in Japan. A number of carved stones outside Shinohata houses commemorate an ancestor's pilgrimage. A group of two or three friends would save up for years, or sell off a bit of forest land, and set out one winter to 'do' the eighty-eight shrines of Shikoku, 200 miles away, or even the thirty-three shrines of West Japan at an even greater distance. It could be the accomplishment of a lifetime; a memorial stone would be commissioned and neighbours regaled with reminiscences for months if not years afterwards. There was even a regular pilgrimage 'club'. Mount Akiba – a lively pilgrimage centre (well equipped with hotels, brothels, souvenir shops, and other recreational facilities) about three days' walk from Shinohata – possessed at its peak a magnificent shrine whose talismans were particularly good for warding off fire. Unfortunately the talismans expired in twelve months. (Or, to put it another way, the god did not continue to exercise his benevolent influence if people could not bother paying him the elementary respect of an annual visit.) So every year two emissaries of the village were commissioned to go to Akiba to get a properly blessed talisman for every house in the village. Money was collected from every house through the year – enough to provide for the (male) emissaries' expenses. (Women were not allowed on the mountain.) The money left over paid for a modest annual village feast to welcome the emissaries' return, to hear their stories, share out the talismans and draw lots to decide who was to go the following year.

It was, I was told, with little trauma or even discussion that they decided at the 1967 party to give up. Hardly anyone still alive then remembered the days when the journey was a perilous one on foot, though for many of the older generation their train journey to Akiba remained a highlight of their middle years – since overshadowed, however, in the last affluent decade, by numerous coach trips to beauty-spots all over Japan. For the young, they realized, Akiba was a bore. They bought fire-extinguishers for their houses and did not care whether they had an Akiba talisman in their god-shelves or not – or even whether they *had* a god-shelf or not in some cases. And for those who did still care – Kanetake's wife, for instance, who had never forgotten that her house burned down in 1913 just two months before her father was due to make the pilgrimage – the Akiba god, through his priest, promised to run a reliable mail-order service for talismans.

The luxury coach – air-conditioned, stereophonic, and always equipped with a fragile, delicate, high-school-graduate conductress of impeccable diction and exquisite politeness – transformed ideas of recreation in the early sixties. The Co-op, the fire brigade, the Women's Group, the Silkworm Co-op, the neighbourhood group using up the tax prompt-payment premium, almost every organization in the hamlet provided an opportunity for a trip.

    – Have you been on any trips lately, auntie?
    – Yes, I went on the Silkworm Co-op outing.
    – Where did you go?
    – Hawaii.
    – Hawaii! My, that's quite a trip!
    – Ha ha! You see. He believes it! No. We went to the Hawaiian Herusu Sentaa in Fukushima.
    – Health Centre? What's that? A kind of sanatorium?
    – No, it's a lovely place. You can't imagine. There are these big baths all set in great greenhouses and full

of palm trees and pineapples, and the whole thing looking entirely natural. And then there are pin-tables and
bowling alleys and restaurants, and a theatre where they
do Hawaiian dancing. My, we were tired! Thirteen
hours on the bus! But it was worth it. That's how we
went to Hawaii. And then last year we went to Expo 70
in Osaka. Everybody was organizing a trip to Expo.
There were about six to choose from and some people
went three times. I went on the one to Kyoto for the
temples, then Expo, then Awaji-shima in the Inland
Sea. I always remember Awaji-shima from the Hundred Poems game. Do you know the Hundred Poems
game we play at the New Year, when you lay out all the
cards with the second half of the poems and somebody
reads one of the first halves and you have to grab for
the card with the matching second stanza? I don't suppose I could recite more than ten of the poems now,
but I always used to like the one that was about Awaji-
shima, and I'd always wondered what sort of place it
was.

The poetry game and the Japanese version of badminton
traditionally played at New Year, skating on a frozen flooded rice
field in winter with skates of sharpened bamboo, illicit bathing
in the irrigation pond in summer (dangerous, parents said,
because you could get caught in the weeds, panic and drown) –
such is the stuff of reminiscences of childhood, of what constituted fun. Then there were the rarer treats: the circus which ran
up its great bamboo and mat building in the next village and
brought bareback riders and conjurers and an amazing boy who
could lean over backwards until his head appeared between his
legs and then walk around on his hands – and they would have
the show at 10 in the morning so that people could come from
four or five hours' walk away and still get back home before
dark. Then, the counterpart of the mid-winter New Year's
holiday, one of the two yearly Settlement Days when one paid
off debts and gave servants their wages, there was the mid-
summer Bon holiday, the All Souls festival at the August full
moon when for two or three nights running there would be
dancing; the outside circle this way, the inner one that, round

and round the frantic drummers, Kanejirō's buxom widow blooming in the atmosphere of controlled sexual excitement and everyone conscious of the electric charges between Sanetoshi's eldest and Kentarō's girl every time the circles brought them together – and the young men jumping into the drummers' circle to take their show-off turn at singing, each vying to outdo the last in voice-power and intricate tremolos.

> Firm, firm your promise. At the Ujijami shrine. Until
> the stone gateway, Rots away to nothing.
> Firm they seem, but have a care. Melt they will and run
> away. Snowmen and Promises.

There is a certain nostalgia for these older pleasures even in these days of television on eight channels and enough money in people's pockets for shopping expeditions to the prefectural town to be a major form of entertainment – a nostalgia particularly, perhaps, for the community nature of many of the old pleasures. Already, the private car and the family expedition are gradually eclipsing even the modern village outing. The luxury coach had passed its heyday by the early seventies. To be sure, there are new forms of community activity: there is a men's soft-ball team and a women's soft-ball team playing an inter-hamlet league in Kakizaka's town district. All ages can play – they have to, to make up numbers in communities with so few young people, and the ingenious device of setting a minimum number for the sum of a whole team's ages ensures a certain fairness.

The women's dancing class that Shigeyasu threatened not to let his wife go to tries to keep alive the tradition of the midsummer 'All Souls' Day' Bon dances. But with its rather self-conscious, folksong-society-preservationist tone, a Bon dance in the 1970s hardly has quite the savour of earlier occasions. The dances may be more intricate – taught as they are by the (subsidized) teacher supplied by the Social (= Adult) Education Officer in Kakizaka township – and the loudspeaker music may be rather more sophisticated than the rude country drummers, but with fewer young men and women in the village – and most of them town dwellers back home for the holiday, half-strangers to each other already – there is a staid middle-aged air to the

affair. And the records which the Social Education Office supplies at reduced rate – ballads about sixteenth-century warrior
heroes of the district – are a poor substitute for the often bawdy
couplets the young men used to sing. The snows of yesteryear
replaced by cotton-wool, I would have thought, though several
of Shinohata's middle-aged men as well as women have learned
the words of the new ballads with apparent enjoyment and
pride.

Although the Social Education Officer is entitled to take all
'cultural activities' as his province, he is suitably modest in his
pretensions and there are a good many hobbies and pastimes of
considerable skill and refinement which continue without benefit of his promotional activities. There were a number of keen
players of shōgi – Japanese chess – for instance, who met in
each other's houses. There was a circle of poets organized by an
eighty-year-old ex-mayor in Kakizaka township to which one
or two people in Shinohata belonged. They wrote 'haiku', the
seventeen-syllable poems, rather than the thirty-one syllable
'waka'. (Just as one could map Japan, according to the dominant intellectual game of the rural gentry into 'shōgi' areas and
'go' areas, so one could chart the 'haiku' areas and the 'waka'
areas.) The Kakizaka area had always been a haiku area. One of
the chief disciples of Bashō, the father of haiku, had been born
in the district, and the Hachiman shrine still preserved on nicely
carved boards hung up in the outer sanctum the record of a
grand haiku party held there in the 1850s – some fifty poems
written on the subject of mist. In the grounds of Shinohata's
decaying temple was another small meeting hall in an even
worse state of disrepair. (It had once housed the shrine of a
minor Shinto god, protector of the temple.) The weeds were
growing through the floor but on the wall there still stood the
record of another haiku party held in March 1916. Then the subject had been horses. A fading ink sketch of a galloping horse
adorned the middle of the board, and on either side were some
fifty haiku about horses, the feel of a sweaty flank, the tinge of
anxiety as one's child goes off to the woods alone with a horse
for the first time, presumably to collect firewood, an autumn
valley viewed from horseback riding along a ridge, the prayer
to the Kannon-Buddha-in-Horse-head-Guise when one's horse
is poorly. Haiku writing is a sociable affair, not a matter for

solitary inspiration or tranquil recollection. The Master of Ceremonies announces the subject. One thinks, one drinks a little, perhaps, one writes, perhaps asking for advice as to whether one has the reference to the season in a permissible form or whether such and such should be deemed an appropriately haikuable word, one reads one's poem with appropriate diffidence and the group's acknowledged leader – or perhaps a guest judge – chooses the one or two poems he deems to come closest to the 'essential spirit' of haiku for special praise. In 1850 and 1916 these prize poems would be written slightly set apart on the commemorative board. In 1975 they would be published in the Kakizaka Town Newsletter.

Others have more solitary hobbies. One or two Shinohata men are keen bonsai experts, cultivators of miniature potted trees. Most houses, in fact, have a few such trees (and are not always sure of what species) but the experts spend a good deal of their leisure time carefully tending a large array. Masatoshi (a married-in son-in-law who worked in an agricultural experimental station) had fifteen kinds of pine trees and almost as many maples. He could chat endlessly about the problems of raising that one from seed, about where he had found this one in the mountains, about the various styles to which their branches had been trained – this one the 'long dragon' style, that one the 'littérateur' style – and about the rather fancy poetic names he had given to his most developed trees, and why.

A few Shinohata people breed carp – dazzling creatures, some of them, in gold and silver and mottled orange and black – but none does it in quite the style of the bean-curd merchant who supplies the village shop. He has a fine collection in a special deep pool near his house in the prefectural town, some of great age whose price can only be mentioned in whispers. He has another twenty or so boarded out on the other side of the prefecture where the water is one or two degrees warmer in winter and contains some special trace element apparently good for carps. His sideboard displays a fine collection of trophies marking his success in local carp shows and a considerable collection of carpological literature. It is apparent that carps are a serious business. One of the books was by the president of a famous women's college who has discovered a way of calculating the age of carp and has identified one of his own as 217 years old. There is an aura of solemn spirituality about many recreational pursuits in Japan and nothing seems to thicken that aura so much as the presence of money. The president seems in his book a little over-conscious of the fact that Japan's most famous carp-lover was the Prime Minister, who had recently been deposed for being so corrupt that not even he could get away with it. He had added a little English postscript to his book describing the enthusiastic public response to a broadcast he had made about carps.

> Whereas it is said that this is the most hard-boiled age of human history, I was overjoyed to find that there are many persons of refined sentiment and tastes in this country, and was deeply impressed with the feeling that Japan will never go to ruin . . . In [our material] age, I find nothing more precious than the people who put a tasteful, sympathetic and nature-loving life before the longing for great wealth . . .
>
> The love we feel for a carp is nothing different from the love we feel for our neighbours. It is unwise to judge a carp's value by the price people put on it. We often hear a person say that his carp has $350's worth, and I cannot help feeling that such a person is boasting of his own money power. He might as well enjoy the sight of a $350 roll of banknotes floating on the water.
>
> Let me ask you to love your carp with pure and innocent heart. It is at such a moment and at no other that a man of abominable spirit, like me, is a step nearer to God. It may be called a religious atmosphere we are enveloped in without knowing it.

14

In the Service of Community, Nation – and Self

Among most men in most of human history it has been taken as axiomatic that the family, the community, the hive are not just abstractions but living realities of far greater importance than the individuals who compose them – separately or in sum. The idea that the individual should be the starting point, and that social arrangements are the result of a social contract for mutual convenience, justified and worth upholding only as long as they serve that individual convenience, is a relatively new one even in Europe. It has even more tenuous roots in Japan. Japan had its enthusiastic translators and admirers of Rousseau in the 1870s, but the period when they had control over the ideological air space was short-lived. The newly systematized national communitarianism of modern Imperial Japan, particularly in the 1930s, had no place for that kind of individualism.

Now those particular pressures are gone, and there are some signs of change. For example, the membership basis of Shinohata's Women's Association has changed. Once it admitted one member and only one member for each household – normally the house-head's wife or widow – and everybody who was eligible belonged. In the late 1960s membership was put on an individual basis. Two or more women from the same house could join and nobody bothers very much any longer that from one or two households no one is even a nominal member. Once,

in other words, the Women's Association was primarily about
duty – about participating in the web of mutual services in the
village which were based on the principle of reciprocity between
households – household levies of so many days' labour, entertainment rosters in which each household had its turn, and so
on. There was also the larger duty to the State when the same
household levy system was used in war-time to impose savings
bond quotas and knitting quotas. Duty required only that each
household should be represented. The newer Women's Association is less about duty and more about pleasure and personal
convenience, a chance to go on outings or play in the soft-ball
team, or to take part in dancing classes, an outlet for sociable
instincts.

More family atomism in leisure life, more differentiated hobbies and tastes, much greater diversity of occupation, less
homogeneity of life-styles – these things are certainly making
Shinohata less of a beehive. But the days of the salaried fire
brigade and headman are still some way off. Shinohata can still
act as one when its collective interests are at stake.

The Kakizaka town council is elected not on a constituency
basis, but on a single list. If all Shinohata voters vote for a
Shinohata candidate he can be assured of being well placed
among the sixteen candidates elected. And since the most con-
tentious issues decided by the town council are how much of
the road subsidy goes to this hamlet and how much to that,
whether the new clinic will be sited near this hamlet or near
that, it is important that Shinohata should be represented –
important therefore that it should be a *community* decision as to
who shall stand and that *all* of Shinohata's votes should be
mobilized to support him. This was how one of the 'elders' of
the village, one of the five or six senior people who decided
most things behind the scenes, described what happened at the
1955 election.

> When the election came along it was obvious that we
> ought to get somebody in the hamlet to stand. The
> question was: Who? Sometimes the matter is discussed
> at the annual general meeting of the hamlet, but the
> elections were not fixed when we had the meeting this
> year, and in any case it is a tricky business discussing a

thing like that unless it is pretty well decided before-hand. Usually somebody drops a hint that he wants to stand, but this time, apart from Hanzō, who is far too unpopular, nobody made a move. A few of us got to-gether and discussed it, but none of us wanted to stand. I have got enough to do without being a councillor. Katsunori said he wanted a quiet life. Gontarō [the ex-landlord doctor] would stand for mayor, but he wouldn't consider being a councillor. Toshitada is a good chap, but he gets tight too easily, and too much of that reflects on the hamlet. We thought of several people and eventually decided to try Sakuji [Hidezō's father, the former railway engineer]. He's not much of a man, nobody particularly likes him, and he never says very much, but he said he'd think about it. Apparently, when he went home and told his wife there was a row. She wouldn't hear of it; said they'd lost enough money when he'd been secretary of the local branch of a credit union which had turned out to be a fraud, and a fine sort of councillor he'd make anyway. In the end he walked out of the house in a huff and disappeared.

He didn't come back for days, and nomination day was getting closer. Meanwhile we persuaded his son, and with his support we managed to talk his wife round. Still he didn't come back. We sent telegrams and phoned all over the place, but by nomination day we still hadn't tracked him down so we borrowed his seal and went and registered his candidature in his absence. Eventually we found him in one of his old haunts in Tokyo, and he soon came back pleased as a schoolboy to know that he was a candidate.

It was a difficult compaign. Because we were late starting, most of the other candidates had got ahead, and a lot of people in the hamlet had already promised their votes thinking that nobody from here was going to stand – people who'd been asked by relatives in other hamlets, that is. And then there was Senkichi down the road in the next hamlet [ex-landlord chair-man of the Village Land Committee who immediately after the war had started a Socialist Party branch, now defunct]. He was offering 500 yen per vote whereas most of the candidates were only giving 300, and Sakuji decided that was all he could afford.

However, five or six of us divided the hamlet up between us and made sure who would be responsible for whose votes. One trouble was Motonori [the impoverished hamlet orator-bully described in a later chapter]. We decided that we had to let him in on it, since he could do positive harm if we slighted him by leaving him out. However, we only gave him his brother and his other neighbour's household to look after, and handed him the 2,100 yen for the seven votes. We were a bit suspicious, though, and checked up afterwards. Sure enough, he had only given his brother half the money he should have done, and kept the rest for himself. His brother was angry; he thought he'd been insulted by being offered such a small amount. However, we decided it would do more harm than good to make an issue of it with Motonori and Sakuji had to take round the extra money to his brother and the other neighbour.

It was hard going, but a lot of people rallied round. The youth group stood on guard at the entrance to the hamlet every night, and just followed round everybody who came soliciting votes from other hamlets – didn't say anything, of course, just stood ostentatiously outside each house they went into to show that they had been observed. In the end we pulled it off. Most people realize, anyway, that unless they have a pretty close relative standing somewhere else in the village their first duty is to the hamlet. The night before the election we totted up the number of votes we'd got, and sure enough, the actual number was within two or three of our estimate. Some people in this hamlet, though, will promise their votes to two or three candidates and take money from them all. It's a dead loss being the official sponsor of a candidate. You get nothing from your own man, because, after all, you're doing it for the good of the hamlet, and nobody else comes near you. Just think what I missed. Five votes in this household, say I collected from two candidates. 300 yen a vote – I could have spent three or four days at a hot spring.

Election techniques have been refined since then – and have become more expensive. Around 1960 youth out-migration meant that the Women's Association had to be formally mobilized as vote-guards. Bonfires were lit at all the entrances to the village so that the identity of suspicious, possibly vote-seeking strangers could be easily established without actually shining torches in their faces.

Technological progress brought further hazards. The arrival of the telephone in 1967 robbed the defence forces of some of their effectiveness – but not definitively. You can at a pinch use the telephone to reinforce a promise, but the initial request for a favour has to be done personally; you have to show a man the light of sincerity shining in your eyes if you are to have any hope of persuading him without his feeling that he has been got at. (The former mayor of Kakizaka, a man of considerable influence after twenty years in office, complained about the constant trips he had to make to Tokyo to 'fix' things for various local people with central government officials. 'Most of them were really no problem at all; could have been settled on the phone in two minutes. But somehow you can't do that; you really have to do people the courtesy of going in person.') By the time of the telephone, anyway, few people were still coming on foot. Village guards had to be waiting in cars, and it was not so easy to tell which were stranger cars at night.

It is hard to say whether the payment for votes has become more, or less, important. There was never any question of the vote being anything other than secret, of course. One relied entirely on conscience for assurance that promises were actually delivered. Payment for a vote was, rather, a formal recognition of one's indebtedness to the voters for their support – a frank acknowledgement that you wanted to be elected more than *they* wanted to have a representative, an indication that you were not so lacking in a sense of propriety as to want something for nothing.

By all accounts, the 1974 election was the most lavish yet. Kanashige was the hamlet chief at the time, and Kanashige is a go-getter who takes, his neighbours think, an egotistical delight in running things and in pretending to unorthodox opinions. His story:

This business of having a sponsored Shinohata candidate: really it's bad. It's a flagrant violation of individual freedom. And especially when you look at the people who stand – most of them are only doing it because they've got a daughter to marry off or are looking for a bride. It sounds good if you can say: 'her father's a local councillor'. A lot of these old men are 'kettle councillors'. They sit there in the meetings and don't understand a word: probably they've got the documents upside down. Section 9, Paragraph 6. They can't even find their place. So they just sit turning over the pages, looking grave. Then when the meeting's over and the saké comes out – we serve saké in big aluminium kettles when there's a big party – then they suddenly liven up and are full of good spirits. That's what we call a kettle councillor . . .

The trouble with the councillor elections is that you can't *ask* somebody to stand. After all, its going to cost a man over [a thousand dollars] for parties and whatnot – and maybe as much as two. It depends on how many candidates. Last time there were twenty-three candidates for the sixteen seats so it was tough. Since you can't ask, you have to wait until somebody lets on that he wants to run. As hamlet head I got the five kumi chiefs to sort out possibles and there were two. In fact they both wanted it like hell, but one said that he would only do it if it was necessary and there wasn't anyone else, and since he was the less well liked anyway, we decided on the other one, Tsunashige. Then Chikayoshi, the first one, got upset: wanted us to promise that he'd have his turn in four years' time and got really mad when I said: how can I promise you that? I'm only hamlet chief for one year!

My approach to the whole thing was simple. Trust: that was it. I told everybody: I have absolute faith in the people of Shinohata. I am confident that there won't be any Shinohata votes leaking away to other hamlets.

So you can rest assured that as far as we in the Election Headquarters are concerned we don't listen to rumours. Even so, rumours are hard to stop. The village was buzzing with them. People would come in and say: It looks as if that family's breaking away and giving its votes to so-and-so. And you really couldn't entirely ignore it; you'd have to work on them somehow. My, it was quite a week from the nomination day to the election. As hamlet chief, of course, I was Campaign Director and I'd go up to the Election Headquarters, Tsunashige's house, after breakfast and not get back until after supper . . .

That it was quite a week, was the universal judgement.

More than a week, actually; it got going well before nomination day. Poor Tsunashige's wife. All the neighbours and relatives had to go and help her out. I went nearly every night. Morning, noon and night people'd be there – until midnight or one in the morning for the whole week. Thirty or forty men of an evening. First you'd put out some tea cakes, then it would be saké and then some meat to go with the saké and then it would be rice to go with the meat and the meal would go on for hours. People who hardly ever eat meat at home would be there packing it in. Not that everybody really wanted to be there. You really had to go. If you didn't, or if you didn't hang around and be feasted, there'd be rumours: 'So-and-so hasn't been seen since a week ago and somebody saw a man they'd never set eyes on before going into their house! I'll bet he's promised his vote to someone else: he doesn't dare show his face.' Wouldn't have been so bad if Tsunashige was a party-type, but he isn't; he doesn't much like that kind of thing. But still he had to be there and drink with all his guests all day and all night. And the expense! Everybody takes a bottle of saké along as a 'jinchū-mimai' ('Gift to the Fort in Siege'), but what's a bottle of saké compared to all that food and drink! Must have cost them eight times as much as what they got. And then on top of that they had to give money. About 500 yen each I think it was. Other candidates were doing it and Tsunashige was told that if he didn't it wouldn't be showing proper respect and gratitude to the village. You don't have to take it to your relatives, of course, but that's still a lot of money, on top of all the feasting. One man in another village apparently cut out all the feasting of the men. He just went from house to house and gave money to the women. More certain that way, he said.

Part of the trouble of course was our dear Campaign Director. It was a tragedy for Tsunashige that the election came in Kanashige's year as hamlet chief. He's so forceful. And a sly one too and as sharp as they come. Nobody really knows where his own vote went to really; there were all sorts of rumours . . . And so overbearing. He doesn't mind how much money he spends providing it's someone else's. He doesn't have a **car**, but he got somebody to drive him around. As Campaign Director, he said, it was his duty to pay a courtesy call on all the other candidates – to collect information about the competition, really. And he'd come back and say: 'So-and-so's serving beer and raw fish. It's what people expect nowadays, after all. You can't say beer and raw fish is overdoing it, these days. Meat and saké really isn't good enough. People will think you're being stingy . . .' He was the one, really, who insisted on handing out money too.

If one is looking for the modern equivalent of the old shrine festivals, it is not so much the tame modern affairs with electric lanterns and contrived sumō bouts and a few old cronies tippling in the outer shrine that one should look to, but the elections. And, although none are the occasion for quite such excitement as the town council election, the elections of the mayor, the prefectural assembly, the prefectural governor, and both houses of the Diet are similar occasions in the sense that although the feasting may be less intense, Shinohata loyalties are called into play. The system works quite naturally through a pattern of interlocking patronage relationships common enough in the Japanese countryside, but perhaps more pronounced in

Shinohata because of the hamlet's geographical isolation and solidarity and because of Taifū-sama – the 'Mr Typhoon' of 1959 which brought such prosperity it acquired an honorific suffix, thanks to the mayor's astonishing success in getting relief funds. Where rice fields had disappeared beneath several feet of boulders and sand, every inch was cleared, or, if the debris was too thick for that, a new rice field was built on top of it with truckload after truckload of good earth imported from elsewhere. And the cost per acre was some seven or eight times the going price of good agricultural land. Any mayor who could talk the lordly Tokyo bureaucracy into such uneconomic folly, such beautifully lucrative employment-creating folly, was clearly an extraordinary mayor.

Indeed, the mayor was a man of considerable personal charm and presence, a mountaineer and leading light in the national mayoral association, a man whose three terms of office were marked by many bold initiatives. He played his role as a fixer, but could distance himself from it: see himself by other standards. ('That subsidy he got for the fire brigade, and another one for extension of the clinic. He fiddled it. Dishonest really. He was telling us one day when we were drinking. A wrong thing to do, he said: very wrong. But, he said, I take all the responsibility. It was for good motives, and I'll carry the can.') But for all the mayor's own personal 'arm', his skill, he obviously could not do these things without friends, and to keep friends he had to mobilize votes in their support. It was well known that it was Mr Masuda who had 'stripped off a layer of skin' (that is, not just his shirt) for Kakizaka over the typhoon – Mr Masuda, one of the MPs for the multi-member constituency to which Kakizaka belonged, and at that time a Deputy Minister (a Deputy Minister of some clout since his waggon was hitched to the faction of a leading contender for the next prime ministership).

After all, I figured, as headman – and Mitsuyoshi, our councillor on the town council, agreed with me – that if we are going to do anything for Shinohata we've got to co-operate with the mayor and support the candidate he's supporting. What I did: I said to everybody at the hamlet meeting before the general election: Look.

We've got to give the mayor our support and every
household should give at least one vote to Mr Masuda.
Some of you work elsewhere and have obligations, I
know; some of you will be expected by your union to
vote for the Socialist Party. Well, that's fine. That's
perfectly understandable – provided we have one vote
from each household for Mr Masuda. That way we
won't have any rumours and recriminations about
people falling out of line, and there won't be any
trouble in the village. And that's the way it went. Of
course you can't be sure because the votes are counted
on a township basis: Mr Masuda knows how many
votes Mayor Shinobu got him from the township, but
not how many of them came from Shinohata. Still, I'm
sure we did our bit. It's all beautifully organized. When
the elections are coming up the mayor quietly arranges
things in advance. Every hamlet forms a branch of the
Masuda Support Society and the village headman becomes the branch chairman. You don't have to pay
anything to join – well, maybe the branch chairman
contributes a hundred or two hundred yen, but you can
be sure they get that back one way or the other. And
then after the election the whole organization evapor-
ates. Of course, our Mayor Shinobu was replaced by
Mayor Katō between the last two general elections, and
Mayor Katō has a different pipe up to the centre, so this
time we had a Kanemoto Support Society instead of a
Masuda Support Society . . .

Both Masuda and Kanemoto, of course, are official candidates of the Liberal Democratic Party, but in Japan's multi-
member constituencies they are thrown into competition with
each other, and naturally belong to different factions within the
Party. It is not quite true that the personal support societies disappear between elections. The village branches might do so,
but I remember going to the second gala meeting of Mr
Masuda's Support Society in the prefectural capital several
years ago. It was just after Mr Masuda's immediate patron had
been elected Party President and Prime Minister. Clearly great
days were ahead for all Mr Masuda's friends and relations. The

Kakizaka township office jeep, the mayor's car, the ambulance-bus that belonged to the clinic and the public works truck were mobilized to take every member of the town council and the headmen of all twenty hamlets to the meeting. I went with Norio and Katsunori, both of whom undoubtedly counted as informal elders of Shinohata, but since they did not occupy formal positions in township affairs did not rate a free ride that day. (Norio, as a local notable, was on Masuda's personal mailing list, though, so he did get regular greetings cards from him at New Year and Midsummer. Also a telegram when Masuda's patron was elected Party President (hence Prime Minister): 'In happiness at realization of Kanda Presidency and thanks your continued support, Greetings. Masuda, Deputy Minister of Construction.')

Not being members of the official party we had to go by bus, and we had to stand in a long line in the sweltering lobby for the chance of shaking Mr Masuda's hand – though the bottle of orange-flavoured milk we were all given, and the cotton handkerchief to wipe the sweat away, did somewhat alleviate our discomfort. Norio was certain that Mr Masuda recognized him because of the warmth of his greeting and because he said: 'It was good of you to come out', a phrase which could be construed as meaning 'to make the trip', indicating that he knew we had come from afar. A wide-eyed foreigner to show off was also not a bad thing to have in tow, either. So it was in some hopes that we loitered after the meeting was over, but it was no good. Nobody invited us to a party; we had to buy our own modest little binge of noodles and saké and forlornly take the bus home. The trouble was that in the press we completely lost sight of the Kakizaka official party. Otherwise if we had been able to get close enough to the mayor to look him in the eye he would have been bound to invite us along. It subsequently appeared that the official party went off to a rather splendid restaurant kept by an ex-Kakizaka man. Mr Masuda appeared in the course of the evening, said a few words of thanks to them for coming so far and presented a few bottles of saké for their delectation. They got home very late and very drunk.

Politics in Shinohata *is* about roads and bridges and schools and irrigation channels and the gentle art of getting central government subsidies for these things, but it is also about personal ambition. Any discussion of the individual and the group

in Japan must take account of the way in which demonstrative
community spirit can be a means to self-advancement. And any
discussion of recreation and leisure pursuits must take account
of the pleasure that some men get from running things or taking
part in the running of things, persuading, manipulating, gently
pressuring, forming combinations, working out mutually bene-
ficial exchanges, making speeches, being the centre of attention.

> Yes, of course, it's been quite interesting being on
> the town council. I think I can say we've had a very
> good share of the roads and irrigation-ditch budget.
> Yes, partly it's done in open discussion in the commit-
> tees, partly you fix it with the mayor. What kind of
> bargain? Well, we'd never, for instance, talk about the
> mayor himself: we'd never threaten not to vote for him
> or anything like that, but, for instance, suppose the
> mayor starts talking about the Prefectural Assembly
> elections. There's so and so belonging to the Masuda
> faction that's putting up, and he hopes we can work up
> a good few votes for him in Shinohata. Well, provided
> there's no particular reason for us to have anything
> against the man, I say: Well, I'm sure we can get people
> to co-operate; people are quite well disposed towards
> you, Mr Mayor. On the other hand, of course, they're
> all very concerned about the subsidy for the children's
> playground, and it might be pretty hard to persuade
> them to vote for Mr so and so if they are disappointed
> over that . . .

Hidezō had, as I mentioned earlier, been a notably activist
headman, full of projects, forcefully inspiring donations from
his fellow villagers for this and for that. Perhaps his greatest
coup was the new 300-metre underground culvert for the
Fushiki irrigation channel: nearly a square metre in size and of
very solid concrete. This was no mere local operation. It was
not simply a matter of wining and dining prefectural officials
and channelling a little more than one's quota share of subsidy
in one's own direction. This was high-level stuff, involving big
names at the centre. His description of the affair went as follows. (I should explain that half of the members of the House

of Councillors to which he refers are elected on a single national list, with each voter having a single vote and the seventy-five candidates with the most votes being elected. TV personalities and popular women's leaders tend to top the poll, beneficiaries of the more impersonal mass appeal politics of Japan's cities. But a good many of those elected even on this national list get there thanks to older types of networks.)

The old culvert was leaking all over and it was obvious we were going to have to replace it. It would have cost us several hundreds of thousand yen per household, but the House of Councillor elections were just coming up and I knew there were some plans for building a forestry-cum-tourist road through the woods at the back of the village, somewhere near the culvert. So the obvious thing to do was to get the road routed right over our culvert, so that they'd be forced to destroy the old one and build us a new one for free. It wouldn't be so difficult fixing the surveyors, but there was still the question of whether the plan would go ahead at all. Well, luckily Takenobu's brother works for a big construction company in Tokyo and he invited me to lunch at the Diet with Hoshimaki, who was a former Ministry of Construction official, standing for the Councillor's election. He was obviously going to be on the Construction Committee if he was elected. So I presented him with our petition to the Ministry of Construction for a subsidy. And he said: 'Right, I'll see to it.' But of course that's not the end of it. You've got to do your part. With these chaps you go along with your petition and they say: 'Ah yes, and where are you from?' and they've got the vote breakdown in their drawer and they look it up, and if your village delivered them a decent number of votes, it'll be: 'Right, leave it to me!' If not: 'Well, I'll certainly see what I can do, but you know . . .' So we really had to work at it. We aimed to get 300 Hoshimaki votes from this township. In the end we made 290 which wasn't too bad: good enough to press the point anyway, so I went back to him after a decent interval, and we got our road. I was still a bit bitter about those ten fugitive votes, though. Some people who promised me a vote must have voted for someone else. That's the dirty part of democracy.

The road, as it stood in 1975, did not follow the most obvious contour, but its coincidental running with Shinohata's culvert did not make it *too* obviously unnatural as a road. It was, it was true, a rather curious quarter-mile stretch since in one direction it ended in nothing and in the other in a fine wide concrete bridge over Muddy River, exactly fifty yards downstream from the equally fine and wide concrete bridge which was built fifteen years earlier with the Mr Typhoon Reconstruction Funds and nowadays bears traffic of approximately two lorries a day (itself a replacement of several generations of wooden bridges from one of which Tomiyo's grandma had lost her horse – in the days when people *were* constantly going up to the mountains). I was assured, however, that although there was no activity at present – the 'oil shock' had upset many things – there really were plans for a very fine tourist road some twenty kilometres long.

Hidezō should with luck 'make it' as Shinohata's councillor next time round – at a younger age than anyone in living memory. Too much of a hustler to be much liked, people had to admit that he got things done.

The beauty of the Japanese passion for organization is that this is no spectator sport. The capacity for speech-making and chairman's solemn formality, the taste for running other people's lives, is widely diffused in rural Japan. In 1955 I went through the savings accounts at the Co-operative for the village to which Shinohata belonged before the local government amalgamations. For a village of 401 households there were no fewer than 177 organizations with an account at the Co-op. There has been some pruning and amalgamation since, but still in 1975 the fifty-five house-heads in Shinohata shared between them the following list of offices, most of them rotated after quite short terms.

Hamlet Chief, Vice-Chief and Past Chief.
Head of a kumi (and ex-officio member of Hamlet Council).
Fire Brigade Chief and Vice-Chief.

President of Child Welfare Society.
Chairman/Member of Crime Prevention Guidance Committee.
Shrines Committee: Chairman, Vice-Chairman.
Shinohata branch of Primary School PTA, Chairman, Vice-Chairman.
Shinohata branch of Agricultural Co-operative, Chairman/Kumi Leader.
Old People's Society, President.
Shinohata electee on Kakizaka Town Council.

At least with some of the most important of these jobs, the satisfactions were not simply the satisfactions of accomplishment, of doing something for the village, but also the pleasure of hobnobbing with the great, of being involved in the same power-game as the people whose faces appeared on the television sets and whose manoeuvres are reported in the papers. The world of conservative politics is a world where 'arm', that epitome of manliness known as 'strength when the chips are down', 'jitsuryoku', are the qualities most admired. For the Support Society meeting I mentioned earlier, Mr Masuda had got the Foreign Minister to come and grace the occasion with what was billed as a Special Lecture. He did indeed say a few well-chosen words. Japan, he could say it with some pride, was firmly with the Free World. She was not in the valley of neutralism. She stood proudly on the hill. He'd recently had a talk with the Russian Ambassador, Federenko. There had had to be plain speaking. They had ended in disagreement but mutual esteem. He had sent Federenko some bottles of saké. Federenko had replied with vodka and caviare – and delicious stuff it was too. There was nothing to fear with these people: one just had to be firm. Though he had to say that the violent student demonstrations which had disgraced Japan that summer made his job difficult. Japan was in danger of being looked on as no better than Korea.

He felt he could say these things frankly because everybody there was a friend of Mr Masuda and any friend of Mr Masuda was a friend of his. And lucky were the friends of Mr Masuda. Mr Masuda and the Governor of the Prefecture, Mr Kondō, were a formidable combination. Ruefully, he had to confess that they were a more formidable combination than he and the Prefectural Governor in the neighbouring prefecture where he had his constituency. After the great typhoon they had managed to get funds amounting to almost exactly 90 per cent of their request. But how much had Masuda and Kondō got? 94·7 per cent! It's no fun having to acknowledge when you're beaten, but you had to admire their skill.

He was not allowed to get away entirely with such friendly modesty, however. The said Governor Kondō reminded the audience that although, of course, everyone hoped that Mr Masuda might be a minister in his patron's cabinet, Prime Minister Kanda had a lot of debts to those who'd supported him, and he'd had to ask Mr Masuda to wait his turn. As for the Foreign Minister – now there was a man of power. Of course he'd been returned to the Diet seven times in successive elections. Mr Masuda so far only four times. And the difference counts. Why, the Foreign Minister, quite recently, but before he became Minister, was able with a single telephone call to stop the Party Transport Committee in its tracks, get a crucial meeting postponed, and in the end come out with a solution much more favourable to the central zone. So they must all look forward to the time when Mr Masuda, too, had been tested in the fire of seven elections.

Along with the uninhibited admiration of power goes, too, a total acceptance of loyal deference to those who have it. Mr Masuda in his speech to his supporters dwelt at length on his close relations with his patron, the Prime Minister. He spoke of himself as 'playing the role of a wife' to him. Just one example of the kindness and warmth with which Prime Minister Kanda recognized his services: after the crucial election for the Party Presidency, Mr Kanda told him of the great pile of congratulatory telegrams, some from people in Mr Masuda's constituency whom he did not know personally. 'Did you get any?' he asked Mr Masuda. A great pile. 'OK. Bring them along to me. I'll send the replies.' And that was just what he did. All at his own expense and, moreover – and here the evidence of real thoughtfulness – he'd sent them in Masuda's name.

This is not feudal politics. It owes little or nothing to the sort of deference which the forelock-touching provincial voter still pays to the scion of a great aristocratic family in some English rural constituencies. Mr Masuda was a man of amiable, bumbling, and clearly plebeian demeanour. He did not move with graceful confident ease. When he broke into a beaming smile it was as if he shyly discovered that he was overdoing it and seemed consciously to push his face back into place and button up his lips.

As the mayor mentioned just now, my father worked all his life for this city, but as a humble clerk. It was not an easy life we led, especially for my mother. I have no words to describe the sacrifices she made for me, to see that I got a good education, that I could study and get to high school and then to the university and into the Treasury. I'm not from any of the great clans and famous houses, and yet today I get full encouragement from cabinet ministers . . . If I become a cabinet minister myself, I've no wish to throw my weight around. Nor am I interested in making a lot of money. Only recently, at last, have I been able to get a house here in my constituency, but actually, thanks to the help of friends, it only cost me some [$600]. I'm not out to make a fortune: all my children are girls anyway, there'd be no one to leave it to. If I do make any money I shall leave it to start a society for the elimination of corruption from politics or something of that sort.

Really, I can't tell you how grateful I am to you all. I've no brothers, no relatives here to help me. So I need your help, and I'm proud of your help. Nothing makes me more proud than the overwhelming support I receive from people who have nothing to do with my family. My Support Society is the voice of the voiceless, the organization of the unorganized. I am just the medium, the means, dear friends, through which you can be involved in the politics of our Japan.

Politicians, of course, are expected to be corrupt, but there is corruption and corruption. Taking a voluntary donation from a contractor is rather different from taking a kickback the size of which has been contractually haggled over. Taking a kickback from a contractor who uses inferior materials so that the dam breaks in the next typhoon is altogether different from taking a kickback from a contractor who does an honest job. A trip by the Kakizaka council to 'study' sewage-disposal techniques which involved half-an-hour at a sewage plant and a luxury expenses-paid weekend at a resort hotel might actually cause a scandal and get written up in the provincial newspaper, whereas if they spent a good couple of hours at the plant and stayed only one night, drank only a modest amount and hired only a few geisha, no one would consider it anything out of the ordinary. 'Big men' deserve a certain latitude and indulgence. They have to keep up a certain style and they are bound to have a lot of dependants if they are really big men. And if they are really sincere in their duty to look after their dependants, they will need rather more resources than the ordinary man.

National politics, for most Shinohata citizens, is a matter of the doings of 'big men'. Who is in and who is out in the ruling Liberal Democratic Party: that is where the real interest of politics lies, though about the issues of national politics they are often not at all badly informed and can talk in terms of rather more sophisticated abstraction than most of the world's farmers are capable of. But often there are ambiguities and inconsistencies. I once met Takenobu clipping his hedge with the meticulous care of a man who rebuilt a family living out of nothing by arduous charcoal burning after the war and who deserved the retirement to which his son-in-law's earning power now entitled him.

> Well, we haven't seen you for a long time. How are things in England? Tell me, Professor, what do you think of Japanese democracy? Do you think it's all right? or has it gone off the rails? Things are pretty bad between Japan and Korea these days aren't they? Bad place Korea, no democracy there – absolutely none. That's statism. Yes, you're right, a kind of dictatorship. But don't you think Japan needs a touch of dictatorship too these days? That's what I think. Things are getting out of hand, don't you think? What's the standard of living like compared to England? They say it will take twenty years before we overtake America – that's what Mr Sato, the Prime Minister, said.

You're lucky to be able to travel all over the world. I wish I could too. Just to compare things. There may be some things that Japan is better at. Before the war when I was in Korea on irrigation works – you know we built an enormous dam that made a lake bigger than Lake Biwa and irrigated thousands of acres and produced electricity too. One of our men who'd been around said it was a better job than anywhere else at the time. We put a lot of work into Korea, you know. And all wasted. Nobody appreciated it. All we got for it was resentment. It was the worst time in my life coming back from Korea at the end. Never be on the losing side: that's the golden rule – that's what that taught me. Still I guess we deserved to lose. The Americans go about things rationally, not like us Japanese. Japanese soldiers throwing themselves at tanks with a box of grenades strapped to them! Americans would never do that. They'd calculate that human lives are scarcer than ammunition so you should treat them as precious. That's really rational.

What about our Self-Defence Forces? Hopeless! They'd never win a battle: they've got all flabby and Americanized. They've never been properly toughened. They're all in it for the money. If ever there was a war they'd scatter to the four winds.

There is a good deal of mild nostalgia for the beehive disciplines, the unambiguity of authority, the certainty of purpose of pre-war Japan. The respect for authority has by and large remained. I recall a lengthy worried first meeting of the Crime Prevention Guidance Committee in Shinohata – a body set up to promote citizen co-operation with the police. Apart from keeping an eye open for high-school children who might be glue-sniffing up in the woods and consulting as to who should tell their parents, there did not seem to be all that much co-operation which needed promoting, but there might be occasional need for house-to-house message passing. Normally, for the Co-operative or the township office, this was done by means of a circulating clip-board – one in each kumi – which one read and passed on. For more important things, each kumi chief would make a quick tour of his twelve or thirteen houses with a verbal message. But there they were in a dilemma. There were five kumi, and the police headquarters said that for a hamlet the size of Shinohata the Crime Prevention Guidance Committee should consist of four members. Four of the kumi were represented, but not the fifth. What to do? Was it better to divide the fifth kumi between them? or to establish entirely new circuits? The debate dragged on. No one made the obvious suggestion that they might appoint a fifth member of the committee. The Authorities had said that Shinohata needs four. So that was that.

Bureaucracy in metropolitan Tokyo may have had to learn to cope with the radical challenge of anti-authoritarian mistrust, but hardly in Shinohata. If there is still respect for the Authorities, however, there certainly is not the same spiritual unity and emotional attachment to national leaders which characterized pre-war Japan. One or two Shinohata houses had formal pictures of the Crown Prince and his bride, but the Imperial family aroused little interest. When I got there in 1975, it was just after a state visit by the British Queen.

My, that Queen of yours, what a marvellous woman she is. Such a pleasant way with her; always smiling and behaving so naturally. That's what our Royal Family ought to be like, they were saying the other day in the papers. They ought to break through the chrysanthemum curtain and mix with the common people a bit more – especially the Crown Prince and Michiko – too much to expect from the old Emperor. But it never goes like that with us Japanese. Always so stiff and formal; no smile, nothing relaxed about it. Well, it's not so long ago that we would have to make a deep bow just to the Emperor's photograph. Not even his photograph: at school there was something almost like a little shrine which contained the Emperor's photograph and the Imperial Rescript on Education. We used to have to bow whenever we passed that.

England always has the Queen on her stamps, doesn't it? Never in Japan. The idea of licking the back of the Emperor's face and putting your thumb on his nose! Still we did once have some commemorative

stamps for the Crown Prince's marriage with his picture on it.

That was a great parade she had, too, wasn't it –
through the streets of Tokyo. Ticker-tape or something
did they call it? You can't imagine the Emperor ever
standing up in an open car like that and looking so
happy. But I suppose they wouldn't do that for the
Emperor – you only do it for guests from outside, don't
you? Can you imagine anybody doing that sort of thing
for our Emperor? Can you imagine anybody doing it
for any *Japanese* Emperor?

There was a certain bitterness about that last sentence. Few
peoples in the world are as nationally self-conscious as the
Japanese, as preoccupied with what it means to be a Japanese
and what being a Japanese means for one's place in the world –
not surprisingly since not many other nations of unique and
homogeneous culture have been trying for a century to break
in, as racial outsiders, to the white man's club known as the
comity of nations. Perhaps the younger generation is growing
up with few of these complexes – if still with much the same
stereotypes. When I asked the middle-school children to write
some essays for me, one girl chose to write on 'The Japanese'. I
am not sure whether this was a topic I had suggested or one of
the additional topics suggested by the teacher.

I've never thought deeply and seriously about the
Japanese, so this is an opportunity to think about a lot
of things I have heard and so see if I can say what sort
of being the Japanese is.

To start with, we have got one peculiar habit which
is to imitate others. I wrote 'habit'. Of course, if everyone in the country was to pay attention, we could break
it, so I think it could be called a habit, but you might
say: 'But why should we, what's wrong with the
habit?' And I agree. There is nothing wrong with it
except that wherever you go in modern Japan today
you see 'horizontal letters' – foreign words and names.
Of course when the foreign word is exactly the *mot
juste* and there is no Japanese word to express the idea,

that does not count as the habit of imitation. But often people use a foreign word even when there is a perfectly good Japanese word meaning the same thing, and they only do it because they think it's clever and makes them sound important . . .

We Japanese have got these peculiar aspects, but we also have some very good aspects. First we love and care for Nature. Secondly, we are very polite and considerate of others. Thirdly, we are very serious about our work. Of course this is to make a living, too, but it is also because we think it is morally proper that we take so much pains. Finally we have a tendency to avoid taking extreme attitudes; we don't think it is right to speak out aggressively. These are the ideas that have occurred to me as I started thinking about the Japanese. Of course I am one too, and I can find these things in myself, so for me too writing this essay was an opportunity for reflection on myself.

15

Nature and the Numinous

Life in Shinohata, it will be rather obvious by now, is sober and organized. Men have been looking for a long time to see if they cannot, by taking thought, add a cubit to their productivity or their long-term security or their arrangements for avoiding conflict in the regulation of their affairs. The water-watch roster, for instance, which all those who have rice fields irrigated from the Fushiki stream work out each year – a roster which gives a man, over a season, exactly the number of turns of duty proportionate to his acreage under rice – is of very considerable antiquity: the sanctions built up against cheating, against flooding one's own field out of turn or giving it more than the regulation dose are so strong, so well internalized and so neatly reinforced by the system of doing the water-watch in constantly changing pairs that a sociologist who insists on discussing the possibility of cheating is looked on as adding yet further proof to the belief that foreigners have devious suspicious minds.

Life in Shinohata, then, in the words with which a Japanese eighteenth-century philosopher thought about the basic Hobbesian problem, is a matter of 'artifice' and not of 'nature'. It is not lived on an instinctual, elemental plane. It is hard to say, even, that Shinohata people are close to nature. What do they say when they ask whether so-and-so's new baby is a boy or a girl? One might expect earthy metaphors of mushrooms and split-peaches, redolent of ancient phallic cults and the fairy stories which the folk-tale collectors so assiduously gather from octogenarians and publish in their many-volumed collections. In fact one is more likely to hear instead the metaphors of urban, military Japan, 'cannon or battleship?'

To be sure, one should not overstress the point. Not everyone's contact with growing things is entirely mediated through noisy smelly machines. Some people still have the feel of that tenderness and intimacy with living things that one glimpses if one watches an old lady handling her silkworms, or a man opening up a bundle of rice seedlings with an appraising eye before he bends back down again to resume the rapid work of pushing them into the soft mud in a carefully arranged pattern. There are the men who tend their miniature trees with great expertise; there is Shigeyasu, the devoted fisherman, who will tell you, with so much enthusiasm it makes him stutter, just how to catch the right kinds of fly for river trout by scraping the underside of rocks with a loofah; there was the wayward and much lamented Motonori, who was wise in the ways of local adders, could catch them in his bare hands and pickle them in saké to make a potent aphrodisiac. But there is only one man who still lives and works in any real sense close to nature and that is Wataru, Shinohata's last surviving woodsman.

Every village has its family of good-for-nothings, and Wataru's family was Shinohata's. Heavy drinkers, lazy, quarrelsome, violent, always hard-up. The four brothers (Wataru was its third)

> used to fight like mad. You go to other houses and you often see the paper of the sliding doors broken through, but in their house you would find great holes even in the slatted frame – smashed up in their fighting.

And yet they were close. When, in the 1950s, the eldest brother inherited the parental house and his three younger brothers had moved out, none of them wanted to leave the place that was home. They built themselves huts at the top of the village and scraped a living heaven knows how. By the seventies, Wataru was the only surviving member of the family in Shinohata. His two younger brothers had died first; one in a road accident caused by his own drunkenness, the other – who was almost blind from drinking the wood alcohol stolen from the army's dumps at the end of the war – with mysterious suddenness. His elder brother and sister-in-law had died soon after. Their numerous progeny had all left home and lost touch. Only their eldest son, Wataru's nephew, occasionally came back for funerals and to look after the family graves. He had been drawn to the bright lights of highway culture, much as the 'disreputable poor' of Tokugawa society used to be drawn to the glamour of the inn-towns on the great trunk roads – the subjects of so many of Hiroshige's prints. A century ago he would have become a post-horse groom or a professional gambler's tout. Now he was a drive-in waiter-dishwasher. He was said to have difficulty holding down a job: a few months and there would be a row and he would have to move on to the next drive-in. By now he had worked his way from drive-in to drive-in all the way down the valley to within a few miles of the prefectural capital. But he *had*, contrary to all expectations and at the age of thirty-seven, finally managed to find a bride. An insurance agent, strategically placed as insurance agents are to play the role of marriage broker, had managed it – a woman a couple of years older than himself, to be sure, but a sensible lady who seemed to be having a sobering effect on him. Perhaps he would settle down. Perhaps he would become the second member of the family to achieve respectability.

Wataru had been the first, though still not quite a hundred per cent first-class citizen. Everyone agreed that he was quite the most worthy, pleasant and reliable of the four brothers. But still no one had nominated him yet for the job of hamlet chief. That endorsement of full citizenship had not yet come. His photograph was not there in the village hall along with almost every other one of his elders and contemporaries – and by now quite a few of his juniors. Wataru had a shy diffidence about him that made one realize it would be cruel to put him in a position of having to preside over village meetings – and who knew how cruel it was *not* to press him to do so?

Wataru's days were spent in the woods. Once he would have begun before dawn the long trek to his kiln in the upper forests and come back at night with forty-five kilogrammes of charcoal in three neat twig-woven bales on his back. Now his days begin in a much more leisurely way and they are spent in less exhausting work. Mostly he is occupied with clearing the under-brush on tree plantations – those that belong to the village or to the Hachiman shrine, or to the commuter 'salary men' among his neighbours who have no taste for spending their Sundays in such labour. Lately he has also occasionally been commissioned by the hamlet council to clear the paths which lead up to the higher reaches of the forest, ten or fifteen miles back towards the ridge of the mountains – a job unthinkable twenty years ago when constant traffic along the main paths took care of under-growth and overgrowth alike.

But now Wataru has the forests to himself. There is little to be heard except, very occasionally, the ring of his axe and the twang of his saw, much more commonly the loud ugly whine of the gasoline motor on his back-pack connected by a flexible drive-shaft to the vicious rotor blade which is now his main tool. There is nothing quietly romantic about the way Wataru communes with the forest.

Sometimes, though, he takes the odd hour from his labours to go, for instance, looking for nests of wild bees. They hold little honey, but the larvae in their spiral cells – even the ones almost fully formed and ready for take-off – are delicious and fortifying. But finding a wild bees' nest, buried upside down in the ground, is a difficult art. Preparation begins, improbably, with catching a frog. Boil its meat. Take a small fragment and tie a little piece of white cotton to it. Display prominently. Bees have an irresistible attraction to boiled frog's meat (explain that, students of natural selection!) and when a bee finds a piece all you have to do is to follow it home: the white cotton will stand out against the leaves and distinguish your homeward-bound bee from other bees.

And then there is hunting: plenty of pigeons and woodcock; occasionally pheasants introduced from Europe a hundred years ago. And, in contrast to Mediterranean villages, in Shino-hata shotguns are rare. Wataru, who has had a fully paid-up shotgun licence for thirty years, does not have a great deal of competition.

The year before last he got a wild boar; once the scourge of Japanese agriculture, then almost extinct, now on the increase again as Japan's farmers withdraw from their forest hinterlands.

The wild boars come for the Irish potatoes. Otherwise what do they live on?

> 'I don't know what you call it. There's a kind of vine with purple leaves. They dig that up and eat the root. Or they go to the rivers and dig up river crabs and eat them. Or acorns. Or the leaves of nara and kunugi trees. Much the same as bears, though the bears also have luxurious tastes: the last five years they have been for the peaches in the village, and the chestnuts, but most of the time they live far back in the forest. They eat bees' nests, too. They smell them out.'

Wataru, the twentieth-century woodsman with the rotary blade, was better informed about the animal life than about the vegetable life of the forest. Most of the plants around him in the forest were just miscellaneous underbrush. Once, the forests were a famine reserve; a source of food that could just hold body and soul together for a few emergency months. That was a long time ago.

> 'Famine foods? I don't know. I have never eaten them, but I have heard people talk of it. Old people. Arrow-root I think it was chiefly. It's a kind of vine with a root. Then there is a sort of rhubarb and fern shoots and then the bush with little clusters of black fruit that we call cod's-eye. But I don't think you can eat that. Then of course there are the akebi berries which are sweet and good. We used to gather them when we were children, but nobody bothers with them now – except for the people from the town occasionally; they sometimes come picking them for a Sunday outing.'

For Japan, less than one generation separates the birth of the middle-class cult of the natural food and adaptation to the environment from the days when peasant poverty bred a thrifty determination to exploit everything available for free.

Not that the middle-class cult of nature is a new thing to Japan, even if its recent environmentalist expressions are just another part of worldwide 'international advanced industrial society culture'. A millennium ago the Heian aristocracy had its regular round of outings and festivals and poetry contests for the picking of this and the viewing of that. And through subsequent centuries, too, Japanese gardens and gardeners had kept some of those attitudes alive. A gardener from a neighbouring village summoned to tend Norio's trees, chatting over tea:

> When I was training in Nagano it was only the best and richest houses that had gardens. Of course the town gardens are the best ones to bring on. There's a difference between town gardens and country gardens. Town gardens have tall trees and around their base, on rising ground to the back, bushes to give a kind of mountain background. But here in the country you have got real mountains for your background so you don't need that . . .
>
> The pace was different then. In these old houses there would nearly always be a retired grandfather, sitting out on the verandah watching while you did your spring pruning. And he'd tell you off if you worked too fast. A good gardener was expected to be properly dressed with proper socks and straw sandals. You would approach the tree, select a branch, work over it for half an hour and then come back and sit on the edge of the verandah and gaze at it thoroughly, as if you were working out your next move. The masters liked that. Time meant nothing to them – or money either.
>
> A tree like that pine you would do twice a year. No secateurs: you never used secateurs. In the spring you carefully pinch out all the shoots that are going out of line, and then by the autumn there's hardly anything long enough to need cutting: you can just pinch out again. But people now let their trees go. They think if they get you along for a couple of days every two years you can really keep a tree the shape it ought to be. It's secateurs now.

Respect for the life-force was, I suppose, one way of describing both the attitudes gardeners were expected by their aristocratic patrons to show towards their trees, and the feeling the ordinary villager had towards growing things and living things. And with respect went a certain amount of fear. Most houses in 1955 had at least one family of swallows through the summer, its nest spittle-stuck to the roof beam in the main living room or the kitchen. Everyone waited for the day of their arrival, counted the eggs, watched the progress of the young and marvelled at the way the fledglings fought for the food and the tireless devotion with which the parents fetched it. People left their outer rain-doors open two inches at night so that the swallows could start foraging at dawn if the family was not up. If you *didn't* get a pair of swallows to nest in your house you were worried and fearful of impending disaster. And if you got two nests you were sure of good luck. But swallows don't quite go with the trim modern vacuum-cleaned houses of 1975. 'All those droppings all over the place. They really are a nuisance.' A few families keep their swallows. The majority drive them out and keep them out; even callously knocking their incipient nests off the eaves when they try the outside of the house as second best.

The Shinto tradition allowed everything that grew or helped growth, everything that was part of nature, to be impregnated with the numinous, to be a 'kami', to use the word for which 'spirit' is perhaps a better translation than 'god'. Their kami deserved respect – respect which took a variety of ritual forms, ranging from formal worship with offerings of rice and water to a cursory bow when passing. Wataru still minimally recognizes that the 17th of every month is the day of the kami of the forest, once the monthly holiday of all forestry workers. That is to say he allows himself a bottle of saké or beer for his lunch that day.

But the forces of the numinous are also dangerous forces. Younger people are not easily frightened. Most would readily plant their rice on the fourth or the ninth of the month (or the fourteenth, nineteenth, etc.) and ignore the superstition that rice planted on four and nine days would end up being eaten at a funeral. A good many have no idea of the supposed identity of the protector god of their own house who is supposed to inhabit the little stone shrine in their back garden – even if they do take the trouble to decorate it with a pine branch at New Year – or more likely to put up one of the pieces of paper the shops sell with a pine branch painted on it. And although they fob the kami off with this mean substitute, they rarely bother their heads with the thought that the god might feel cheated and visit his vengeance on the family. For older people, however, who grew to adulthood in an era when man's control over nature, his health and himself *was* much more tenuous than it is now, and whose lives are bringing them close to the great climactic contact with the numinous which is death – for the older people things are not so simple.

Toshitada's grandma is pretty bad now: this leukaemia is a terrible thing. You know, when she first became ill, Masayoshi's grandma – the eighty-year-old – went in, and she told them she knew what was wrong. It was all because of Toshitada's cutting down the big cypress they had behind their house. He did it without any kind of prayer to the tree, and just at that time the White Dragon kami from Kurokawa shrine was resting at the top of the tree and suddenly – bang – he was rudely disturbed. So he was angry. So Masayoshi's grandma undertook to go and find out what best to do, so she went to the shrine at Kurokawa and when she came back she said that they should have somebody go regularly and do a proper prayer and leave a proper gift and the old girl would get better. The kami had agreed that he would see to it. That was the message she got, anyway. So they did, and the old lady got better.

But then she was bad again. So they asked Masayoshi's grandma what to do. She was cross. I knew it would happen, she said. I told you it would happen. You didn't do a proper thank-you visit to the shrine when the old lady got better. The god must be angry. She went to the shrine again for them, but she was gloomy when she came back. 'It's just as I said. It's because you didn't do a proper thank-you pilgrimage. You should go on praying, but it may not be any good. The kami said he couldn't take any responsibility now, not now that things had got to this point.' I expect Masayoshi's grandma already knew by this time that it was leukaemia.

The old lady went into hospital but the doctor said
they couldn't do much for her, they said she might as
well go home and drink tea with her friends. I took her
some rice cakes last night. I didn't think she would
manage to eat them, but she did. In fact she seems to
have got better since the doctors gave her up.

A number of elderly widows in the district are specialists at
communing with the spirits. Their messages are not always
trusted however.

Matsuji's old lady had terrible arthritis and they
called in an old prayer lady. She went into a trance; it
was supposed to be the spirit of one of the family's
ancestors; she started shrieking and even beating the
old lady, and kept on saying, 'Give her some woodland
and then I'll be all right', meaning, presumably, that
they should make over a piece of woodland to her, the
medium. They were really frightened and decided that
they did not want any more to do with *that* prayer-lady.
Then they went over to the Kōbō cult. The whole
family was very keen on that sort of thing. Their son
used to go to the Kōseikai centre in the next village on
his way to work every morning, praying that he would
find a bride . . .
But Akira's old lady was different. She was a remarkable old lady. She went blind soon after she came as a
bride, about four years after, in fact, but she was very
clever and she soon adapted. She started a mill and
worked it day and night – flat mill stones for the wheat
and a mortar for the rice. It was amazing how she could
work that thing and sift the flour that came off the mill
stones without being able to see a thing.
She had a marvellous memory too. Not being able
to read, she memorized all sorts of sutras and she was
in great demand for wakes and memorial services when
people didn't want to have the expense of a priest. She
was good at divining too. I remember an old man who
came up to see her from Kamata. He'd lost 200 yen. She
said some prayers and screwed up her eyes and said:

'Look about you.' Sure enough; he'd been intending to put it into his hanging sleeve but had put it inside the lining instead and it had worked down to the bottom of his kimono.

We got Akira's old lady in to advise us about that Fudō-san up there on the shelf. [A rather finely gilded and painted two-foot image of the fierce defender of Buddha's law, The Unmovable, sitting against a background of flames, sword in one hand to quell all demons, and a rope in the other to bind them.] That was brought here by the ancestor who founded our house, six or seven generations back. He was a yama-bushi ascetic who came to settle here. We've still got all the yamabushi things in the store-house, the little black lacquer cap they wore and everything. When I came here as a bride my parents suggested that since I didn't know the proper way to pray to Fudō-san I ought to take him back to the Fudō shrine on Mount Narita. But then Akira's old lady came and said prayers all day – she knew so many – and she said: 'No, Fudō-san doesn't want to leave the house.' So I was afraid that if I did take it back something terrible might happen. So instead we just shut him up in the store-house.

But then last year we had that accident; we had a trailer on the motor tiller and it started to run backwards, and the old man got flustered and forgot about the handbrake and shouted 'Jump!' and I jumped into a telegraph pole and fractured some ribs and hurt my spine and was several months in hospital. So we wondered if there was anything wrong, and we got an old lady from Tabata to come and get rid of the evil influences just in case. She said this house would never flourish as long as we shut Fudō-san up in the store-house, so we brought him out and cleaned him up and put him up here and put those white streamers up, and every day I offer up water and burn some incense. But I still don't know what are the proper prayers to offer up.

She also said that the lane into the back was the Devil Gate of this house and we shouldn't use it as an entrance and let people come in and out. If we did, she said, the luck that was coming into the house would just turn round and go out again. I don't know whether there's anything in it. But anyway, to be on the safe side, we blocked it off.

Who was she? A lady from Tabata who's been a devotee of Kōbō-sama for a long time. Yes, well, I did wonder whether she should know anything about Fudō-san. It is a different Path, after all. A Shinto god or a Buddha? Well, I think Fudō-san is a Buddha, but I don't know about Kōbō. In real life Kōbō was a famous priest, wasn't he, so I suppose he ought to count as a Buddha, but I'm not sure. I've never thought about it.

Nor is there any reason why she should think about it. A rough distinction is made between kami – Shinto gods whom one worships with a handclap, and hotoke – Buddhas *or* the spirits of dead ancestors – for whom one places one's hands quietly together in prayer and for whom sutra-recitation is appropriate, but by and large it is only Westerners with ethnocentric notions about religions being something you 'belong to' one at a time who would be much bothered about such niceties. At this level of magical assurance against bad luck, reassurance in tribulation, 'just-in-case' attempts to influence in one's favour those things which *do* seem to be a matter of chance, kami like the village protector shrine, the ujigami, and hotoke like Kōbō or Fudō, are hardly to be distinguished; all are possibly useful points of contact with a world beyond. The other kind of hotoke are the ancestors of the family. Rituals for the ancestors have much more important ethical implications with their symbolic affirmation of family and filial duties. But the ancestors too can be prayed to in the same manipulative spirit, and, in fact, most of the fears of the malevolence of spirits centre on ancestors who (projections, perhaps, of guilty feelings about some lapse in filial duty) are thought to take exception either to their descendant's ritual devotions, or to the way they are running their lives, squandering the family's property, or failing to sustain the family's prestige in the village. Some of the new sects of post-war Japan have, in effect, specialized in laying the ghosts of disgruntled ancestors, and built up a large following thereby, particularly of anxious, not to say neurotic, middle-aged women. They have devised elaborate rituals to give new posthumous names to the family's ancestors and re-write all their tablets for the family shrine. They offer new and uniquely efficacious prayers, too, and some of them – though this applies much more in the cities than in the countryside – congregational sociability as well.

Some of them also have ethical doctrines of some degree of sophistication. The connection between religion and ethics has been an off-and-on thing in Japan. Shinto priests almost never, and Buddhist priests only in some sects, have stepped beyond the role of ritual practitioner to assume that of moral guide and guardian. That job was largely left to the secular realm – to the head of the family and community, to the Confucian scholar and in modern times to the school. Nevertheless, these luck-manipulating, dark-force-allaying rituals are not entirely lacking in ethical content:

> No, I really don't bother with the ancestors. I never pray at the altar or offer incense. My wife goes up to look after the graves. But I'm not worried. After all, I've got nothing to regret. I did all in my power for my mother and the house. I got her a doctor when she was ill and bought a lot of expensive medicines. I wouldn't think I'd be subject to malevolent spirit attacks.
>
> Generally, I'm not one for praying. A lot of people go in for it though. They think they'll get something out of it. But that isn't what praying is supposed to be. Really the whole idea of praying is to pray to someone known for his fine actions, so that you can somehow make yourself a fine life like the kami you are praying to.

He was doubtless echoing an idea he had heard at school: the pre-war state authorities did indeed try to inject a strong ethical element into their refurbished Shinto. But there are also older traditions. Some Buddhist priests, too, used to preach homely folksy sermons once or twice a year – though no question there that any concern with morality should be at the expense of a magical approach to ritual.

When I was a little girl I remember the festival of the Great Perfection of Wisdom Sutra as being a really exciting occasion. A whole group of priests would come and their voices as they recited the sutra in chorus sounded really splendid. And all the old men and women would be nudging and shuffling up on their knees to get as close as they could to the Buddha and they would listen and pray and feel really 'arigatai' – really overwhelmed with goodness. Afterwards there would be a sermon and then a red-bean rice feast. Of course, only quite rich and respected temples could afford to have so many priests come. You should see the Shinkanin temple at Musashi village. It really is a splendid temple. There's a famous pine tree called the Dancing Crane Pine that is now a national treasure. I used to play under that tree when I was a girl.

What sort of sermons? Oh, I don't know. About filial piety and honesty. Yes, honesty . . . To be honest and healthy . . . Do you know the saying: 'In this un-reliable world, take tōfu as your guide [tōfu is the bean-curd which comes in white soft cubes]. Be serious [mame de is a pun for 'made of beans']. Be square [i.e. honest]. Be soft [in dealing with others].' Don't you think that's a good rule? That was the sort of thing.

The moral cohesion of society owes even less to specifically religious institutions in Japan than in most other industrial societies. Likewise the diffusion of scientific medical knowledge makes religion less and less relevant to health. Once, prayer was as reliable a cure as most competing alternatives. You grew old, you had a stroke, you survived half-paralysed and people said of you: 'Ah, poor man, he's had his time. I wonder how long it will be.' And all you could do was pray. But now, if you talk to, say, Masasada, one of the more valetudinarian of Shinohata's seventy-year-olds, he will tell you all about the difference be-tween animal fats and vegetable oils, cholesterol, the effect of salt, what alcohol does to the small blood vessels, and probably even recite to you his blood pressure readings for the last four of his weekly check-ups. Standards of health care seem very good in Shinohata village. Apart from the clinic service with about a dozen beds for in-patients at Kakizaka township centre three miles away, the doctor comes once a month to Shinohata to check blood pressure and urine. Preventive medicine is given due importance. In fact, the chief medical officer at the clinic recommends in one of the 1975 issues of the Kakizaka Township Newsletter that every home should have its blood pressure testing apparatus.

> A fifty-year-old man who had been 'in human dock' for a comprehensive medical check-up came out as pleased as punch to be told he had the body of a thirty-year-old – and then, that evening, died suddenly at a party. The fault lay in the fact that what they tested was the body at rest; they did *not* test the reactions of the human body eating and drinking rich food and wine at a party . . .
>
> It would be quite a good thing for every house to have a blood pressure apparatus just as everyone has a thermometer, so that members of the family could keep a check on each other, especially at abnormal times. During sexual intercourse some people's blood pressure goes up 90 points. So, a man with a pressure of 160 can go up to 250 at which point there is danger of a cerebral haemorrhage, so that taking the blood pressure in the home is quite important . . .

But still there remain things the doctors do not know (even if their skills do extend to checking their partner's blood pressure while making love). Illness is still fearful; diagnosis is uncertain. There remains the element of trust. There is still room for the charismatic healer, though he is likely, now, to be a modernized one who has assimilated – at least a pop-version of – the science on whose fringes he operates. He is likely to have more in common with macrobiotic foods and Canadian Air Force exercises than with traditional 'prayer ladies' and their trances. And he is likely to have his roots in town rather than in the country.

It was not a Shinohata villager but the visiting insurance agent whom I overheard proclaiming the virtues of his particular 'teacher'.

– You look very well, Mr Omura. You've put on weight.

– Yes, thank you. I wasn't very well four years ago. That's when I gave up alcohol and started doing exercises. I feel really fine now. I used to be 55 or 56 kilogrammes and it wasn't quite right, you know; I felt there was something lacking – physically. Now I'm sixty-two and that's just right.

The exercises are very simple really. Five minutes. You can do them lying on your bed. They were developed by Teacher Nakayama in Hachiōji. He's a very wise old man who's been doing this all his life. He believes, you see, that it's just a matter of mobilizing the life-forces within you. Everybody has enough power to overcome illness if only it can be mobilized. It all has to do with giving free play to the autonomic nervous system . . . the body's self-healing power. And he has extra power of his own, too. Even as a boy of thirteen, when one of his friends had hurt his arm and his mother was going to take him to a hospital, he said: 'Wait.' He felt the arm, touched it – and it was better.

It's amazing how simple it all is. To start with you just sit up straight, then relax with palms up and empty your mind, slumping forward a bit. You'll find, then, that quite naturally your body starts a gentle circular motion, and as this begins you then expand the motion with your conscious mind. It's strange, you know, that everybody has a different motion; some go more forward and backwards than from side to side; some are irregular; some fast, some slow. Teacher Nakayama can tell from this your basic physical tendency – what sort of illness you are likely to suffer from . . .

He then went on to describe some of Teacher Nakayama's cures like turning round a potential breech baby by talking to the foetus, and curing athlete's foot . . .

It's really quite simple. You just lie flat on your back and then you just put your weight on your shoulders and your back and raise your bottom in the air. Then, with the fingers of both hands you press the bone in each groin. If you've got athlete's foot one or the other is bound to hurt. You then press harder for just twenty seconds. Then you flop back and relax completely on the floor. And that's it. That's the cure.

16

Harmony and its Tensions: The Day the Fire Brigade Went Fishing

The first night of Nobufumi's roof-raising parties, it will be remembered, was a stormy one. People were calling each other 'black-hearted bastard' and other such nasty names.

> It's amazing, really, how some people change when they're drunk and surrounded by a lot of people. They seem to go out of their mind, sometimes, but they know really that they're safe, because if they provoke the other chap to violence there are enough people there to keep them apart. And the next morning they'll be all smiles and greet each other as if nothing happened. But the one who spoke his mind will know the other one will remember what he said. He'll have got his point home. In fact people – you could see it – often used to come to a party with the express intention of picking a quarrel and getting something off their chest. It doesn't happen so much now, though. There aren't so many village gatherings for one thing.

The 'harmony of the village' has its cost. Underneath the placid landscape there are geological faults – a personal incompatibility, a clash of economic interest, a belief that one has been cheated – along which tensions build up which require occasional release. Shinohata, in that sense, is a relatively quake-free zone and has become more so: the tensions rarely become unmanageable, a good deal more rarely than they used to. But, to hark back again to the 'nature' and 'artifice' distinction, the 'harmony of the village' is a product of artifice. It is not maintained without a good deal of conscious self-restraint, the careful avoidance of possible sources of tension, and purposeful, even frantic, efforts at mediation whenever conflict breaks out into the open – as happened when the fire brigade went fishing, of which more in a moment.

One source of difficulty is the mixing of neighbourly relations with economic contractual relations. Neither a borrower nor a lender be – nor buyer and seller. A widow and her daughter who made most of their living by dressmaking in 1955 tried to avoid doing anything for Shinohata neighbours. Neighbours might expect a concessionary rate: might gossip about grasping people if one charged the ordinary market price.

Tenancy was another cause of some awkwardness in the post-land-reform period. Traditionally there were clear long-established (and by any reasonable standard exploitative) norms – it was accepted that landlords took half the crop. But there have not been such clear market rates since, and for a long while, in fact, there was an unenforced legal maximum rate which, in spite of its being by common consent unrealistically low, the prospective tenant might take – or be thought to be taking – as having some validity. The uncertainty led to considerable awkwardness. The 'stiff-necked' Sanetoshi who had rented out an upland field for 3,000 yen a year for ten years felt that with inflation and the general rise in rents the tenant should have come along and offered him the 6,000 yen or so that he believed was commonly being paid for new leases now. He was also a little upset that, in the eighth year of the contract, the man was planting chestnuts and assuming the lease would be renewed. But, between neighbours, it was awkward to say anything. Affluence, of course, makes this reticence easier. One does not so easily forebear to press one's economic advantage in a bargain when one is close to subsistence. That is one reason why conflict is less common now.

Apart from transactions of this kind which have in the nature of the case to be overtly bargained, it is sometimes difficult to know the dividing line between the ordinary obligations of neighbourliness and very special favours which require special requital – and how much requital. Differences in assessment, behind-the-back mutterings about niggardliness or ingratitude, can easily result. And for some, the careful avoidance of such relationships is the answer. Chikayoshi had considerable mechanical experience in factories and in the army.

> Repair my own tractor? No. If you do that you end up 'clever-poor'. All the neighbours start coming to ask you just to take a look at their machine. They think nothing of it. They're not particularly grateful. You lose a lot of time and you use up your spare parts.

'A great man for service to the community – when it shows, not otherwise' was one neighbour's comment on Chikayoshi. But the point is that even Chikayoshi's grudgingness was accompanied by sufficient recognition of the obligations of neighbourliness to make it difficult for him to give himself the benefit of his own skills without sharing them with his neighbours.

Conflicts over more substantial matters like the ownership of land (the boundaries of forest land are often very unclear and the hills immediately behind Shinohata are a chequerboard maze of tiny plots) are usually settled eventually by a go-between's mediation. I have heard of only one dispute ever being fought through the official civil courts – by the implacable O-Sada when she was twenty years younger than I described her in Chapter 2.

Similarly people prefer not to make an issue of the rare real offence – of theft or arson. Most people know something of the story of the burning down of Katsunori's house in his grandfather's day, sixty years ago. It was generally believed that it was the work of the neurotic old lady next door, mad with jealousy at the way Katsunori's house was flourishing under his grandfather's headship, when her own, in the hands of her rather uninspired son, was declining.

> It was envy, I suppose, that's about the size of it. But in our house, well, what was the good? Our house was burned down, after all. You get somebody arrested for arson and that only causes more trouble. So in the end we just had it registered as an accidental fire. But everybody knew. In those days you were liable to a fine for negligence if you burned your house down with an

accidental fire, but we weren't given a fine. That shows that everybody understood.

It is a far cry from those Mediterranean villages where vengeance is a central value and feuding that which gives life its zest. But, of course, not everybody is so perfectly controlled that he can see his house burned down and exercise such politic restraint. There are exceptions, people who have little or no scruple, and they can profit considerably from the scruples of others.

The role of licensed bully in Shinohata society is a curious one. I have known two. One is the richest man in the village, the ex-landlord, of whom more in the next chapter. The other was Motonori, who during the period when I knew him was probably the poorest man in the village.

Motonori was born poor, younger son of one of Shinohata's poorest families; in fact the closest Shinohata had to a 'low-caste' family: it had occupied the semi-hereditary position of servants to the Shinohata priest. Numerous were the stories of Motonori's delinquencies too. He had gone to work in some kind of family enterprise in Hokkaido. He returned at the age of twenty-one for his triumphant entry to adulthood, his conscription medical, magnificently dressed in long overcoat with fur collar and voluminous sleeves, a splendid hakama skirt below, a new kimono with silken sash. He made a great impression – until the police arrived two days later accompanied by his previous employer who had come all the way from Hokkaido to reclaim his stolen property. Motonori disappeared thereafter into the towns, but the war and the destruction of the towns brought him back to a hut in the corner of one of his brother's fields. Had his kleptomania been cured? Some were sure it hadn't. *Somebody* had broken into Morishige's storehouse and taken half the large stock of fine kimono Morishige had bartered for black-market rice. And soon after the same thing happened at Shijūrō's. And there was the affair of O-Sada's old lady's best coat – her funeral haori. O-Sada's old lady was the oldest inhabitant with the black-painted teeth mentioned earlier. She was a raconteur of no mean gifts. Alas, I missed ever hearing her version of the story and got it only second-hand.

You know the way the old lady talks: 'I came back from the funeral,' she said, 'and I was just taking my haori off when who should come but Mieko wanting me to go up to the shrine, so I thought this old lady shouldn't ever say no to going to a shrine, and off I went and put my haori down in a corner without properly putting it away.' And she came back and it was gone. So she went to pray to Kōbōsama and sure enough Kōbō came to her in her dream and said: 'A man with bushy eyebrows. Came from the south.' Well, there was only one person that could be, and she told everybody till Motonori got to hear of it and he came along. My, he could be fierce with those thick bushy eyebrows. You should hear the old lady tell you how her stomach intestines turned upside down. But actually he was smooth: 'Look, old lady,' he said, 'I don't like being falsely accused. Will you come with me to a diviner so that we can get this thing sorted out?'

So they went – right across the valley and up to Kataoka on the other side. 'I've never been so frightened in all my life,' the old lady said, 'as when we were going across the bridge. I was sure he was going to push me in.' But they got there, anyhow, and the diviner did his business and said the haori had gone for ever and it had passed to the hand of a woman. So the old lady said: Nonsense; she didn't know any woman with bushy eyebrows and the diviner was unreliable and her Kōbō was better and anyway she'd seen Motonori whispering something to him just before they started, and it was all a put-up job. And all this time Motonori, the usually fierce Motonori, just went on quietly pleading – which the old lady said was sure proof he was guilty.

(For those interested in evidence and verification, that was the 1955 version. The same informant's 1975 version had the old lady going to the diviner alone – graphic description of old lady setting out, bent double, supported by her tall staff, her lunch box tied in a wrapping cloth and hung round her neck – only to see, as she arrived, the wily Motonori, who had obviously been fixing things, slipping out of the diviner's back door.)

But Motonori, for all his poverty, had a great gift – his eloquence. Combined with craft and effrontery it was a winning combination. More, it was half a livelihood. During the last stages of the war, people started doing all sorts of unpatriotic things they were somewhat shamefaced about, like selling rice on the black market. They did not escape Motonori's eye. He would put on his most portentous manner and go to offer them a lecture on public morals, the duty of the citizen – and the inevitability of being found out and inviting the wrath of the authorities. He would come away loaded with 'hush gifts'.

After the war, as he gathered years and gravitas, his power in the village increased. He was known, tolerantly and half fearfully, as the Shinohata MacArthur, or – for the effect of his bushy eyebrows was now enhanced by a shining pate – as the Bald-headed General. Still his sole worldly possessions were a hut in the corner of his brother's field, now a vineyard, and a small plot of land on which he grew exotic flowers, all carefully labelled, and kept rabbits which he weighed every day, recording the results on graph paper. He was always happy to discourse on the underlying aims of US foreign policy or the causes of juvenile delinquency, was always unhurried, and always gave the impression of enjoying life greatly. He pieced together an income from various sources. He organized, in those pre-television days, periodic film shows in the village hall. (As a social service to raise the cultural level of the village.) There were those happy days in the forests, gathering bees nests and catching the adders which he pickled in saké and turned into a highly marketable aphrodisiac. Sometimes, with great dignity – but with a certain unmistakable firmness – he would tell Katsunori's wife, the voluntary welfare officer, that his property-lessness did indeed qualify him for poor relief benefit, and that in these days, when rights were as important as duties, and duties as important as rights, he would be obliged to accept it. But above all, as a source of income, there was his eloquence. A ticklish debt to be collected? A son in trouble with the police? Is Kentarō moving the boundary stone in the forest to take in a few saplings that are really yours? The Shinohata MacArthur was always delighted to be of service, and if he thought that your subsequent thank-you gift was too little, he would always be perfectly open and frank about it.

Democracy, too, brought its blessings in the form of frequent elections. Motonori's eloquence was so convincing that no conservative candidate (unless forewarned) could ever have doubted Motonori's claim to be able to deliver a full twenty-five votes, nor questioned what he said about money: that of course there was no question of selling votes, that it was a matter of mutual esteem, that the candidate was well known not to be the sort of person so devoid of a sense of propriety as not gratefully to acknowledge favours done to him, that the loyalty of those particular voters was a shining example to all, given that so many candidates were operating in the very same village and quite openly buying votes – and for as much as 300 yen too . . .

And it was not only with outsiders that Motonori's eloquence was effective. With Shinohata's other bully, the wealthy Gontarō, he ingratiated himself. Gontarō's coercive style was bluster, somewhat high-pitched and uncertain and clearly needing the backing of his wealth to be effective. Motonori's, by contrast, came from inner sources, a resonant voice, a sturdy physique: he had gravitas. Gontarō recognized this and responded to Motonori's ingratiating approaches. With his backing, in 1955, Motonori became one of the two co-opted members who, together with the chief, past chief, and next year's chief designate of the hamlet made up the hamlet council. From there, at the end of the year, he became chief agent for Shinohata's candidate in the Kakizaka township elections – for fear, everybody said, of what he could do to the campaign as spoiler if he were alienated by being denied the post. (See the story quoted earlier about the way some of the money entrusted to him went astray: not a word of reprimand was addressed directly to Motonori.)

It was his membership of the hamlet council which ensured that Motonori should play a large role in the affair that began on the day the fire brigade went fishing, an affair which revealed all the consternation which open and widespread conflict can cause in Shinohata and how difficult it is to mend things once the integument of harmony is broken.

It all began one sleepy July afternoon in 1955. Many people were, in fact, asleep, enjoying a siesta inside their mosquito nets, away from the flies. A few were pottering at after-lunch chores in their back yard; even fewer out in the fields. Somebody with keen hearing caught the ringing of a distant bell. In a matter of seconds rather than minutes, the bell of the next hamlet was ringing too and by then the man with the keen hearing had reached Shinohata's fire tower and he too began to pull at the bell rope, tolling out frantic emergency peals loud enough to get the siesta-takers out of their mosquito nets. Everyone between twenty-five and thirty-five years old in the village rushed to the fire hut (those out in the fields dashing home first so they could seize their blue and red happi coat and braid cap and appear properly dressed). The hand pump was wheeled out, and they set off at a trot down the stony path, the fire pump with its iron-hoop wheels and crude springs bumping behind them. They were directed from hamlet to hamlet towards the source of the original bell which proved to be a village at least forty minutes away. But it was a minor blaze. The Shinohata detachment was only half way there when it was greeted with the disappointing news that the fire was out. The youngest member was left in charge of the pump. The others went on to offer fraternal commiserations, to see if there were any lessons which the Shinohata team should learn from this experience of its fellow firefighters – and to share in the 'purification saké' which the owner of the half burned-out barn was bound to provide to anyone who turned up in a red and blue happi coat.

And that was all very well, but by the time the Shinohata brigade had got back to the village and stored the pump away, they were all stone sober again – which is no way to round off a day of public service. Fortunately it was found that the fire brigade budget (at that time a sixth of total hamlet expenditure; see page 208) could stand another party this year. Or at least it could stand several bottles of sweet-potato shōchū, but as for anything more substantial, a few tins of pilchards were the best that could be managed. Someone had a bright idea. There was a moon; there were fish in the Muddy River. Why not a riverside barbecue?

They set off for the woods behind the village to the point where a broad irrigation channel branched off from the main river. Fishing, in Shinohata, is an essentially pragmatic affair, the purpose being to catch fish rather than to exercise arcane skills. 'When one catches the fish, one does not question the trap' as Chuang Tzu is supposed to have said to a fellow philosopher in China in the fourth century BC. The fire brigade had a simple method. They cut off the water leading into the irrigation channel, and with a few minutes' tickling in the remaining isolated pools between the rocks a respectable number of modest fish were soon being roasted on wire spikes over a crackling fire.

The trouble was that in their excitement the fire brigade forgot to adjust the weir and send the water back down the channel again. That would not perhaps have mattered very much except for the fact that the channel did not just supply irrigation water to Shimogawa, the next village down. It was also the source which fed the channels running past each Shimogawa house that gave cooking water and washing water to every villager, that fed their water wheels and the creaking battari hammer machines that pounded rice.

So there was some consternation in Shimogawa when the familiar sound of rushing water died away and the creaking battari gave one last final thud at the rice meal and lapsed into silence. The vice-chief of the hamlet called on the chief for consultation. They decided that duty demanded an investigation.

They had not gone far upstream when the sound of raucous singing gave them an inkling of the cause of the trouble. When they arrived on the scene and peered from behind a tree there was no need to use their electric torches to recognize in the light of the fires the braid caps and the blue and red happi of the Shinohata fire brigade. They noted also the presence of the chief, the two vice-chiefs and one or two of the ex-chiefs, now advisers, of the Shinohata fire brigade.

They considered the situation. They were two and sober. The enemy was fifteen and intoxicated. Discretion and optimism both suggested that the dam would soon be removed in any case and the best thing would be to go home and sleep on it. And sure enough, after an hour or so, the brooks began to rustle again and the battari once more took up its wheezing, thudding, creaking work of pounding the rice.

At six-thirty the next morning the headman of Shimogawa visited the headman of Shinohata to make representations. He described last night's happenings and lodged a formal complaint. In what precise terms he lodged his complaint, however, no one will ever know. Therein lay the source of the whole turmoil into which the village was about to be plunged.

It was unfortunate that the incident should have happened in the year when Katsuo was headman of the village. Katsuo had many estimable qualities, but he did tend to take his duties and himself rather seriously. Not surprisingly, perhaps, since he had spent the greater part of his life as a naval officer and navies generally expect their officers to take their duties and themselves seriously. He had not, he said, much wanted the job of headman. It had been part of his family tradition not to take office ever since his great-great-grandfather had died of a heart attack on the very day the village archives passed into his hands. But people were so insistent, and he felt that perhaps he should set an example by discarding old superstitions . . . Having taken the job he carried out his duties with meticulous conscientiousness. The accounts were a model of careful bookkeeping. He carried out a stock-taking of village property, recording the last chip on the last tea cup. He kept a log-book, which recorded every happening in the village which should legitimately come to the headman's notice. He saw to it that the dignity of the village was preserved in all its external relations and always put on a collar and tie to greet the meanest sanitary inspector from the Prefecture. And he was careful to follow democratic procedures. The protest from Shimogawa was clearly not one to be dealt with on his own sole responsibility. He called a village council.

The meeting lasted five hours. Tomezō did not say very much – he never does, which is why he was for a period such a successful village mayor. Nor did Saburō, the deputy headman and headman designate for next year who before the land reform was a tenant farmer and had not quite got used to the idea that his new position as a relatively prosperous owner-cultivator gave him a voice in village affairs. But five hours was hardly sufficient to give full scope to the eloquence of the Shinohata MacArthur.

It was on such occasions that Motonori came into his own. His gloss on Katsuo's hesitant explanations of the seriousness of the situation was, as he retailed it to me the next day, pure eloquence. The concomitant responsibilities which go with all rights in a situation of social co-existence; support and be supported; the duty of man to neighbouring man and of village to neighbouring village; the evils of egotism and irresponsibility; the importance of water in the social and economic conditions of Japanese rural communities; the ideal of public service embodied in the Constitution of the fire brigade; and, of course, democracy – all these were dealt with at length. On these matters he carried the meeting with him, but there was a practical question to be decided. The honour of the village had been besmirched. Should they require that the fire brigade chief submit a written apology duly signed and sealed with the promise of future good behaviour? Or would a verbal apology suffice?

Moderation eventually prevailed. Perhaps it would be too much to treat a grown man of thirty-five as a delinquent schoolboy. A verbal apology was deemed sufficient and at six-thirty the next morning a delegation including the penitent and abashed fire brigade chief visited the headman of Shimogawa to express its deepest regrets.

But by the time the fire brigade chief returned to the village there was anger, not sackcloth and ashes, in his heart. The gentle old headman of Shimogawa had expressed embarrassed surprise at their visit. 'Oh, but no really . . . This is very polite but you shouldn't have . . .' The truth was revealed. Katsuo's talk of 'strong protest' was pure invention. Sticks were being made out of needles. Katsuo was throwing his weight about. Doubtless it was all spite. He had never forgiven the fire brigade for the incident after Gorō's wedding two years before. What if some of the lads were singing songs up and down the lane and were a little tight? And what if they did dispute the right of way with a truck driver who came along? How were they to know it was Katsuo's firewood they were throwing off the lorry? A reasonable man would have realized that such things happen after weddings and forgotten all about it.

Within an hour after his return the chief of the Shinohata fire brigade had presented his resignation. The district chief of the township fire brigade system was my host Atsushi, so I was strategically placed to observe the events. The letter of resignation was a rather splendid affair: neatly inscribed on a roll of the paper used for pasting on partition doors with a new brush and in the blackest of ink. 'Watakushi gi,' it read, in the most formal of epistolary styles, 'isshinjō no tsugō ni yori . . .' – 'The undersigned, for personal reasons, is desirous of relinquishing his post as chief of the Shinohata fire brigade and requests that you will give due consideration thereto.'

Nor did matters end there. That evening the fire-bell summoned a general meeting which soon decided to express its solidarity with its ill-treated leader and by midnight two more pieces of shōji paper were in the hands of the district chief, one bearing the joint resignations of the three vice-chiefs and another – for the proprieties of status-distinctions were strictly observed – that of the entire rank and file, imposingly rounded off with thirty-four signatures and thirty-four thumbprints. The evening ended with a procession bearing braid caps and blue and red happi coats which solemnly wended its way to Katsuo's house to request that he, as headman of the village, should take over responsibility for this village property which they would no longer be needing.

A little intemperate abuse when drunk at a party is one thing; sober, open, implacable hostility and a situation of deadlock is quite another. One or two people such as Motonori clearly enjoyed themselves, but most people, and certainly those involved, were distinctly unhappy.

For four days, formally and unofficially, Shinohata had no fire brigade. The district fire brigade chief and other respected elder villagers joined in attempts to mediate, and by the end of the third day they seemed to be successful. The chief and the three vice-chiefs, now somewhat chastened, had been persuaded that their gesture having been made the time had come for a settlement. They agreed to call a meeting of the fire brigade the next morning and recommend the withdrawal of resignations.

But the young bloods of the fire brigade were far from chastened. Nothing less than an apology from Katsuo would suffice. Katsuo appeared and refused to apologize. He withdrew in high dudgeon at the very suggestion, giving the other members of the village council to understand that he washed his hands of the matter and they must do the best they could.

Forty able-bodied men spent eight hours of that fine working day in tense discussion. In June, to be sure, there was not so much urgent work to be done in the fields, but many of them were sacrificing a day's paid work in the forests or elsewhere. Plenary session disintegrated into small groups and re-coagulated again. Fractional elements took time off for base-ball practice but always came back. And, as an indication of the seriousness of the situation, nothing stronger than tea passed the lips of a single one of them.

Eventually it was Motonori's eloquence which saved the day. He had not read his ethics textbooks at school in vain. Har-mony, co-operation, give and take, the best of motives often misunderstood, high spirits of youth, understanding the other man's point of view, the danger of allowing private emotions to interfere with public duties. Perhaps, he was not saying there was, but it is possible that . . . a certain malice . . . some exag-geration . . . It became clear that he was apologizing. And by four o'clock in the afternoon the desire for some sort of solution was general. After all, either one is working or one is sitting around. And if one is sitting around one wants something stronger than tea to sit around with. Resignations, it was agreed, should be withdrawn. A forage party was despatched to the Co-operative and within half an hour hands had been clapped as a token of mutual accord and a happy fire brigade and a happy village council were gulping tea-cups full of shōchū, eating sembei piled on sheets of newspaper and prising pilchards through the jagged lids of tins.

Peace and harmony prevailed in all hearts except one. Katsuo, who had earlier retired from the negotiations in high dudgeon, remained in it for the rest of the day, and when he heard that an armistice had been reached on the basis of an admission by his fellow councillors that he had been in the wrong his dudgeon became higher. He had been betrayed; the principle of collective responsibility had been infringed; right had given way to might. He would resign. There was a technical difficulty because he had no one to hand his resignation to. He could do no more than delegate his powers to his deputy with the intimation that he no longer intended to fulfil the functions of his office.

Most people were inclined to the view that having made his gesture Katsuo would eventually resume his duties. But they reckoned without his obstinate sense of rectitude. He insisted that he had been doing no more than follow what he conceived to be his duty – to lead the delinquent spirits of the fire brigade

into paths of decency and sober citizenship. And that the council which at first supported him should have apologized on his
behalf was shameful and irresponsible. His indignation was
unbounded.

Every night the other members of the council waited on him,
but not even the eloquence of Motonori could turn him, nor the
prestige of the elder and respected members of the village
whom they enlisted in their support. The distress level, though
somewhat lower than when the whole fire brigade had resigned,
remained high. Divisions grew as people took up positions.
There were those who supported him; the fire brigade were a
bad lot, they said, all right as individuals, but when three or
four were gathered together in their braid caps and their happi
the devil got into them. Katsuo had done the right thing and he
had been shamefully treated. But the general feeling was critical.
No doubt there were faults on both sides, but Katsuo was
carrying it a bit far. He should know that a village is different
from a battleship; there are times when you have to bend to the
general will, when it is no good 'sticking out horns', 'putting
on corners', or 'refusing to bend your backside'.

Inconclusive day followed inconclusive day until the time of
my departure came round. I had spent a month visiting every
house asking about experiences in the land reform, and I had
been contemplating holding a party in the village hall to say
thank you for everyone's co-operation. But that required the
approval and co-operation of the headman.

Discussing the matter with my host, Atsushi, it seemed
that we might turn the occasion to advantage. Perhaps,
if Katsuo could be persuaded to preside at my party as headman,
that might prove the turning point. I must go to see Katsuo.
My speech was carefully rehearsed. I especially liked the phrase:
'that which has a beginning must have an ending' and used it
several times. Katsuo, as headman, had presided at the meeting
when I explained myself to the villagers soon after I arrived.
Katsuo was the only one who – as headman – could preside at
the party for my departure. I spoke of the sadness of leaving
with the thought that all was not well in Shinohata, of how
much I was indebted to him for all his instruction, for the way
he had smoothed my path . . .

But Katsuo was not easily moved. He stood in an attitude of

deep contrition. He was sorry, truly sorry, that this should have happened to mar the delight of my visit, that I should carry away such an unfortunate impression of village self-government, that certain turbulent elements should have behaved in such a way that . . . I must know the whole story and how he had felt compelled to take responsibility for the outrage committed against Shinohata; how he had resigned in token of his awareness of the deficiencies in his own leadership which had allowed such deplorable events to take place. He could not apologize too much. He would, however, be glad to attend my party. 'But, as headman,' I insisted. He would say no more than that he would consider the matter.

When he arrived at the hall I thought perhaps that his formal black kimono, contrasting with everyone else's shirtsleeves, meant that the point was won. But clearly it was not so. He carefully avoided the top position. Ignoring the urgings of the other members of the council, he sat three places down so that the deputy chief and ex-mayor Katsunori were between him and where I had been placed in the 'co-top' position. However, the fact that cushions slide on the tatami mats gives seating positions a certain flexibility. Tomezō got up, ostensibly to supervise the placing of the bottles and casually pushed his cushion back out of the way. The deputy on my side pulled and Motonori on the other side pushed. Katsuo was now only two positions down. Every one was assembled. The bottles were unstopped, heaps of multicoloured rice cakes were piled on the newspapers. There was an air of expectancy. The deputy stealthily got up and reinserted himself lower down. The gap was unfortunate, but Katsuo was now indubitably in top place. The members of the council sought Katsuo's eyes. Motonori nudged him. The buzz of talk died away and all eyes flickered from the bottles to Katsuo and from Katsuo back to the bottles.

It was too much for him. But he had too much dignity to show that his opening remarks were made under protest. As the evening wore on he even began to show a certain heavy jollity. In my honour he sang 'God Save' as he called it. (The navy, he explained, had always been close to British traditions.) He looked on with an air of almost benevolence when turbulent spirits of the fire brigade began singing ribald ditties. Perhaps it was only the effect of the synthetic saké grade four but I felt sure that reconciliation had been achieved.

My illusions were somewhat shattered as Katsuo accompanied me home. He was glad I had enjoyed my stay. It had been nice having me. The people of Shinohata were nice people – most of them. There were, however, delinquent elements, the members of the fire brigade, for instance, a tough and irresponsible lot, a menace to respectable citizens – some of them, even – and he lowered his voice as he spoke the words that had sent people to gaol and brainwashing thought-reform in the 1930s – 'had bad thoughts'.

I later heard that it was a full fifteen days before Katsuo eventually 'bent his backside'. Four bottles of grade-four saké left over from my party had come in handy to celebrate the outbreak of peace.

I saw Katsuo again only once, several years later in the Kakizaka clinic, two days before he eventually died of stomach cancer. Neither the disease nor the bits of apparatus plugged into him had robbed him of his dignity.

democracy they have been collected according to a nicely calculated formula – 40 per cent by equal levies on all households,
30 per cent according to the previous year's local government
income-tax assessment, and 30 per cent according to the
property-tax assessment. (There is no secret about these
assessments, incidentally; the township office gives them to the
hamlet chief as a matter of course and no one objects. The lack
of what in other societies might be valued as 'privacy' is part
of what it means to be a 'member' of a community like
Shinohata.)

The formula takes account – partially – of differences in current financial standing, but I never caught any suggestion that
the higher contributors claimed any superior rights by virtue
of their larger contribution – any more than a progressive
national income tax is commonly argued to give the higher tax
payers the right to a second vote.

Similarly, no one had a prescriptive right to be a headman of
the village any more. Exactly when is not quite certain, but it
was probably before the end of the last century that the old
Tokugawa system of hereditary headmen gave way to a system
of annual rotation. Even so, before the war, perhaps not as
many as half of the house-heads could have aspired to the
honour of becoming headman. They could not hold their heads
high enough for that. Besides, they could not have afforded it.

> Father was elected headman at the age of twenty-
> nine, which was young even for those days, when there
> were not a lot of houses that could afford to do it. It
> was no fun being headman then. When you were
> elected you had to have the whole village to your house
> for a party: there was no village hall then. We had to
> cook mountains of rice and prepare all sorts of side
> dishes and provide saké. There were no hamlet funds
> for entertaining then. Money was so precious in those
> days: ten yen was all you got for a bale of rice . . .

Greater affluence, a greater concern for equality, the citizen's
hall, the practice of budgeting modestly for hamlet parties out
of communal funds – all these innovations of the post-war
years had made a big difference. To be sure, I remember Saburō
telling me when he was elected in 1955 – and telling me with

considerable pride, because until the land reform he was almost entirely without land and would never have dreamed of becoming headman – how he had been saving up to buy his own thresher, but was holding off now because being headman was bound to cost him a certain amount of money. But the expense of being a headman is a burden which no one need be much daunted by. Nowadays the position is open to all. The office circulates largely on a seniority basis, usually coming to a man around the age of forty-five – though Wataru and Shigeyasu are well over fifty and still uncrowned, and Hidezō was appointed at the age of thirty-nine. The difference, anyone in Shinohata would tell you, is a matter of personality: Wataru, with his slightly wild-man shyness, has not sought the job; Shigeyasu has, but with the sort of clownish lightweight eagerness which confirms his general reputation for tipsy unreliability. Hidezō, on the other hand, was a keen Shinohata man, solemn and public-spirited, full of plans for hamlet development works. It is *also* true that Wataru belongs to a family of traditionally very low status and Hidezō to one of the former landlord families (Shigeyasu's was of middling standing). It seems highly unlikely that ancestry has much to do with it, however, except in so far as their family's standing in the village at the time when they grew up probably had a good deal to do with the shaping of their personalities, respectively cramping or enlarging their conception of themselves, their self-confidence and their capacity to give an impression of gravitas.

In all the formal institutions of Shinohata, then – all those things that are explicitly regulated by people sitting down and consciously taking decisions about them – the principle of equality of citizenship reigns supreme. The trouble (*mild* trouble, as we shall see, but still trouble) lies in certain conventions which, although highly formalized, are not of the sort that people normally sit down and take decisions about, and which consequently have rather greater inertia. There are certain patterns of relations between families which fall into the category commonly called 'patron–client' relationships, and which were established and took their conventional forms before the dawn of the age of equality.

They date from a time when it was taken as axiomatic that men are of unequal worth and that in all social microcosms hierarchical order is proper order. But further – and this was what distinguished Japan from many other societies – they reflect the assumption that the proper relationship between those of high and those of low status is not one of aloofness, or avoidance, or impersonal exploitation, but of paternalism and dependency – that archetypal relationship of feudal societies which consists in the exchange of benevolent protection on the one hand for loyal service on the other.

There were two kinds of such relationships, the first being part of the kinship system, and the second a 'pure' kind of clientage.

The former is very simply related to the primogeniture inheritance system which became almost universal in farming communities from the seventeenth century onwards. Primogeniture *inheritance* is not quite right, of course, given the notion – a little more explicit in Japan than among the British artistocracy, though the similarity is great – that property belongs to the 'house' and that what is passed on from father to son is not property but the headship of the house. The headship normally passed to the eldest son (or to the 'adopted husband' of an eldest daughter if there were no sons). What happened, then, to younger sons? At a time when death rates more or less kept up with birth rates, a high proportion could hope to be adopted – that is to say they could hope for an heirship and eventually headship of an existing family unit which happened not to have sons. An alternative was to set them up in an entirely new family, a cadet branch of the existing main family. This was the preferred solution, in fact, for families which had a lot of land. A small proportion – rarely as much as a third – of the family's land would be allocated to the new cadet branch of the family. It would have built for it a modest house. The branching might take place when the younger son married (usually at a fairly advanced age), sometimes even later, after he *and* his wife had lived in and 'done service to' the main house for anything up to ten or fifteen years.

The relationship between the 'great house' and the 'new house' (as they are called in Shinohata) continued in principle for ever. The house-heads were brothers in the first generation, first cousins in the second, and umpteenth cousins in the ninth, but that made no difference. The tie was not a tie between persons, but between households. It was also a tie with an inbuilt inequality. The 'new house' remained for always ritually subordinate. After the first generation it had its own ancestors, but more remote common ancestors were commemorated in the shrine at the 'great house' and it was there that the family from the 'new house' went on feast days to pay its respects both to the ancestors and to the ancestors' most direct lineal descendant, the current head of the great house. Everything fitted together nicely if the new house remained economically dependent on the great house, too – and since it started life on an exiguous allowance of land, the odds were that it would. The principle was that the great house must remain strong, so that it could always be a source of strength and leadership for all its new houses. And indeed, in many northern villages one used to find large and solidary 'clans' made up of a great house and anything up to twenty new houses, some of one or two generations standing, some claiming to have branched fifteen or more generations back. Usually, a precondition for their keeping their close-knit group character was that the great house retained its economic supremacy and *could* dispense benevolences of one kind or another to the subordinate new families, a favourable tenancy, say, or an interest-free loan, or help in fixing a creditable marriage. These benevolences gave the great house the right to command the labour of its new houses, often on exploitative terms, and thus retain its economic supremacy. It was the sort of self-sustaining system that gladdens the heart of functionalist sociologists, whether of the Marxist or non-Marxist persuasion.

It was not quite perfect, however. As a system of mutual support and social security – or alternatively of exploitation and false consciousness – it had its merits, but also its flaws. When the head of the great house is a gawky teenager and the head of a new house a venerable old man, there can be strains in the respect relationship, though sufficient differences in wealth can take care of that problem. Much more problematic is what happens when the differences in wealth themselves alter. A dissolute improvident house-head for one generation, and the supremacy of a great house could be entirely wiped out. Much less dramatic shifts over a few decades gradually made some new houses richer and some great houses poorer. Thence discordance and cognitive dissonance. The ritual and social sub-ordination of the new house implicit in the unchangeable genealogical facts clashed with the economic reality that if there was any economic dependency it was the great house which was the supplicant. Subtly to recast the genealogical facts was one common way out, but not necessarily an easy one unless the great-house was in such straits that whatever grandmother went on saying about what she very clearly remembered having heard from her grandmother, the house-head was prepared to shush her up, swallow pride and accept a fictional subordinate status in the hope that the *nouveau riche* in the new house would be generous when accorded great-house status.

It was probably because of the awkward inflexibility of these great-house–new-house relationships – the fact that one tended to get stuck with them long after they were really useful for economic, social-security purposes – that in the region to which Shinohata belonged there had grown up a secondary pattern of patron–client relationships which did not depend on a kinship 'charter'. The words used for the two sides of the relationship mean literally 'parent role' and 'child role', but since almost any translation sounds bizarre, I shall use the Japanese words 'oyabun' and 'kobun'.

These oyabun–kobun ties were essentially like great-house–new-house ties in terms of rituals and respect *and* economic dependency, but were entered into by choice, by an act of 'commendation' on the part of the kobun – to use the closest equivalent European term, the word which describes the formal act by which lesser feudal lords put themselves and their lands under the protection of a greater lord and accepted a vassalship from him.

Most ties of dependency and service in Shinohata, at least over the last century, were concentrated in these oyabun–kobun links, rather than in the great house–new house relation. This did not mean that great house and new house considerations entirely lost their importance, but they were important mostly for pure status reasons. Shinohata people, especially the older generation, are very susceptible to pride of ancestry. One ex-pression of the new affluence is a rash of large stones of Chinese black marble in the village graveyard – expensive imports recently costing anything up to $2,000. One family had had the whole of its ancestral roll carved on its stone, going back several generations to the late eighteenth century. Others had more modest stones 'to all the ancestors of the XX family' and rested their claims to antiquity on the sheer number of traditional mossy commemorative stones in the family plot, sometimes backed by theories, à propos of the more illegible ones, that according to a certain professor at such and such university, stones of such a particular shape could not be less than 300 years old. New houses normally started their family grave plots fairly close to their great house's plot, but if the branching had taken place many generations back, there was no clear proof from the graveyard as to which was which, and in one or two cases rivalry for the status of great house resulted.

However such rivalry was not usually carried to open confrontation, but confined, rather, to the nobbling of third parties for bitter complaint about the rival's pretensions. I once came across Hisayō (whose stories of her family's great fire and rebuilding I told on pages 30–31 in the graveyard running her finger in the faint grooves of a memorial stone trying – for the umpteenth time without success – to read the name. It was a monstrous story, she told me, after some hesitation. This was a very, very old stone. Once it used to be in her family plot. One day she came to tend the family graves and was alarmed to see one stone less than there should have been in her family enclosure. She looked around. Sure enough, there was a stone that looked familiar in Kanetsugu's plot adjoining hers. Kanetsugu's family was an old new house of her family, though actually they claimed that *they* were the great house and hers had been a new house. So now they were resorting to gravestone theft to prove their point. She had gone away steaming, but uncertain what to do about it. The next time she came the stone had been properly cemented to a base in the next plot and looked as if it belonged there. What could a poor widow do? Nothing, absolutely nothing, except come up here occasionally and light a stick of incense to her poor stolen ancestor. Kanetsugu would see the incense sticks. He would know ... If only she could make out these faint illegible characters ...

The other well-known rivalry in the village concerned two families both of which were among the pre-war top four upper-crust families. Here the basic facts seemed not to be in dispute.

Hidezō's was the great house; O-Sada's family was founded as a branch new house some six generations back. But according to O-Sada,

> The trouble was that our founder – he was the third son – was a fine person, much better than his older brother who took over the great house. And their parents loved him – our founder – much better. They would come across here to the new house for their meals; they would even come over to go to the toilet, and they were constantly staying overnight. But when the father was dying, the elder brother came and insisted on carrying him – he was unconscious by then – back to the great house so that he should die there and not give rise to any dispute as to which was the great house and which wasn't. Our two houses have never got on since. What made it worse was that when they divided the new house's portion of the woodland, they divided each separate tract into two, so that the new house would have a fair share of all the trees at different stages of growth. The result was constant disputes. When they went to cut the undergrowth and leaves to put in the fields, whichever one was the first would cut into the other's land. In my great-great-grandfather's time he dug holes all along the boundary and buried bales of charcoal as markers, but it still went on.

Apparently, however, the two households still kept up some ritual contact for several generations and tended their graves together. A definitive break in that occurred two generations back over a wedding. The great house advised the new house against alliance with a certain family, but the new house went ahead. The great house could not suffer to have its authority flouted in this way and broke off relations.

Both of these families were also, being rich, oyabun families, and the relative number and loyalty of their satellite kobun was probably a more important ultimate determinant of their overall 'standing' in the village than the question of which, by genealogical fact or by moral right, was the great and which the new house.

The oyabun–kobun relation was one with many facets, both formal and informal. But the central one, the act, as it were, by which the existence of the relationship was publicly displayed, was the part played by the head of the oyabun family when a son of the kobun family married. At any proper wedding feast somebody had to 'take the oyabun's seat' – to act as master of ceremonies. He might also play a greater or lesser part in the marriage negotiations, not as match-maker, but representing the interests of the kobun family in negotiating through the match-maker. But the essential thing was his public appearance at the wedding – and also at funerals, when he would greet guests on behalf of the mourners and give the kobun family general advice on the appropriate food and drink to serve. He would also (a very common facet of patronage relations in Mediterranean societies, too) act as a kind of 'godfather' to children born in the kobun family, deciding on their names and ceremonially inscribing them on a piece of rather special paper in his Sunday-best calligraphy. Another part of an oyabun family's ceremonial job was for the mistress of the oyabun household, in the days following a wedding in the kobun family, to walk the new bride around the village, introducing her formally to all those who had given wedding gifts.

There was a material reason for the involvement in wedding and funeral feasts. Oyabun families were the only ones in the village rich enough to have the necessary crockery and lacquer ware and cushions for these large parties. Lending these to their kobun was an essential part of their role.

The relationship would be formally and publicly established at a kobun's wedding, but it would be – if less publicly – re-affirmed by formal visiting at New Year and the Bon Festival. The house-heads, or their wives, or both, would exchange visits to burn incense to the ancestors, sip a cup of tea and chat. But the kobun househead would make the first visit, the gift which the oyabun took would be greater than the one he received, and it was more acceptable for the kobun's househead's visit to be returned by the oyabun wife than vice versa.

There were proper forms of speech, too, which made clear the inequality of the relationship. Members of kobun families would call the head of their oyabun family 'o-tōsan', the polite word for father. His wife would be 'mother', and their children, irrespective of age, 'elder brother' and 'elder sister'. Members of oyabun families, on the other hand, at least adult members, would address anyone belonging to a kobun family by his given name, without polite suffix – a practice with such clear authority-asserting implications that there was a special word for it – like *tutoyer* in French, but always in the sense of disparagement rather than intimacy.

These were the external trappings of a hard economic core. Party crockery was not the only thing that the oyabun might lend the kobun, but also money for medicine, and rice when the family food supply ran out six weeks before the harvest (the latter at no interest, the former at interest but generally less than market rates). The oyabun had wealth, power, self-confidence, *savoir-faire*. They were much more likely – until the late nineteenth century at least – to be able to read and write. They could guide their kobun through the dangerous tangles of dealings with the village office, the land and taxation authorities. Some oyabun, it was said, kept their kobun's 'signature seals' (the 'chop' that has to go on all legal documents) and simply acted at their discretion on their kobun's behalf. If a kobun got in trouble with the police – caught for gambling, say, or fighting – his family would turn to the oyabun as the obvious one to go and 'moraisageru' him – a curious word meaning 'to secure release from custody on the informal guarantee of a social superior', literally, 'to get back down'.

All the oyabun families were landlords, and most of the kobun families were tenants. Sometimes kobun rented their own oyabun's land, but this was far from being the norm. In fact, one of the jobs of the oyabun might be to intercede with a landlord if his kobun, the latter's tenant, had grounds for asking for a reduction or postponement of the rent.

And the pay-off? If ever there was a wedding at the oyabun's house the family could be assured of a host of willing, cheerful servants. For special jobs like a re-thatching they need pay nothing for labour. Even for regular field work, an oyabun family could claim first call on the labour services of their kobun, even at the busiest season, when the kobun might prefer to be working on their own fields. The oyabun family could expect a few days of this labour 'service' to be free, though how many days from each house had to be nicely judged according to the degree of their dependency. (Though a good meal for the helpers at the end of the day – with liberal doses of saké – could help to redress any imbalance.)

The other part of the pay-off was less tangible. Deference is always flattering. In the muted rivalry between leading families in the hamlet the number and loyalty of one's kobun were major criteria for claims to status. And in open conflict such as might arise over irrigation or management of the shrine or anything else whatever, the loyal support of a cohort of kobun could be decisive.

Like all other important relations in the village, of course, it was a relation not between individuals but between households: it continued through the generations, but unlike great-house-new-house relations, it *could* be broken off. If an oyabun family lost all its wealth, or if it gave good cause by excessively arrogant or exploitative behaviour, a kobun could seek a new oyabun when next a son married.

Such, in outline, was the oyabun–kobun relationship. Inequality – inequality of 'condition', or of intrinsic worth – was of the essence of it, reflected both in ritual and everyday social contact, and in the asymmetry of economic exchange. It was one which entailed duties (of a different kind) for both sides, but it was not supposed to be *about* duty. On both sides, it was expected to be maintained by 'genuine feeling', the spontaneous desire to protect on the one hand, to serve on the other. Somebody in 1955, telling me of the sad decline of these relationships, made this clear when he said that what was wrong nowadays was that people kept up these customs as a 'mere matter of obligation'. Spontaneity was possible – or it was possible to expect it – because the inequality involved was not thought necessarily to be a demeaning, irksome inequality. The Japan of the mid nineteenth century was not a society in which a man felt essentially diminished by being 'anybody's man but his own'.

England was such a society once. Shakespeare, presumably, did not feel ashamed of his humble deference when he dedicated his poem to the Earl of Southampton: 'What I have done is yours, what I have to do is yours; being part in all I have, devoted yours . . . My duty . . . is bound to your Lordship.' But England changed. Johnson felt ambivalent enough about pat-

rons to define them in his dictionary as 'wretches who support
with insolence and are paid with flattery' and within another
century the patron had altogether disappeared from the literary
scene, significantly at a time when the political and economic
supremacy of the aristocratic patron class was being curbed by
the popular franchise. Tocqueville, bemused by the French
Revolution's pursuit of equality and its institutionalization in
American society, saw a trend towards greater egalitarianism as
a deeply rooted social movement of long standing, 'an unques-
tionable sign of God's will'.

Certainly Japan has changed, too – remarkably so in the last
hundred years, but even before that there were signs of some
of the equalizing processes that one can discern in Europe's
history – even if they were a long way from affecting village
life. The growth of education, for instance, emphasized the
non-coincidence between 'talent' as manifest in scholarly
achievement, and hereditary rank. As the political crisis of the
nineteenth century deepened, there were calls for 'the appoint-
ment of men of merit' to high office: urgings that the claims of
'order' and 'hierarchy' must give way to the need for government efficiency.

And so, when the great political changes took place and
Japan was opened to the West in 1870, some of the most
popular authors to be translated were Rousseau and Mill and
Sam Smiles. 'Heaven did not create men above men, nor set
men below men,' began the preface of Fukuzawa's *Encouragement
of Learning*, the most influential book of the Japanese enlighten-
ment. And if you go to his birthplace, that is the phrase you will
still find inscribed on the slabs of chocolate on sale at the
souvenir booths.

Probably more important in the long run was the embodi-
ment of the principle of citizen equality in the new institutions
of modern Japan. The formal abolition of traditional class dis-
tinctions between a warrior nobility and the common people
was the first milestone. The birth of a conscript army was another; so was the creation, in the 1870s, of a unified school
system leading from elementary school to university – something Britain did not fully achieve until 1944 – and then only in
the public education sector. It was an open system; meritocratic
principles of selection were strictly enforced for entrance to

higher education, the professions and the civil service. And in that competition – because it was competition in terms of new 'imported' school knowledge, not in terms of mastery of a traditional family-transmitted culture – the handicap of the poor and lower-status groups was probably less great than in European societies which evolved with greater cultural continuity.

These changes set in train an irreversible movement. By the third decade of this century the notion that in some important political sense men had equal rights had acquired, as Marx said of bourgeois Europe, 'the fixity of a popular prejudice'. In 1925 the enactment of universal manhood suffrage recognized the logical consequence of universal conscription and universal education. Army domination in the thirties and forties repressed liberty and individualism, but did not reverse these egalitarian trends. 'All Japanese are equally children of the Emperor' was the slogan, and 'equality of sacrifice: equality of effort' was the principle which justified the removal of social discrimination against former outcast groups and the reduction of landlords' profits.

Then, more recently, the creeping egalitarianism of the pre-war period gave way to the galloping egalitarianism of the immediate post-war years of the American occupation. The change in the tenor of press and radio commentary was remarkable. One heard no more of 'loyalty', 'patriotism', 'service'. 'The dignity of man', 'human rights' were the new hurrah words and 'feudal', 'patriarchal' were the new boo words. According to the letter columns in the newspapers, a husband who refused to let his wife go to flower-arranging classes, the father who insisted on his teenage daughter being home by 11 o'clock, were 'feudal': the word could be used to decry any resented exercise of the privileges of superior age or status.

The tone of the mainline mass media soon became less strident as the occupation ended and the new conservative government set about 'correcting its excesses', but the new ideas of equality and citizens' rights were well enough rooted for the backlash to be a minor one. The late sixties, too, with a new wave of Naderite consumer movements and local citizens' action groups, represented something more solid than the frothy enthusiasm of the immediate post-war years. For one thing, it was founded on a new affluence and a higher level of expectations,

a higher level of the perceived 'right' of citizens. The Japanese of the 1960s could afford to equate 'dignity' with not being 'feudally' subordinate to any man, because hardly anybody was so close to the poverty line that he was forced to trade the acceptance of subordination for a livelihood.

These changes in the ideological climate at the metropolitan centres inevitably affected the ideological weather in Shinohata. Take the school and conscription, for example. Oyabun's child and kobun's child went to the same school and sat side by side, and neither nature nor a complaisant teacher could always ensure that the oyabun's child came top of the class. To be sure, Gontarō, the eldest son of the richest oyabun family, was the only child in his class at the village school in 1910 who wore the hakama divided kilt which was supposedly regulation wear – but which no one else could afford. He was also the only one who went on to middle school. But even Sanetoshi (the stiff old disciplinarian of page 82), who was in the same class and who will tell you that Gontarō came third in his class in the middle school and is a genius, cannot suppress the memory that at the village school Gontarō could not do his sums as well as many of his peers from kobun families.

And after school came the army. It was not always the oyabun youths who came back sergeants, nor kobun youths who remained inglorious second-class privates. The suspected arson story of Katsunori (page 268) needs filling out in two respects. Just before the fire Katsunori's father had returned with a fine battle record from the Russo–Japanese war. His father had made the most of it by putting up a rather splendid lych-gate with stone pillars carved 'To commemorate victorious return'. The neighbouring family, whose madly jealous old grandmother was suspected of burning their house down, was Katsunori's family's oyabun – from which family nobody had gone to the war.

One does not have to read the sociologists' theories about the origins of egalitarianism in social differentiation and the emergence of multiple non-congruent status rankings, to see that this sort of thing might well put oyabun–kobun relations under a strain.

At the same time, economic changes tended to drain oyabun–kobun relations of that element of mutual material benefit which, however infrequently called to mind, gave an extra zestful fillip to the spontaneity with which both parties to the relationship met their obligations.

It is clear enough that the oyabun came to have less to gain. The present generation of oyabun family house-heads had all been to a middle or higher school and – until the bombing, food rationing and threat of land reform drove them back to the village – lived in the towns. Their fathers, as they got older, had gradually reduced the amount of land they farmed themselves and let more out to tenants. They had no need to have first call on the labour of an army of kobun.

Moreover, even for the members of the parental generation (and *a fortiori* for their town-dwelling sons) the modern age had brought a widened sphere of activities. As leading lights in their own hamlets they were naturally drawn into the new local government institutions. They could aspire to be a member of the wider rural district council, chairman of the district agricultural association. New wider reference groups made them less dependent for their self-esteem on the submissive deference of kobun families in the hamlet.

The gradual progress of money rationality probably counted too. In the late nineteenth century Shinohata was still partly a subsistence-and-barter economy. The furtherance of the switch to a money economy made people more accustomed to the idea of buying labour by the piece. To oyabun it came to seem preferable to buy a day's labour for 200 yen rather than to purchase it at the expense of diffuse, and possibly in the end more costly, obligations.

Things changed from the kobun's point of view too. To begin with, rising incomes, especially with the expansion of silk production, made them less dependent on the starvation-security safety net offered by the oyabun's granary. By 1910 nearly every househead was literate, and had no need of an oyabun to interpret officialdom and its bureaucratic forms to him.

How different oyabun–kobun relations were in 1940 from what they had been in 1890 I have no certain means of knowing beyond a few clues. There was the story of Tsunashige's father, who said on one of the occasions when Gontarō's father called for a labour-service work party, that in this day and age oyabun could afford to pay for labour. The remark reached Gontarō's father's ears and the Tsunashige household suffered excommunication. One or two pairs of comfortably-off owner-farmers had, by the 1940s, reached a 'mutual oya' compact whereby they reciprocally performed the ceremonial oya role for each other. It was around 1910 that one of the kumi neighbourhood groups bought its communal set of crockery and lacquer ware that made it unnecessary for the kobun families to be beholden to their oyabun for the loan of the basic equipment for a wedding or a funeral. What does seem certain is that former kobun came to attach greater value to the luxury of not having to 'lower one's head' to anyone, and more of them came to enjoy a sufficiently secure well-being to be able to afford that luxury.

After the war the basis of economic dependency was eroded much more rapidly; the land reform substantially equalized incomes; the spread of medical insurance reduced the damage which a prolonged illness could do to a farm economy; the rapid rise in agricultural prices in the mid-fifties made farmers better off. What had been the luxury of not having to 'lower one's head to any man' was economically within reach of everyone. It *could* become redefined as a basic necessity, a precondition for individual self-respect. Would one expect it to do so automatically because, as Matthew Arnold claimed, any system of institutionalized inequality is 'against nature', can only be sustained by some kind of coercion and will rapidly wither away as soon as the coercive pressure is removed? Or is freedom from subordination and personal dependency a taught and not a basic instinctual need, so that, for example, without all the strident talk of 'individual dignity' in the post-war Tokyo newspapers there would have been no such change in the villages? Shinohata provides no test to offer a conclusive answer to that question since the ideological push to equality was certainly present, as well as the conditioning change in economic circumstances. (And where will one find such a test today – a part of the world where economic change provides the conditions for equality but the influence of outside egalitarian doctrines is absent?)

But, curiously, oyabun–kobun relations have *not* entirely disappeared. Not everyone among the kobun wants to stand on his dignity, and there are one or two who still see personal advantage in maintaining these claims on other people's good-will. The majority do not and would be glad to extricate themselves. For their part, however, some of the oyabun – and for the same sort of reasons of family pride as prompt Hisayo to tell all her stories about her gravestones – are far from keen to let the relationship drop. And in the face of their insistence the Shinohata habit of avoiding confrontation prompts many kobun to humour them.

The trouble is, of course, that the relationship cannot just wither away by mere attrition. There comes a time when a kobun family's eldest son marries. There are only two choices – you do, or you do not, ask the head of your oyabun family to 'take the oyabun seat' at the wedding. And not to do so towards an oyabun who is assiduous about keeping up his side of the relationship does seem like a very unfriendly act.

At least it would to Gontarō, whom I have already introduced several times before as, with Motonori, one of Shinohata's two 'bullies', not to put too fine a point on the capacity for getting away with overbearing behaviour by presuming on one's neighbour's mild-mannered preference for harmony and the avoidance of confrontation.

One of the first times I saw Gontarō in action was in 1955 at a meeting of the hamlet council. (I never did understand why he was there since he was not a regular council member.) The issue was the arrival of Shinohata's first telephone, to be installed in the shop but publicly available. Telephone poles would have to be planted in people's land, just at the time when the machine tillers were coming in, making it even more awkward to plough round obstacles. By rights, some suggested, the owners of the fields were entitled to some compensation. Gontarō delivered himself of a fine piece of forceful rhetoric about individual sacrifice and the common weal. Those who wanted compensation had nasty, small, calculating minds . . . All suggestions about compensation were dropped after that.

'He's just so rude,' said one woman. 'He shouts at people, if they don't do what he says, and, well, he's an "erai" sort of person (a "big" man in the outside world) and people don't like to answer back. So he nearly always gets his way. The only reason he's still the Shinohata representative on the Co-op committee is because nobody's strong-minded enough to suggest that he stand down.'

Whether he was, or was not, erai was a matter of opinion, but Gontarō had indeed spent most of his life outside Shinohata. Before he retreated to the village in 1942, stricken with a stomach ulcer (which for the next ten years, until he was operated on, he was sure was cancer), he had been secretary of the Dental Faculty of a large Tokyo university, having himself graduated in medicine. He still keeps up his connections with the university. The Dental Faculty recently had a party at the Imperial Hotel to honour his seventieth birthday and he proudly shows the photographs: Gontarō dressed up in the traditional seventieth birthday red cap and bib being honoured by some of the great names in dental surgery. (The red cap and bib symbolize entry into the second – quasi childhood – phase of permissive freedom, which some villagers would hold Gontarō had been enjoying for some time already.) He is also ready to use his connections to do whatever he can for local parents whose children are having difficulty in mastering enough esoteric examination lore to get the necessary marks for entrance to a decent university. There are ways . . . gifts to the university memorial fund . . . always glad to fix things for any relative of mine, he assured me at the end of one drunken evening. It might come a bit expensive, though. Something like $35,000 for the Medical Faculty, about half that for dentistry, and mere peanuts for law and arts. (That was in 1970: 'backdoor entrance' for less reputable medical colleges cost triple that figure by 1977, according to the press.)

That particular evening, as the contents of a bottle of Ballantine's gradually shrank (whether Messrs Ballantine had been responsible for the contents as well as the bottle I rather doubted, but the local whisky is also rather pleasant), he happily told me and the tape recorder his life story. He always was, he admitted, somewhat wilful and headstrong.

> 'My parents sent me to take the examination to the middle school but I walked out in the middle of it. I didn't want to go to middle school and as a matter of fact my parents didn't want me to go either. They said they wanted me, the eldest son, to carry on the house in

the village as a farmer, not to be going away, but my uncle – my father's younger brother that is – he was an army doctor. In fact he rose to a very high position in the Army Medical Service. He would have been the Director if he had not been killed in the Russo–Japanese war. Anyway, he persuaded my father that I should be educated. But I didn't want to go, so I walked out of the exams. No school for me, I thought. I wanted to be playing war games up in the woods above the village. It was soon after the Russo–Japanese war and we played war games every day. Of course I was always the general. The other kids around here made quite a fuss of me, being born in this house.

'You can't imagine what it was like in this village. I hardly like to talk about it. The houses – so dirty! Lice were a matter of course. The bedding – why, I doubt if they ever put their bed quilts out into the sun to air. They weren't any longer cotton quilts. They'd stand up by themselves! Didn't bear looking at! And the stink! After the war, when I was doctoring, I would do home visits and as like as not, come back with lice. And the food they'd eat! They used to have what they called "o-yaki" – a kind of burnt dough that was mostly corn meal and millet flour, plus a bit of barley with a splash of bean paste inside. You'd never be able to get it down.

'The owner-farmers? No, there wasn't any difference – they were all like that. Our house was the only exception. You'd go to their houses – to one of our kobun's house, say, and they would show you what they were eating and apologize for not having anything fit to offer you. And now look at them today! Look at what they are selling in the shop down where you are staying: butter, cheese – all kinds of pretentious foods. And, you know, the lower their cultural level the more likely they are to be always buying their kids these fancy cakes and Coca-Cola and milk and all the rest of it. And the kids leave half of it. God! When I think of meals in our house. How we had to sit straight, stiff and formally on our heels – no sitting cross-legged – and with aprons on. Yes, kind of bibs; ours was the only house

that did that, and if you let one grain of rice fall, left
one grain in your bowl, the wrath and thunder was
terrible. No: it was grandmother. Grandmother was
from a samurai family and she knew all about the tea
ceremony and flowers and the whole Ogasawara school
of etiquette. And was she strict! And thrifty, too, by
God! We too ate plain food. There was never pure rice
on the table. We didn't go so far as to mix millet in, the
way the others did, but always barley. For one thing,
it wouldn't have been right, you see, to eat pure white
rice when all the others were economizing so – it
wouldn't have been right towards the other families
in the village, towards our kobun. But we would have
pure rice on feast days when we would entertain the
kobun at the house – and the glutinous rice cakes, too;
they were a special treat . . .'

At this point we broke off for a tour of the house. Gontarō
may have lost most of his rice land in the land reform, but that
still left him with many fine stands of timber on his extensive
woodland. Some of that wealth – since augmented by careful
speculation – has been translated into internal furnishings, anti-
quities and art objects of catholic provenance. The garden has a
'natural stone' (uncarved) lantern of stupendous height made
from three rare and fantastic stones; the lintel that divides his
once earth-floored, now cemented, entrance area from the
'upper' parts of the house is another fine stone. Concealed
lighting above it spotlights the polished carapace of an enormous turtle. Above it, high up in the upper darkness, one can
see the blackened roof timbers, great thick rough-hewn beams,
more substantial, for they support a wider span of roof, than
in any other house in the village.

The rooms seem enormous, one ten-mat room after another.
There are tables filled with family photographs in which the
eminent military surgeon prominently figures. There is a screen
presented to his great-grandfather by the samurai Intendant.
Elegant cabinets, their doors alive with wild iris designs in
Momoyama style, a stuffed fighting cock in brilliant plumage, a
pair of pheasants in mid-flight, both, I am assured, the work of
a nationally famous taxidermist; scrolls with the calligraphy of

loyalists of the Meiji restoration and famous politicians of the Meiji period; a Rodin head, a lacquer box which has (illicitly) an Imperial Household Chrysanthemum crest – made specially for Gontarō's family by Japan's foremost lacquer-ware maker, an exact copy of one made to royal command; hand prints of last year's sumō wrestling champions; numerous screens and pieces of pottery; swords in beautifully gold-flecked lacquered scabbards, one recently authenticated by a well-known antiquarian . . .

We move round to the kitchen at the back of the cemented area, and just as Gontarō has friends at the top of the art world, at the top of the lacquer world, at the top of the dentistry world, so he had a wife of taste and discrimination who had a direct line to the top of the kitchen equipment world. Spotless Formica cupboards, stainless-steel double sinks, automatic heaters. 'My wife finished this just before she died last year. I don't know about these things, but I gather that it's just about the best you can get.'

Gontarō's wife was a city lady, but a lady of grace, beauty and sensibility, as much admired for her charm and her unpretentiousness as Gontarō was viewed askance for his brusque insensitivity. As we went back to his den – what had once been the loom room beside the stable – I noticed, before we sat down again to the Ballantine's bottle, a white poem card set in front of the alcove, rather prominent among the clutter of pottery and brass objects.

> One caught her sleeve,
> but she was not to be stayed.
> Into the clouds she dissolved.

My inquiry brought to Gontarō's face the first flush of unwonted modesty, and embarrassment – and, I think, genuine grief. Self-pity, perhaps, was mixed with bereaved love, but one glimpsed a little of what his normal boastfulness was keeping at bay when he said soberly that he had written many haiku on his wife's death, but that this was the best. And that reminded him that he must ask me to write some poem cards for him, and sign them as a souvenir of my visit: he had a new brush and would rub some ink. If I couldn't write a poem to order, a quotation would do. What about Shakespeare? I fear 'ripeness is all' is probably still being displayed to his guests. (Together, I have no doubt, with some of Gontarō's own compositions, for I apparently started him off on a new art form: the English haiku. When I went back a couple of years later he showed me his latest and wondered if the grammar needed correction.

> Early rising
> Tell the guiding principle
> In his life

The meaning, as will be readily apparent, is that the early riser learns the guiding principles of life without having to be explicitly taught them.)

We went back to his middle school. He had spurned the examination for the leading school in the prefecture. There was nothing for it but back-door entry, via the second supplementary entrance examinations, to a lesser school. In that meritocratic society the knowledge of his back-door entry gave him a complex. But he conquered it. Results gradually improved. Captain of jūdō, champion baseball pitcher. Urged to go to military academy; assured of brilliant career. Parents not about to gamble with life of eldest son and heir. Crisis in the dormitory in final year. Gontarō as leader of revolt. Lived in lodgings. Drink and women: undisciplinable streak. Back home. Intolerable. Determined to shape own future. Ran away. Commerce at Waseda University. Parents refused to support. Worked to sustain himself. But disillusioned with poor teaching after a year. Decided to accept his military service until then deferred by his student status. Parents relented. Put up the 108 yen necessary for him to be a 'one-year volunteer' rather than a two/three-year conscript. But they didn't send any money.

'I had a hell of a year. Everybody else would go off to the canteen, the P . . . what do you call canteens in English? P-something? – PX that's it – everybody else would go off to the PX and I would be sitting unable to go. So I would say "I dislike that sort of thing". I got quite a reputation. Staying in at weekends, too, because I couldn't afford to do anything else. I remember one

officer asking me: what are you doing in barracks on a
Sunday when everybody else has gone? Well, I couldn't
say I had no money, so I said: "Sir, I am conscious of
the fact that unlike most of the others, as a one-year
volunteer, I have only one year to adapt myself to the
military life, so I feel I should use every minute of that
year, one hundred and twenty per cent." He was most
impressed. Silly bugger. They were simple-minded,
these military men, though, I must say, an officer then
was a figure of awe: they weren't two-a-penny as they
later became during the war. But they were simple-
minded. And no wonder, in that sort of atmosphere
where everything revolves around simple obedience,
nothing but obedience. No personal responsibility, no
personal initiative. I couldn't stand that. I am a liberal.
Your Bertrand Russell, is it? Great man. Ninety-seven
years old, a scholar and a pacifist. I am an absolute
believer in Bertrand Russell. And recently, of course,
Toynbee – he was from your University, wasn't he?
Great man. Great on love for mankind. And then in
ceramics there's Bernard Leach. But anyhow, as Bertrand Russell said: "It is because society permits us to
live that we are alive. At the same time we too are
seeking to live. In aim, man and society coincide." '

And so his career took him on through dental surgery to his
medical secretaryship to the bombing and his ulcer and back to
the village to recuperation, some casual doctoring ('until they
started the national health service after the war. Then I stopped
immediately') to his role in the village Land Reform Committee, his directorship of the Co-operative, lately his distinguished
service for the Prefectural Public Safety Committee.
In the middle of our conversation the telephone had rung.
'What silly bugger is that?' He was staggering somewhat by
then. 'Here we are in the middle of nowhere . . . These Agriculture Co-operative Neighbourhood phones. Pah!' 'What is
it? Me? Eat? I haven't eaten all day. What are you talking
about? Nonsense. Come. Come. Bring it here. Mr Dore's here.
Dore, yes. Dore. Don't be such a bloody fool.' He returned,
muttering, to the table, but apparently the conversation was not

conclusive, at least in the mind of his interlocutor. In fifteen minutes the phone rang again. 'Yes, what is it ? Of course. Don't be such a bloody fool! Of course there's nobody to cook for me! Yes, don't be such a bloody fool. I haven't eaten all day. There is nobody to cook for me here. And bring one for the English Professor. You know. Yes, of course you know.'

It was soon after that, but already nearly 10 p.m., when we heard the sound of a 150-cc Honda and Shigeyasu appeared slightly drunk but otherwise his usual, slightly clownish, eager ingratiating self. These were the days before Shigeyasu had graduated to his Toyota Corona GT, but the one period in his life when he had managed to combine work with his major passion, fishing. He was employed at the Trout Hatchery off the main highway. His job was to feed the trout in the breeding ponds, to select those ripe for destruction and transfer them to the muddy fishing ponds, and to bedazzle the clients with esoteric nonsense about fishing techniques which made them feel flatteringly proud of their skills when they eventually caught one. A proper cook did the cooking and provided the rice and saké which rounded off the fishing party's day.

Shigeyasu had a parcel wrapped in newspaper and looked hesitant. 'Come on in, man. Don't stand there looking lost.' Gontarō staggered out to get a half bottle of cold saké: however devoted and loyal, retainers apparently do not drink whisky. Shigeyasu, more at home now he had crossed the threshold, went to the cupboard for a couple of plates. From the newspaper were drawn two magnificent rainbow trout, professionally cooked by Shigeyasu's specially trained colleague, sweetened and salted, so delicately marinated and roasted that one could eat every bone and the head as well. 'Please eat up. It's the greatest delicacy you will find in this village.'

'Chopsticks, you fool. Chopsticks!' Gontarō yelled. 'Yes, sir. Of course, sir.' Somewhere in the kitchen Shigeyasu finds some chopsticks. He sits down at the table. 'Not here you fool. The other side.' Gontarō is clearly put out by Shigeyasu's lack of *savoir faire*. Why exactly he decides to change the saké bottle I could not surmise but he clutches it and staggers out. Shigeyasu confides in me that I must not mind the doctor. He is slightly ineb . . . inebri . . . intoxicated. Certainly he cuts a strange figure as he returns with the saké bottle: he has put on the red cap and red bib in which he was honoured by the leading figures in Japanese dentistry at his recent seventieth birthday party. The floppy red hat has been clearly redesigned with Western academic robes in mind; it has a comical effect in accentuating Gontarō's stick-out ears.

'Not just chopsticks, you fool! What about chopstick rests? Don't you know about manners, you fool?' Shigeyasu is by now prepared to answer back. 'I didn't think you would need ...' 'What are you talking about? Get them. Up there. No: on the right!' 'Here we are then.' Shigeyasu remains doggedly cheerful as he brings a variety of chopstick rests. 'Which one of you wants the sparrow?'

As Gontarō sinks gradually into his doze, Shigeyasu becomes more eloquent. I really must come to try the fishing. One day when he is on duty. I shouldn't be put off. It's not true that only the long-suffering and the patient make good fishermen. In fact, scientific study had shown that the quick-tempered, the impetuous ... Shigeyasu, when I left, seemed to look forward happily to his final task of putting Gontarō to bed.

One or two others of Gontarō's kobun were also content to assume the servant role, if none was quite as doggedly at his service as Shigeyasu. (Shigeyasu 'has a good nose', someone said in comment, and explained that the term applied originally to game dogs and their ability to seek their prey.) One of these others was Tokinori, who was frequently summoned to act as Gontarō's chauffeur and would suffer to be bawled out if he arrived late. In his case, Gontarō presumed on two things: first that Tokinori's mother had been an orphan servant in Gontarō's house and had been married out from there which put his family, as kobun, high up in the dependency scale; secondly, Tokinori worked in the Agriculture Co-operative and as a Director of the Co-op Gontarō felt he had a legitimate call on his working time. Two other loyal younger house-heads were said to share Shigeyasu's reason for jumping at Gontarō's beck and call: they were interested in land speculation. They had entered the field as brokers in a small way, speculating in local holiday villa land, but later breaking out farther afield. Some years after the evening described above, Shigeyasu told me that he owned a tract of several tens of acres in the northern island of Hokkaido. Gontarō with his experience of the world and his connections in high places was a valuable source of advice and assurance in that dangerous but attractive world where, if one were both shrewd and lucky, fortunes might be made. Injustices survive, Tawney once said, not merely because the rich exploit the poor, but because, within their hearts, too many of the poor admire the rich. Shigeyasu and friends did, indeed, admire the rich. They also hoped to join them. If their fathers admired Gontarō's father as a model of respectable solidity and life-line to firm security, they admired Gontarō as a model of affluence and guide to the end of the rainbow.

In 1955 when I first inquired into these matters, I remember one or two other households where Gontarō was readily acknowledged as oyabun; one was a former tenant and keen hard-working farmer who did a day or two's work for Gontarō every year and valued the opportunity he was given in return to cut green fertilizer and firewood from Gontarō's woodland, because he himself had none. Another was something of a hypochondriac and one of the few people in the village who had some faith in Gontarō's doctoring skills. But, of the sixteen households in the village which were acknowledged kobun of Gontarō's family, the loyalists were very much a minority. A few were quite vociferous in denouncing the whole oyabun–kobun business as cheap-labour exploitation, or worse, a form of trickery whereby, benevolently taking charge of their kobun's business affairs, oyabun had entangled them in debt and then stolen all their woodland from them. Most were clearly slightly embarrassed by the whole thing, and somewhat ambiguous in their account of the relationship.

Gontarō's own ambiguous behaviour was partly responsible for this. In the immediate post-war years he was very much the progressive, much given to talk of the need to consign all things feudal to the limbo of history. He did not go quite as far as the leading oyabun of a neighbouring hamlet, the other landlord representative on the land reform committee, who, having become an ambitious local leader of the Socialist Party, had summoned all his kobun together at a final feast to declare an end to their relationship. And in fact Gontarō's progressive phase was short-lived. By 1955 he was pleased to boast of the number of his kobun and of their devoted loyalty. He had also revived the custom of holding his annual bamboo-grove fencing.

He owned one of the biggest bamboo groves in the district, some four acres of it, producing the most succulent of bamboo shoots. The heads of all his kobun families were invited annually to a day's work clearing up the grove and repairing the fence which surrounded it – a day topped off by a feast at his house. Apparently, with varying degrees of reluctance, nearly all his kobun turned up. There was Katsutoshi, for instance, a man of some gravitas and some weight in village affairs. He had told me that oyabun–kobun relations were a thing of the past, that after the war 'most people with any sense of self-respect had gone along to their oyabun and said they wanted to end the relationship'. Katsutoshi went to the bamboo grove nevertheless.

However, he went to work for only half a day, and he went late to the feast that evening – in fact a messenger had to come from Gontarō's house to urge his presence four times before he set out. When I talked with him later about the party he complained rather bitterly of the predominance of plain filling vegetables and the token nature of the meat dish.

Gontarō did not hold his bamboo-grove party in 1969. It was partly his wife's death, he explained to me, partly because the bamboo flowered that year. (It happens, apparently on a nationwide scale, every sixty or seventy years, and when it does so both bamboo and bamboo shoots are ruined for a year or more.) But he would probably start again. I had another and more sober conversation with him about this in 1970, soon after the evening described above. I had said that I supposed the problem with these oyabun–kobun relations was the fact that they were unequal.

> 'That's it. You've put your finger on it. That's the trouble. Too many just won't agree – too many oyabun, I mean, won't agree to democratizing things. They want to be just like old-fashioned oyabun. They don't live up to their oyabun responsibilities but they just behave arrogantly. "Oi! Come here," sort of thing, and calling people by their name without using -san. I would never do that sort of thing. But some do.'
>
> 'But quite apart from that, surely all these visiting practices – paying respects at New Year and so on – are also not based on equality.'

'Oh, but all those things have just gradually disappeared. Once we used to fix a time for all the kobun
to come at New Year and they'd all stack their regular
gift of a small bale of rice by the door and an impressive
sight it would be. But that's all gone. A few come
individually, but that's the same as between neighbours.
All the old customs have gone.'

'But your bamboo grove. After all, it's your bamboo
grove they come to work on: you don't go and work
on theirs. That's surely unequal.'

'Well, yes, but I don't tell them to. You see, somebody takes the initiative. All the farmers get busy
around that time and so he'd say we'd better fix a day
in advance, and I'd say, well, such and such suits me,
and then it'll all be arranged. But the big question is
whether that bamboo grove's worth it. No money in
bamboo shoots, you know. Absolutely none. But it's
four acres of prime land by the main national highway.
Think what I could do with that: a drive-in, perhaps,
or a hotel, or a sauna. If I was an economic animal I'd
have started it long ago, but . . . you know, spiritually
I haven't lost my baitaritei (vitality) but all the same,
age does impose limits. I think I'll have to leave that to
my successor.'

Gontarō did not revive his bamboo-grove work parties.
Shigeyasu and Tokinori remain cronies. The son of the hypochondriac still gets Gontarō to name all his children. Noritake
told me in 1955 that it was too soon to do away with
oyabun ('a wedding doesn't seem like a proper wedding without someone in the oyabun's seat, and if you are arranging a
marriage and the other party asked who your oyabun was and
you can say it was somebody like Gontarō – well, it gives you a
bit of a lift'). Noritake, arranging a marriage in the mid-seventies,
got Gontarō to act not just as oyabun for him but as actual
negotiating go-between. (Though he paid all Gontarō's travel-
ling expenses, and a thank-you gift of $10 as well.) But Gon-
tarō's health – and vitality – is declining. One sign is his reconciliation with his estranged son who has come back from Tokyo
to live with his father, runs a petrol station built on the very

bamboo grove in question and probably neither knows nor cares who the family's kobun are. In any case the majority of them have drifted away. The fact that so many weddings are celebrated outside the village makes it easier to make the break. Some of the restaurants specializing in weddings provide professional masters-of-ceremonies which provides an excuse for not asking the oyabun. Most of the sons are working elsewhere: their employer, departmental director, foreman, is the obvious one to play the central role at their wedding. I did not hear of any dramatic breaking off of relations; only gentle disentanglement.

So it was with others of Shinohata's oyabun, though among the second biggest contingent – the seven kobun of Hidezō's family – there had been one somewhat dramatic quarrel at the time of the land reform. Mitsuyoshi had been a tenant of Hidezō's family. Hidezō's father, having just come back from his railway engineer's job, was keen to salvage as much of his land as he could and to get it back from tenants to cultivate himself – including the field Mitsuyoshi was renting. Mitsuyoshi sent his mother along to appeal to their oyabun benevolence ('old women are better at this sort of thing'). Couldn't the oyabun release that field for land reform transfer to Mitsuyoshi, and claim instead some of the land that was being rented by other people who were *not* their kobun? Tsuneko, Hidezō's mother, reacted sharply. It was not fair of them to bring that sort of pressure. The family needed that particular land and if Mitsuyoshi was going to talk like that, then they would stop being oyabun and kobun . . . Mitsuyoshi had given in. 'Well, there's no point in living horn-to-horn at loggerheads. In a small place like this where you are always meeting on narrow pathways in the fields . . .' Mitsuyoshi was a mild man.

Some time after I had heard his story, in 1955, I visited Hidezō's house. I mentioned to his father that I gathered he was in favour of getting rid of the oyabun–kobun business. He looked embarrassed. Grandfather, then well over eighty, had chipped in. 'Yes, it's bound to happen. It costs far too much with all these gifts and things.' But Tsuneko again reacted somewhat angrily. The suggestion was taken by her as an accusation that the family was stingy about its obligations. Who had been maligning them behind their backs?

Now Hidezō is house-head. The energetic champion grower of oak-mushrooms, hamlet chief at thirty-nine and tipped to be the next representative on the town council, Hidezō is not inclined to abandon traditional claims to status. But nor is he imprudent enough to assert those claims beyond what the traffic will bear. When I introduced the subject one day he did react rather as if I had referred to a somewhat embarrassing scandal.

> – Well, you know, the day for all that is past, really. But, still, when the time comes, when somebody builds a new house, say, or there's a wedding or a funeral – or say, the other day we had the seventh memorial anniversary for my father – well, they come along. There's one of our kobun that broke off relations in my father's time, but they've started again. It's a pretty silly and wasteful business really, but I suppose – well, everybody needs friends, I suppose. It's like having extra relatives.
> – But it's not really on a footing of equality, is it? You go and sit in the top seat at their weddings, but they don't at yours.
> – Yes, that's right: there's the question of standing. But, for example, we take a 2,000 yen gift for congratulations when a child enters primary school, or gets into high school. But then you find, when the time comes and we have a child entering school, they give back the same amount.

'They're a pretty feudal lot up there, aren't they?' said the barber in Kakizaka town centre when I told him I was living in Shinohata. Perhaps. Perhaps there is a trace of the seigneur even about Gontarō, with his high-pitched voice and his large stick-out ears. Perhaps Shigeyasu's semi-distanced deference is a little reminiscent of Sancho Panza. That may be why they console each other so well – and why they need to console each other. For Shinohata is no longer their village. Modern Shinohata belongs to the solid bourgeois citizenry, the sober men who believe in the virtues of hard work, not speculation, and for whom giving as good as one gets, not having to 'lower one's head', have become elementary conditions of self-respect.

Epilogue

I work nowadays in an Institute of Development Studies. Its business is to pursue knowledge which might be useful to the countries of the Third World which are trying to 'develop'. It was once thought that someone like myself who had spent several years contemplating what has happened in Japan over the last century might have some novel perspectives on the matter. I am not sure that I do, but living among people who are constantly talking about 'development' does prompt certain thoughts about Shinohata which I might otherwise not have had.

To start with, there is that strain in modern development thinking which grows out of a much older 'where are the snows of yesteryear?' kind of romanticism. See what a mess our crass materialism has made of our society: the pollution, the decline of the family, the drugs, the loss of purpose, the loss of simpler, purer pleasures. Let the poor countries learn from our horrible example and seek some *alternative* pattern of development. When Chou En-lai suggests that the Chinese would be happy to remain bicycle-riders for ever, many of our philosophers of 'true development' (car-owners to a man) heartily applaud the appearance of a man of vision.

Such a view would be almost entirely incomprehensible in Shinohata. I say 'almost' because there *are* parents who worry slightly that their spoiled children are thriftless and wasteful, have lost a 'sense of the preciousness of things'. But that is the last dying kick of the puritan ethic, not a romanticization of the simple life in the style of our zero-growthers. Shinohata's citizens are too close to their past poverty for that. They revel in their new-found comforts, and I entirely sympathize.

To be sure, Shinohata was in many respects a much more exciting and exotic village for an outsider to visit in 1955 than twenty years later. There were more colourful characters around; they got drunk more often; people seemed more impulsive and passionate. I doubt if Shinohata will ever again produce an incident as suitable for a Fernandel farce as it did the day the fire brigade went fishing. And doubtless, outside observers apart, Shinohata farmers looked forward, then, to their shrine festivals and drinking parties with much keener anticipation than they do to their far more frequent outings today. Doubtless, too, they felt greater warmth and security and kinship with more of their fellow villagers than they do today, and I am sure there was great satisfaction in accomplishing the lengthy and laborious task of making their own soya sauce, even if it tasted ghastly compared with the bottled product of modern chemical expertise they buy today. But with all that went the long hours of sheer hard grinding toil needed to maintain even an austere standard of living; the work-horse resignation of the young bride combining housework and farmwork under her mother-in-law's unremitting discipline, the anxieties that often attended the business of keeping up dutiful neighbour relations in the imprisoning village community which circumscribed social relations far more conclusively than they do today. For these things Shinohata people have no regret. Even less – for 1955 was already a period of considerable comfort compared with 1935 and *a fortiori* compared with 1905 – do they have regrets for the days when the sanction for not working, or not saving against the bad seasons, was real gnawing hunger; not having food in the house for days at a time.

Nothing that I have seen and heard in Shinohata has made me doubt the virtues of economic growth.

It has made me doubt the current prescriptions for getting it, however. Fifteen years ago those who spoke and wrote about development took it for granted that the only obvious way to a general rise in living levels was industrialization – learning to make those additional things besides food which make for a comfortable style of living and acquiring the capital equipment to make them by machines and inanimate energy rather than by human toil. Nowadays industrialization has become almost a dirty word. Probably the majority of writers, at least the academic writers, on development who concern themselves with industrialization are less interested in promoting it than in highlighting its ill-consequences – the way it creates income inequalities, invites the domination of multinational corporations, etc. Rural development, by contrast, is thought to be an excellent thing: the number one priority which all the international agencies want to back.

Of course there is a lot of sense in giving rural development high priority. Japanese farmers did not take long to acquire the idea of 'improvement'. They have been diligent in their husbandry, cautiously willing to experiment, quick to seize an opportunity of making two blades of grass grow where only one grew before. If their output had not kept up with the growth of the Japanese population – and if the silk they produced had not financed a lot of Japanese capital imports – Japan's industrialization would have been much slower. Nowadays they get more than twice as much rice off each acre as they did a hundred years ago. But the chief factor responsible for that is their enormous use of chemicals made in highly capital-intensive factories. Nor is it the increase in their *own* productivity which makes them so well off today, but rather the way the Japanese economic and political systems allow them to share in the great leaps in productivity made by industry. And the reason why those leaps have been possible in the last twenty years is because of the foundations laid in the 1890s and the 1900s.

Those foundations were laid only because the Japanese did not act according to what have today become the prescriptions of enlightened development strategy: they put the bulk of the savings the Japanese economy was capable of making into industrial investment, not into agriculture. Moreover a lot of the industrial projects backed by government money at that time would certainly never have got off the ground if they had been judged by the sort of cost-benefit project appraisal methods used today. It took the Japanese a long time to learn to use their first steel plant in a way that made it anything like profitable by international standards. But industrialization was their goal and costly learning was the only way of getting there. And in the end it paid off. It was not, perhaps, the pay-off which the designers of the strategy intended. They wanted to make *Japan* strong and powerful, a force to make the nations tremble. They succeeded only in making *the Japanese* comfortably well-off. Although Shinohata people were solidly behind the original intentions, in retrospect they seem to prefer the actual outcome.

But it took a long time – some eighty or ninety years – from the laying of those foundations, and the squeezing of the farmers that made it possible, to the pay-off in the 1960s and 1970s. I believe that the reason why so-called development theory today is in such an emotion-laden mess, the reason why the rate of slogan-obsolescence among its practitioners seems to be constantly accelerating ('take-off to sustained growth', 'balanced social and economic development', 'employment-oriented strategy', 'redistribution with growth', 'poverty-focused planning', 'basic needs strategy', etc., following, one after the other, with bewildering rapidity), is that people cannot – or believe they cannot – afford to wait. The traditional growth strategy with a heavy emphasis on industrialization has, we are told, 'failed'. Failed in what? Failed to transform agrarian Sri Lanka or Ghana into an affluent industrial state in fifteen years? Failed, in the absence of industrialization, to raise the living standards of the Sri Lankan or Ghanaian peasants? The perception of failure seems chiefly to be a function of the unrealism of the original expectations. What is not entirely certain is whether the disappointed expectations are only those of the people who make the running in the International Development Conference Community, people whose enthusiasm for international equality is stronger than their sense of history, or whether there is also a strong sense of frustrated expectations among the poor of the developing countries themselves.

There are some good reasons why the poor in developing countries should feel such frustration, why they should be unwilling to wait as patiently for the millennium as the people of Shinohata waited. Nowadays political leaders in most countries (much less so in countries animated by a strong nationalistic drive like China) claim that the purpose of development *is* popular welfare rather than national strength. They make promises. Unlike the authoritarian leaders of an earlier Japan when the world was younger and still allowed for the possibility of benevolent autocracies, they *need* to make promises to stay in power. Another difference is that better communications, the shrinking of the globe, make life-styles – and income levels – in the modern sectors of the developing countries much more like those of the rich countries than they used to be. Accra is much more like London today than Tokyo was like New York or Paris in 1900. And so internal disparities within the developing countries – between the alien life-styles of the modern sector rich and the peasant poor – become that much more glaring, and glaringly at variance with the rhetoric of equality and socialism which many of the developing countries today profess.

So there are *some* good reasons for thinking that Japan's history is not going to repeat itself very closely elsewhere, and that it is not politically realistic to expect the peasant masses of the Third World (except perhaps the Chinese peasant masses) to wait as long for the fruits of 'development' as the Japanese have waited. What I am not certain about, however, is how far the now widespread belief that 'traditional growth strategies' are 'bankrupt' and 'have failed' is a reasoned response to these political realities, how far it springs instead from the impatience of idealistic development theorists in the rich world who know about compound interest rates in principle, but could never accept intuitively how long the long haul of industrialization has to be.

Whatever the reasons, the doctrines of 'poverty-focused planning' and a 'basic needs approach' nowadays dominate the development field. The emphasis is on immediate improvements in diets and standards of health care, the provision of clean water, decent housing and basic schooling for all. Suppose that this had been the dominant doctrine in Japan in the later nineteenth century. It is a subject that I have often speculated on; most specifically in print some ten years ago when I tried to work out what would have happened if the post-war land reform had been carried out in the 1880s.* For a variety of reasons, having to do with the way new technology spread, the

*See 'Land Reform and Japan's Economic Development – A Reactionary Thesis', in T. Shanin, ed., *Peasants and Peasant Societies* (Penguin Modern Sociology Readings), Harmondsworth, 1971, pp. 377–88. Also *Land Reform in Japan*, O.U.P., London, 1958.

pattern of rural marketing organization, the sources of investment funds, the relations between political stability and the
propensity to invest etc., I concluded that a land reform at any
time after 1920 would probably have hastened the rate of
growth; a land reform – and a shift to more egalitarian patterns
of consumption – before 1900 would very probably have
slowed it. Quite probably, too, to come back to 'basic needs
strategies', massive state expenditure on health, water and education, or shorter hours and better safety standards in factories,
would have slowed the rate of capital accumulation. The people
of Shinohata might only be getting to their first black-and-
white TV sets today, rather than being on the second generation in colour.

And would that have been a bad thing? I just do not know.
What the jargon calls intergenerational distribution problems
are among the most intractable problems of social policy. I
know, personally, the *present* generation of Shinohata people.
As I write this the Yamamoto grandson who is staying with us
here in England has just come home from the expensive English
Language School in Brighton which, thanks to the non-
consumption of the generations of the 1870s and 1900s, his
policeman father can now afford to send him to. It is real flesh-
and-blood friends of mine whom I would be wishing poorer if
I said that the more egalitarian growth strategy would have
been better, and shadowy great-grandfather figures of the past
whom I would be wishing a little extra comfort – which one
imagines (for their presumed degree of subjective frustration is
one element in one's judgement of others' situations) they probably would not in any case have seen themselves as entitled to
expect. It is not surprising that my instinct is to decide in favour
of the former and to conclude that Japan made the right choice.

And I suspect the advocates of a 'basic needs strategy' today
judge by the same criteria; they too weight the balance in
favour of the flesh-and-blood people they know, the people
with yaws and bilharzia they see in the Third World villages
today, not their shadowy competitors, the generations as yet
unborn (and in spite of the fact that, with present population
growth rates, the latter are likely to have worse yaws and worse
bilharzia if the rate of capital accumulation is not increased).

And in fact, I suppose, nobody ever does choose otherwise

and vote against the present generation and in favour of the insubstantial wraiths of the future, as long as they are thinking in the individual utility terms of welfare economics. When political leaders do give their vote to the unborn generations in effect, it is not primarily in individual welfare terms that the choice is made. They see themselves, rather, as servants of some abstract entity, as working for the Nation, or for History. The people of Shinohata know all about politicians who think like that. On the whole they have seen enough of them, and prefer their more welfare-oriented and vote-oriented successors who hold power today. It is one of the ironies of history, though, that they owe their colour television sets as much to the former as to the latter.

Index